# LONDON & SOUTH WESTERN RAILWAY
# ENGINE SHEDS

For
REG RANDELL
A Southern Railwayman

Published by
**IRWELL PRESS**
3 Durley Avenue, Pinner, Middlesex, HA5 1JQ
Printed by The Amadeus Press Ltd
Huddersfield, West Yorkshire

# LONDON & SOUTH WESTERN RAILWAY

# ENGINE SHEDS

BY
CHRIS HAWKINS & GEORGE REEVE

## WESTERN DISTRICT

IRWELL
PRESS

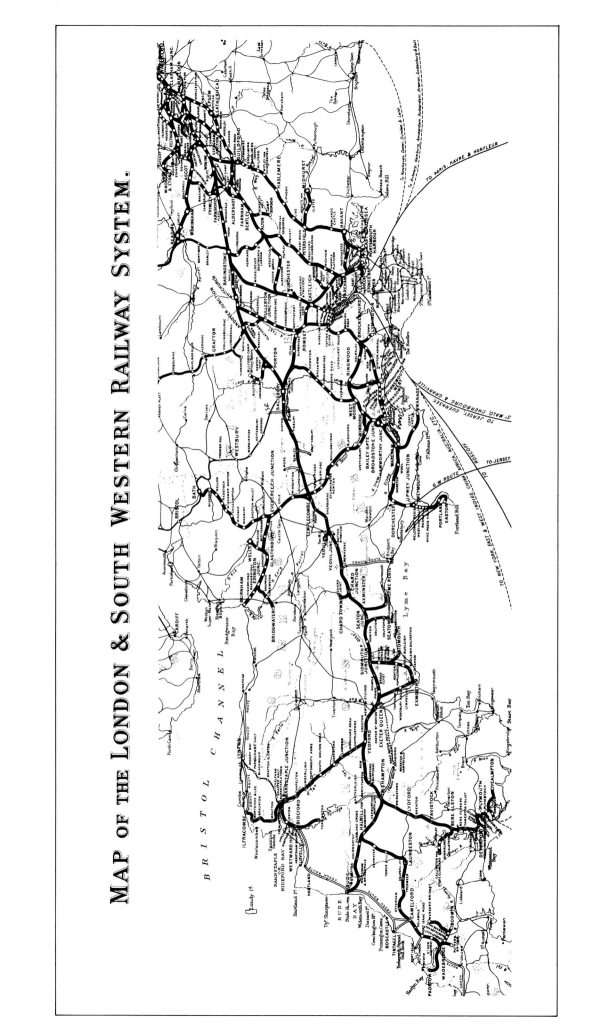

# MAP OF THE LONDON & SOUTH WESTERN RAILWAY SYSTEM.

# Contents

Track plans are all based on original LSWR and Southern surveys and are reproduced to a uniform scale of approximately 2 chains to 1 inch. Structural drawings are again taken from official sources and are reproduced at 1mm, 2mm or 4mm to the foot.

**Plymouth Friary just completed, one of the LSWR 'new standard sheds'. Smaller than most of its contemporaries, Fulwell, Eastleigh, Nine Elms and others it was nonetheless a great barn of a building, an elegant structure rejoicing in a complexity of detail. The new sheds were an emphatic declaration of a new found assuredness and confidence upon the LSWR and whilst every structural nuance was strictly traditional in quality and style, even for turn of the century Britain, the 'new standard' was regarded as something of a** *parvenu*

# Introduction

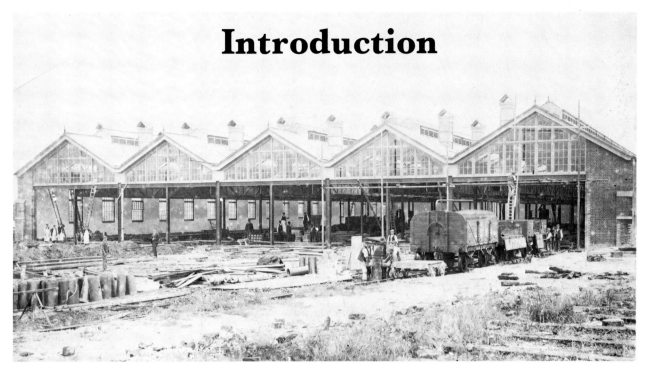

**Salisbury's new locomotive shed nears completion in 1901.**

As the London and Southampton Railway drew near to completion its engineers were faced with the novel problem of engine stabling. The term, which is still used for diesels and electrics to this day, was an odd one, but no accident; the locomotive was indeed *an iron horse*. It was important that it be stabled at the end of the working day and this idea persisted over many decades; engineers continued to argue in their constant battles with Traffic Committees, Way and Works Committees and others for more engine shed accommodation, on the basis that engines were 'forced to stand outside in all weathers'.

As the main lines came haltingly into operation in the 1830s and 1840s no-one was entirely clear as to what sort of buildings might best suit the new locomotives. How were they to be arranged and how might these elemental creatures (it was no accident that many of the names recalled the Classical *Underworld*) be calmed and made safe before the next sally forth? A 'trough' was provided by the Liverpool and Manchester 'at the Liverpool Engine Shed' in 1831, a startlingly new device 'to enable the men to repair them'. The humble engine pit thus came into being, illustrating that the self evident and obvious of later years was at first baffling. Tens of thousands of pits later and not until the 1950s, with diesels, did BR stumble across the (American-inspired) alternative - run the rails on pillars. If this equally efficacious remedy had occurred to the Liverpool and Manchester pioneers, engine sheds throughout Britain would have looked very different indeed.

Every engineer had his own answer to the problem of engine stabling and the period allowed a flourishing of weird and wonderful building, many of them tending to the *baroque* and almost all, it is a great pity, now gone. The task began with several precepts; apart from the idea that all engines should be 'stabled' at the end of the days work, the driver was deemed to be 'in charge' in the literal sense. He would accompany his charge to the stable and see that it was bedded down for the night, no other might drive his engine and he was paid often according to the load. The roundhouse appeared in Britain in these times and was regarded as the ideal, most economical use of space though in all early instances it was far too small. Turntables were crude, ill-balanced affairs (made of *wood* in some cases) and were necessarily small, engines being detached

from the tender for 'berthing'. When the physical principles of the turntable were better understood longer examples became available (the earlier models would simply not function beyond a certain size); engines and tenders could be turned together but this immediately rendered the roundhouses inadequate. The 'bays' were now far too small and in any event explosive growth of traffic usually meant the sites had to be yielded up for expansion of stations (as at Paddington) or works (as at Miles Platting on a progenitor of the Lancashire & Yorkshire.

The roundhouses of the 1840s and 1850s were rightly regarded as astonishing; they were usually very tall in relation to the modest circumference and had a fortress quality about them. The Chalk Farm roundhouse is the only survivor today of this remarkable range of buildings.

The early days of the LSWR and its forebears were punctuated (possibly more than most) by a flowering of such buildings, all marked by a peculiar exotic or eccentric quality. While other large concerns eventually settled upon an arrangement of buildings not obviously removed in construction and arrangement from latter day sheds (the British 'square roundhouse' derives from the 1860s), the LSWR followed a gloriously different path. This is best charted in developments at Nine Elms (detailed in full in a subsequent volume) where almost every bizarre disposition of shed could be found, from the 1830s to the 1870s and beyond. Even the final form of layout at Nine Elms, the great part of the shed which was so familiar into the 1960s, had an eccentric quality, a large straight shed, fixed upon a turntable *and set at 90 degrees to the main line*.

The first shed(s) were put up at the old Nine Elms terminus in 1838, the usual unwieldy combination (a series of plans detailing all of this will be found in the next volume but a description appears in *Southern Sheds* Hawkins & Reeve, OPC 1979, and there is a fine account by Peter Winding in *Railway World* November 1980).

At the old Nine Elms terminus, on the damp ground close by the Thames a collection of buildings grew up, worked in a fashion (largely by interlocked turntables) now long lost to us and certainly the arrangements involved the old ideas of separating the engine from its tender, though at Nine Elms there was no roundhouse like Paddington, Birmingham Vauxhall or Camden. The various small sheds were ordinary straight road buildings though from plans it is clear that engines were manoeuvred (or rather manhandled) about via a series of turntables. It was a year or so before the drawbacks of such a layout became obvious.

The establishment at Nine Elms proliferated in confusing fashion to a gaggle of buildings and on extension to Waterloo these were replaced in sweeping fashion by a huge running shed equipped with *four* turntables, two at each end. Such provision must have been unique in Britain. An even more remarkable building, a great open arc of a roundhouse, served by *two* turntables replaced this strange establishment. This came in the 1870s when every other company had settled down with much more sober, conventional buildings, the sort of straight sheds and roundhouses familiar to the end of steam.

Nine Elms stands as something of a paradigm, if a slightly extreme one, for LSWR shed development. This eccentric succession was repeated at other important LSWR locations. Exeter was relatively simple and straightforward in its development though the eccentricities lurking just below burst forth in the biggest corrugated iron shed (an abject failure) the country has seen. At Bishopstoke (Eastleigh) an almost unending collection of small engine sheds grew up and Bournemouth (the *Bomo* of the Southern) boasted a comparable collection of oddities.

From this sprawling and disparate lot, from the hovel to the splendid, the company forged from the turn of the century a range of solid, well appointed straight sheds, a standard design in solid brick with high and generously glazed gable roofs. The style could be adapted to any size, from the little three road shed at Basingstoke to the vast barn of Eastleigh...

## Of Turntables and other Matters Diverse ...

The Board or its Committees examined and approved almost every detail of the working of the line and the following extracts are illuminating with respect to our subject:

At a meeting of the Way, Works and Land Committee held at the York Road on Thursday 7th June 1849: Present R.E.A. Townsend Esq in the Chair Thomas Smith Esq. - The Minutes of the last meeting were read and approved.

Locomotive Shed Covering
Read Minutes of the Board as to shed covering for the Locomotive Engines and also Mr. Gooch's Report, of which the following is a copy.

10th May 1849.
To the Chairman of the Locomotive Committee,

Sir,

I beg to recall the attentions of the Committee to the very insufficient protection to their Stock of Engines and Tenders, whereby they receive injury and cause very great additional expense in cleaning, examining etc. etc. The numbers of Engines and Tenders will during the present year be 117 while there is only shed room or covering including repairing shops, over the whole line for 78, making the fullest practicable allowance for detaching the Tenders from such Engines as are under repairs and examination - thus leaving 39 requiring protection - of this number 30 will be stationed at Nine Elms and the remainder at Southampton

I have therefore to recommend for the consideration of the Committee that Sheds should be constructed capable of holding the above number of Engines and Tenders and thereby prevent considerable    injury and continual expense to this Department.

I have also to suggest that a plan should be agreed upon for the extension of the Work Shops at Nine Elms to meet the repairs of the greatly increased Stock of Engines and Tenders with facility and economy, in which the present shops are very deficient - I would propose that only a portion of this extension should be — done now, letting the other remain until by degrees they can be done with advantage.

I have gone carefully into the expense of that portion which I think should at the present time have the consideration of the Directors, and find it would cost about £9,500. In this I include -

Sheds at Nine Elms and Southampton for Engines and Tenders.

Making platform round outer repairing Shop at Nine Elms to make it like the inner Shop; enlarging windows etc.

Erecting new Wheel and Tyre Furnace, the present one being too small for the driving wheels of the Engines besides being in such an inconvenient position and so fully occupied for carriage and waggon repairs as to involve great inconvenience and cost in doing the work that can be done there.

Erecting shed for boilermakers and Tender repairs.

The accompanying plans shew the position and arrangement of the various Sheds etc.

I feel it my duty to add that unless this is done, the injury and depreciation which arise to this Stock will be such as to require provision to be made to meet it at no distant period.

I am, Sir, your obedient Servant,

John V. Gooch

Mr. Gooch presented his plans and also Estimate of works at Nine Elms and Southampton between £9,000 and £10,000 and it was recommended to the Board to adopt the same accordingly, and that Mr. Martin prepares specifications in order that the works may be let by public Tender.

It appears from the reductions introduced by Mr. Gooch in the arrangements of these Sheds and by the abandonment of Five Engines and Tenders intended to be constructed at the time the Financial Statement in 1848 was prepared, that the Capital outlay in the Locomotive Department will be reduced considerably below the sum there charged.

Water at Bishopstoke; The like recommendation was made to the Board to adopt Mr. Gooch's suggestion for obtaining water from Bishopstoke from the River at a cost of about £100.

Engine and Carriage Sheds

In reference to the resolution of the Court of Directors of the 15th instant by which the Way Works and Land Committee together with any other Members of the Court who could attend were requested to inspect the Nine Elms Station for the purpose of ascertaining what further accomodation (sic) is required for the placing under cover and the repairing of Engines and Carriages, the following Report was ordered to be entered.

That Mr. Reed, Lord Morley and Mr. Lacy inspected the premises on Tuesday last; being attended by Messrs Gooch and Beattie and accompanied by the Secretary.

That the result of the inspection is to fully confirm the opinion that the existing accomodation (sic) is altogether insufficient for the economical carrying on the inspection of repairs, and the shelter which is necessary to the protection of the property of the Company.

That as regards the Carriages it is proposed to lay lines of rails along each of the platforms of the former arrival and departure Shed - lowering the level of the platforms to that of the other part of the Shed, and providing a movable platform which will preserve the facilities for the departure or arrival of Her Majesty. The encrease (sic) of accommodation for the Carriages it is proposed to limit to this extent for the present; and a very small expense will therefore be incurred.

That the Locomotive Engine Department should have a Shed built as proposed by Mr. Gooch. It is absolutely necessary; and it is the reverse of economy to defer its construction. The only question that ought to be considered is whether the supervision should be left to Mr. Gooch and whether Mr. Tite should be consulted and charged with the responsibility, not only of the building, but of the foundations, which are somewhat difficult.

The proposed Shed will be of sufficient capacity to contain 30 Engines and Tenders.

Mr. Gooch's proposition also includes an additional Shed at Southampton capable of accommodating 12 Engines, also some small addition to buildings for repairs at Nine Elms. The entire outlay for these matters is estimated at £9,500 and as that sum is within the amount estimated in the report of November last, the Court will perhaps exercise a wise discretion in sanctioning the entire proposition.

R.E.A. Townsend

With regard to turntables the LSWR increased the diameters as other companies, from 42ft and 45ft to 50ft and 55ft by the end of the last century and into the present one. 65ft 'tables came as the earlier sizes did, when it became evident that new engines would require them. Each new size 'generation' would be quickly installed at the vital sites, Nine Elms, Salisbury and so on and would become the 'standard' for new installation/ renewal elsewhere. The LSWR was notable in that almost alone (with the Great Western) it employed at many sites (particularly after 1900) the peculiar 'over girder' type of turntable; it saved much expense in the excavation of a pit but was necessarily massive in its construction. Developments can be traced through an assortment of Minutes...

6th June 1883: Stronger description of Engine Turn Table ... should be adopted by the Co. as their standard type. Approved. Tenders to be invited.

21st July 1886: 1st section of North Cornwall Railway Halwill - Launceston inspected on 13th instant by Colonel Rich of the Board of Trade. Plan to show site of a 50 feet Turntable ... which Colonel Rich requires to be provided at the Halwill Station within four months of this date... Standard 50 feet Turntable to be supplied to the North Cornwall Co. at cost price......4th August 1886: Portion of cost to be borne by the North Cornwall Co.

£170.

3rd August 1887: Exmouth Station Engine Turntable. Turn Table at this Station has broken down; the Engineer asks that it be replaced by a Standard 50 feet Table and estimate costs of £645 including fixing and foundations.

Within two weeks ...a secondhand replacement ... being sought and on 28th September the transfer of the 42ft turntable from Exeter Queen Street .. approved at £250.)

Waterloo - Salisbury 8th September 1912. Reported verbally as to the Engine Turntable required at Waterloo Station (North side) and recommend that the one at Salisbury (55 feet diameter) be transferred to Waterloo and that a new one (65 feet diameter) be purchased for use at Salisbury. Approved Cowans Sheldon & Co. of Carlisle price of £870, a duplicate of the Table recently ordered from them.

In terms of enlightenment the LSWR can hardly have differed over much from its contemporaries. Drummond was in the ferocious tradition of his kind, commanding variously respect and loathing, but men like him built and ran the Empire; his was simply the way of the times. The company was by no means the *Gradgrind* of legend and in a harsh age could look after its people, in its own way. The sad tale of G.Reeve (no relation) is a small insight into Victorian staff welfare...

*7th January 1891... G. Reeve, Greaser. £13.10s paid for artificial leg and a foot. Both feet were cut off by a train on the 3rd June last year.*

*24th July 1895: G. Reeve , Greaser. Artificial legs needs repairing. To be allowed.*

*24th November 1897: G. Reeve, Tin Shop Eastleigh. This man's artificial feet, provided by the Company in January 1891, are worn out and beyond repair. Recommend £12 for new ones.*

*6th March 1907: G. Reeve, late Oiler, Exeter. Two new feet required. Approved £12.*

G.Reeve hobbles off into LSWR history with this entry, un-noticed probably amid the 'cripples and not to go' blokes and no doubt with a fierce loyalty to the company, intact.

# LOCOMOTIVE DISTRICTS

The London South Western, for its own operating and accounting reasons, divided the company into three separate districts, London, Southern and Western. They were wholly different in terms of size and traffic etc. but were overall controlled from London, Waterloo. The locomotive depots thus, within each district, are shown below in 1906.

**LONDON DISTRICT**

NINE ELMS
  Fulwell Junction
  Ascot
  Windsor
  Reading
  Leatherhead
  Hampton Court
  Chertsey
  Woking
GUILDFORD
  Ash
BASINGSTOKE

**SOUTHERN DISTRICT**

NORTHAM
  Bishopstoke/Eastleigh
  Andover Junction
  Gosport
  Bishops Waltham
  Southampton Docks
PORTSMOUTH (Fratton)
  Midhurst
BOURNEMOUTH
  Lymington
  Ringwood

  Hamworthy Junction
  Wimborne
  Swanage
DORCHESTER
  Weymouth

**WESTERN DISTRICT**

SALISBURY
YEOVIL
  Templecombe
  Chard
EXMOUTH JUNCTION
  Seaton
  Sidmouth
  Budleigh Salterton
  Exmouth
  Okehampton
  Bude
  Holsworthy
BARNSTAPLE
  Ilfracombe
  Torrington
PLYMOUTH (Friary)
  Devonport
WADEBRIDGE
  Launceston

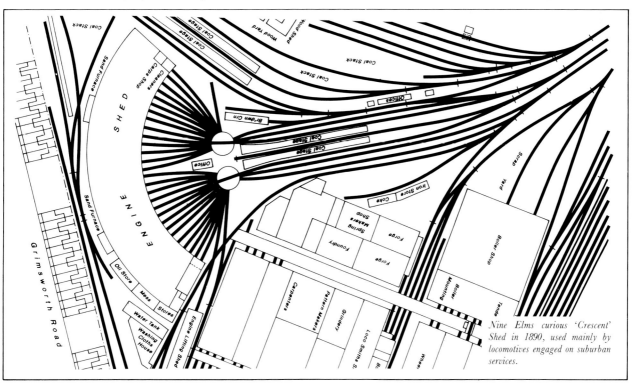

*Nine Elms curious 'Crescent' Shed in 1890, used mainly by locomotives engaged on suburban services.*

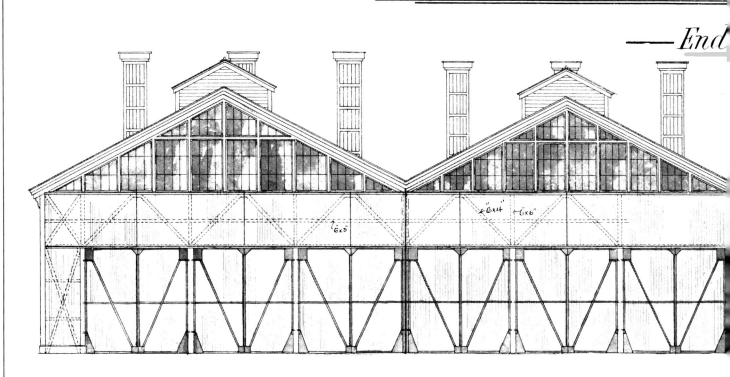

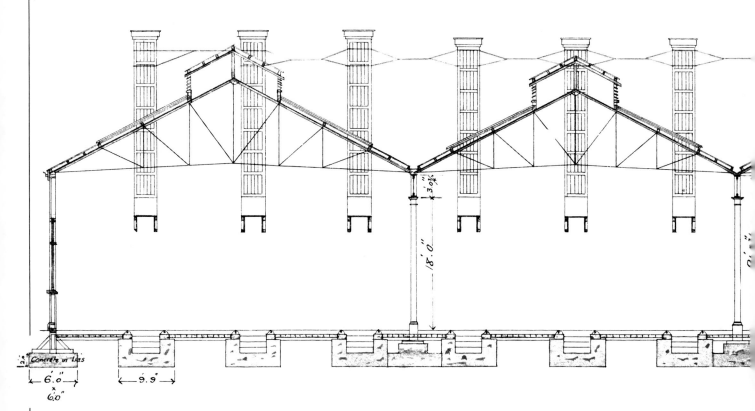

The 'new standard shed' can be traced directly in lineage to the extraordinary corrugated iron affair at Exmouth Junction. The high elegant wooden smoke flues and the gable glazing are the same but ironwork in such a structure was an extraordinary choice. Whether boldness or folly, it was not repeated on this scale and the reasoning behind the almost over-emphasized solid quality of later sheds is not hard to understand.

# NEW STEAM SHED

*Elevation —*

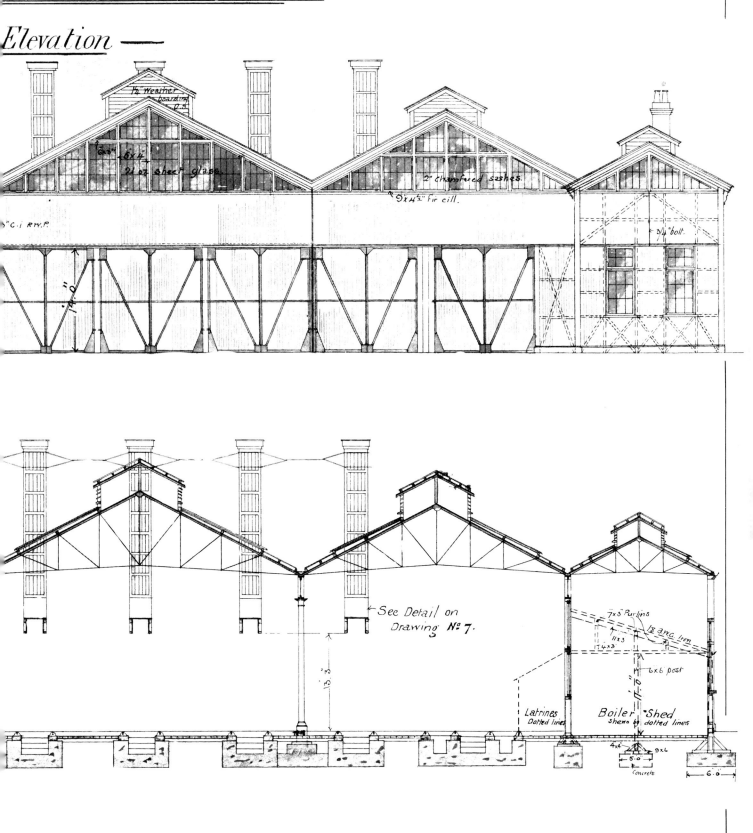

# EXMOUTH JUNCTION NEW STEAM SHED

To open.

To open.

To open.

To open.

To open.

To open.

To open.

To open.

SIDE ELEVATION

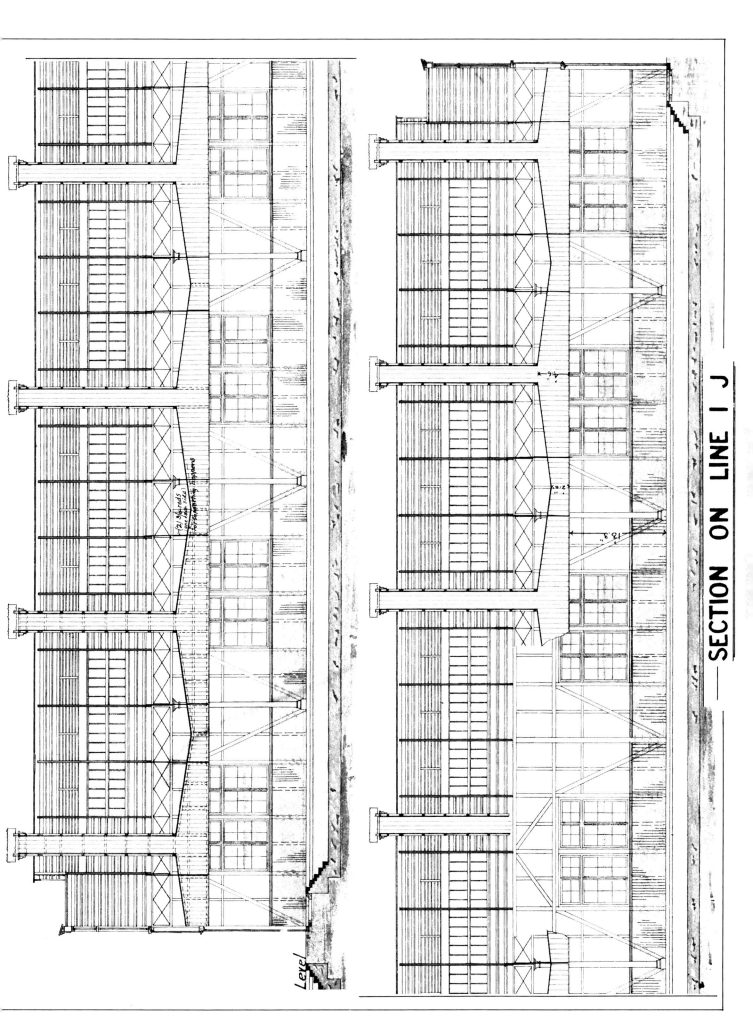

SECTION ON LINE I J

# EXMOUTH JUNCTION

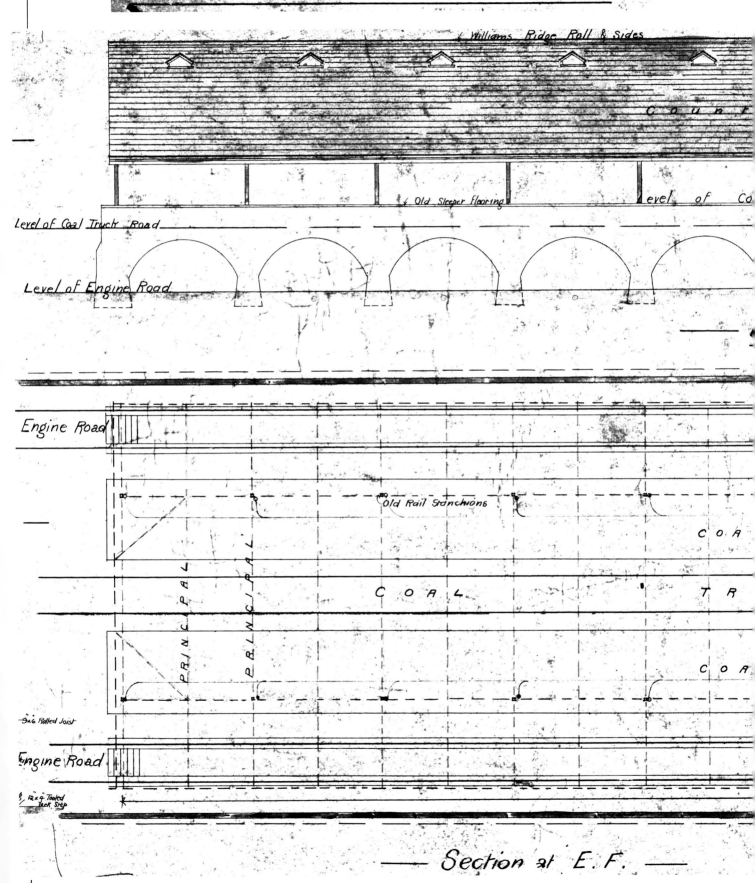

Williams Ridge Roll & Sides

Count

Old Sleeper flooring     Level of Co

Level of Coal Truck Road

Level of Engine Road

Engine Road

Old Rail Stanchions

C O A

C O A L     T R

PRINCIPAL

PRINCIPAL

C O A

9x6 Rolled Joist

Engine Road

⅜ 12x4 Tooled Tack Step

Section at E.F.

# COAL STAGE

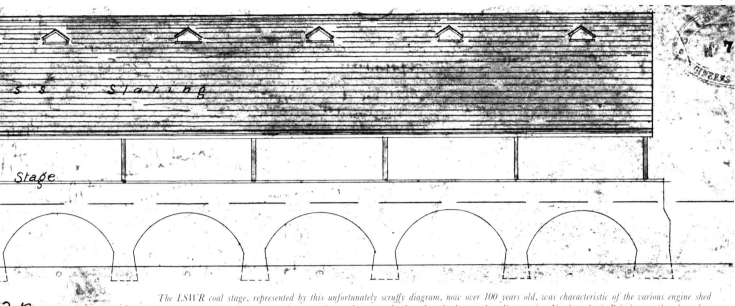

ss Slating

Stage

an.

The LSWR coal stage, represented by this unfortunately scruffy diagram, now over 100 years old, was characteristic of the various engine shed developments within the company: for every advance there seemed to be a throwback to much earlier practice. Nowhere else in Britain were these long, low sheds put up, apparently without recourse to wheeled tubs, cranes or whatever. Anyone shovelling spilled coal from a wooden floor would soon come to loathe the place

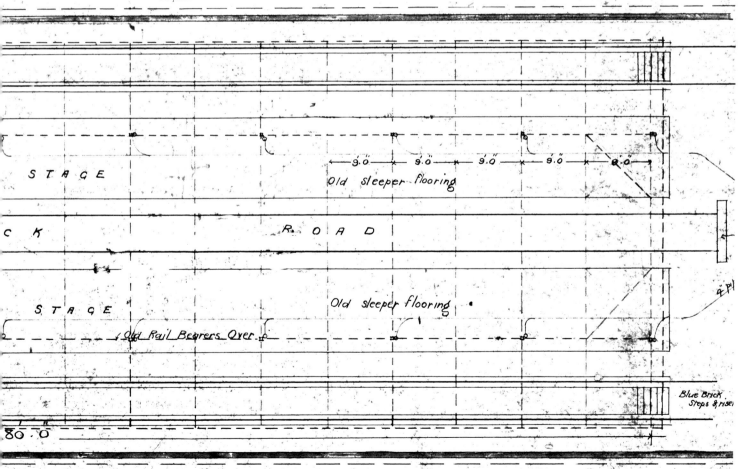

STAGE

Old sleeper flooring

CK          R O A D

STAGE          Old sleeper flooring

Old Rail Bearers Over

Blue Brick
Steps & risers

80'0

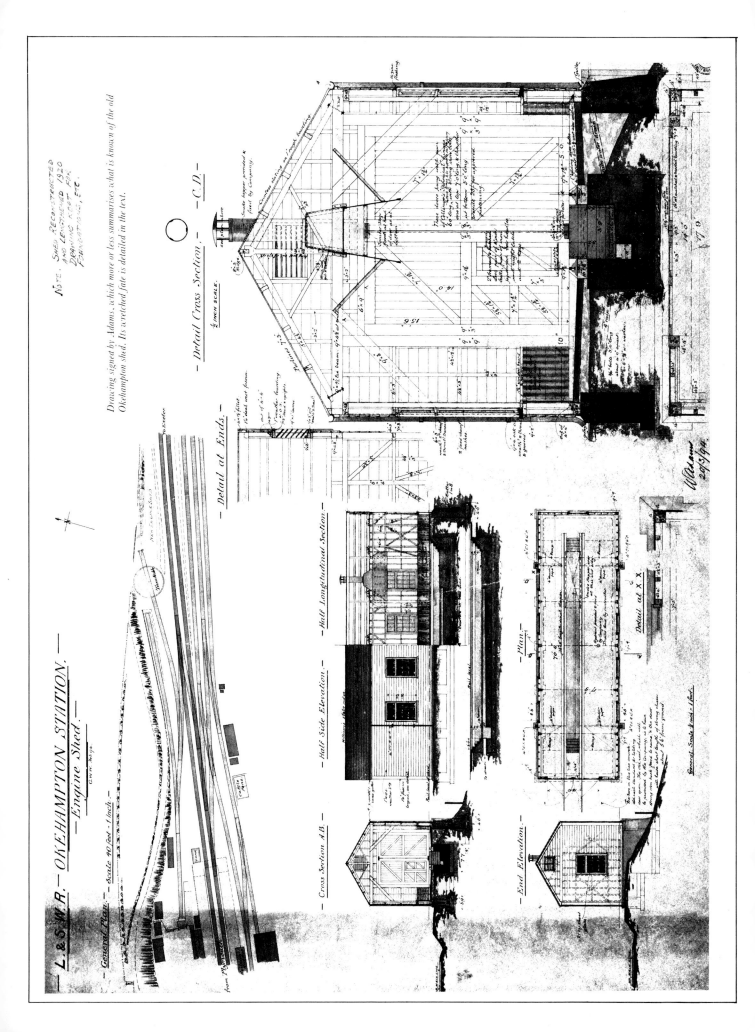

— L. & S. W. R. — OKEHAMPTON STATION. —
— Engine Shed. —
G.W.R. Relays.

— General Plan. — Scale 40 feet = 1 inch. —

— Detail Cross Section. — C.D. —
½ inch scale.

Note. Shed Reconstructed 1920 and lengthened 1927 for Foundations, etc.

Drawing signed by Adams, which more or less summarises what is known of the old Okehampton shed. Its wretched fate is detailed in the text.

— Detail at Ends. —

— Half Longitudinal Section. —

— Half Side Elevation. —

— Cross Section AB. —

— Plan. —

Detail at X X.

General Scale ¼ inch = 1 foot.

— End Elevation. —

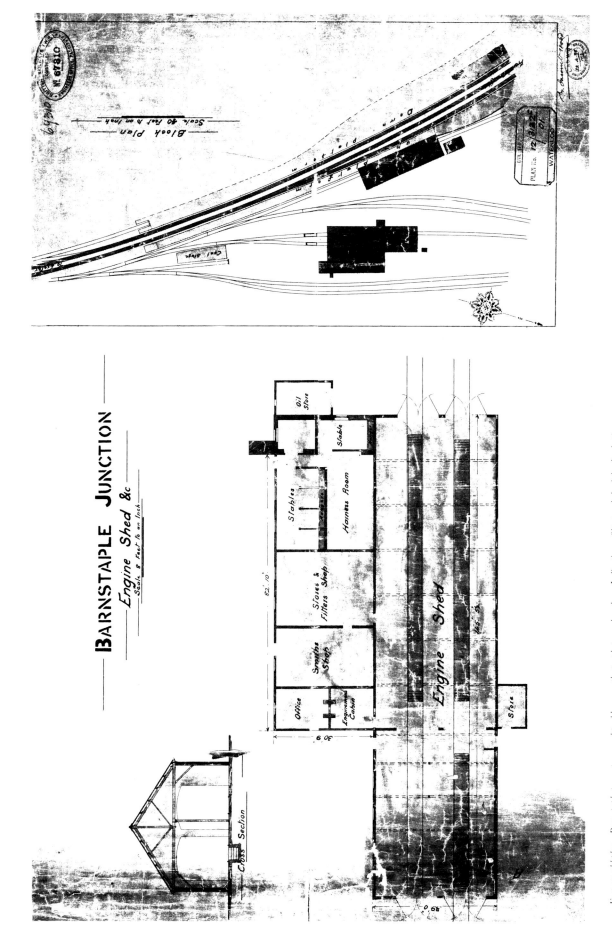

# BARNSTAPLE JUNCTION

## Engine Shed &c

Scale 8 Feet to an Inch

### Block Plan

Scale 40 feet to an Inch

Office

Smiths Shop

Stores & Fitters Shop

Stables

Harness Room

Oil Store

Stable

Engine Shed

Cross Section

*Ever an odd place, Barnstaple presents several problems, as the text later makes clear. Indications of its tangled origins lay in the width disparity of the archways (a trace of the broad gauge?) and the tacked-on extension at the rear.*

# L.S.W.R. FRIARY. PLYMOUTH.

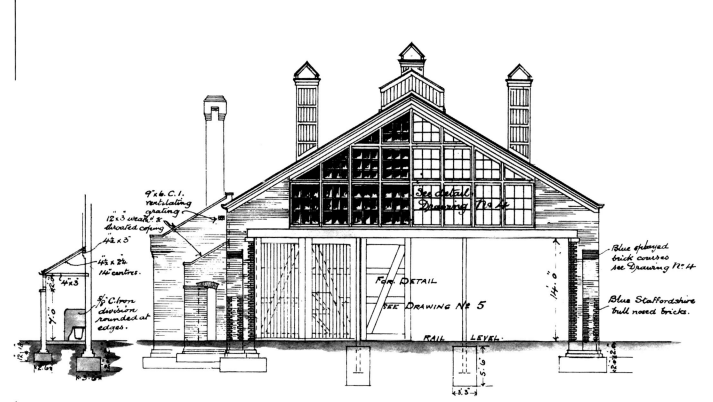

9"x6. C.I. ventilating grating

12"x 3 weath'd & throated coping

4½ x 3"

4½ x 2¼ 14" centres.

4"x3

S/O C.Iron division rounded at edges.

See detail Drawing No 4

For Detail see Drawing No 5

RAIL LEVEL.

14'·0

Blue splayed brick courses see Drawing No 4

Blue Staffordshire bull nosed bricks.

**EAST ELEVATION.**

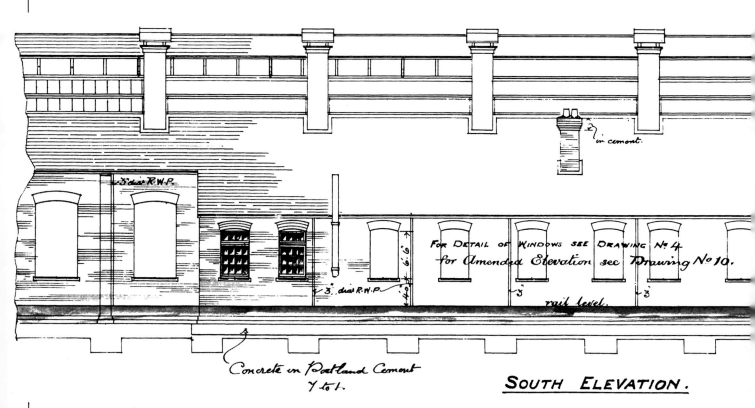

3" dia R.W.P.

in cement.

3" dia R.W.P.

For Detail of Windows see Drawing No 4

for Amended Elevation see Drawing No 10.

rail level.

Concrete in Portland Cement
7 to 1.

**SOUTH ELEVATION.**

# RUNNING SHED.

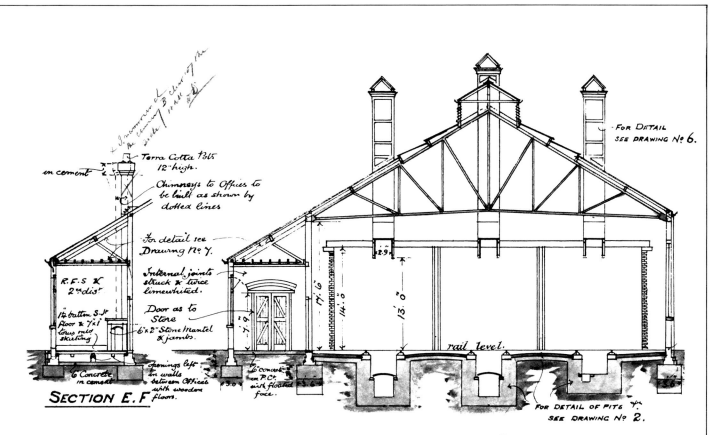

in cement

Terra Cotta Pots
12" high.

Chimneys to Offices to
be built as shown by
dotted lines

For detail see
Drawing No. 7.

Internal joints
struck & twice
limewhited.

Door as to
Store

6" x 2" Stone Mantel
& jambs.

R.F.S.K.
2nd dist

1½ batten S. Jt
floor & 7" x 1"
torus into
skirting

6 Concrete
in cement

Openings left
in walls
between Offices
with wooden
floors.

6" concrete
on P.C. with floated
face.

### SECTION E.F

For Detail
see Drawing No. 6.

12.9"

17.6"

14.0"

13.0"

7.9"

rail level.

For detail of Pits
see Drawing No. 2.

### CROSS SECTION A.B

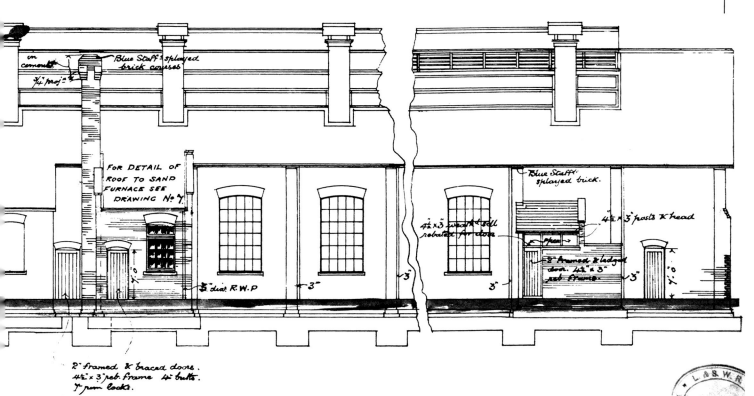

in cement

¾" proj.

Blue Staff. splayed
brick courses

For Detail of
Roof to Sand
Furnace see
Drawing No. 7.

7.0"

3" dia. R.W.P

3"

Blue Staff.
splayed brick.

4½ x 3" wrought sill
rebated for door

4½ x 3" posts & head

3" framed & ledged
door. 4½ x 3"
reb. frame.

3"

3"

7.0"

2" framed & braced doors.
4½" x 3" reb. frame. 4" butts.
7" rim locks.

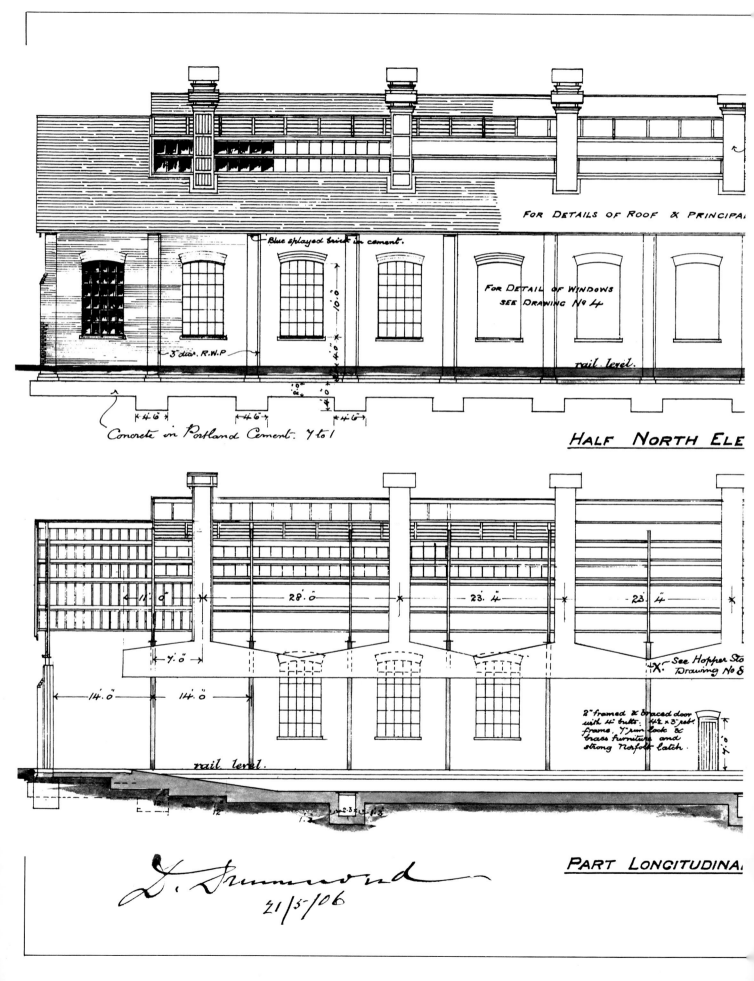

Blue splayed brick in cement.

10.0

4.0

FOR DETAILS OF ROOF & PRINCIPAL

FOR DETAIL OF WINDOWS
SEE DRAWING Nº 4

rail level.

3" dia. R.W.P.

4'6"    4'6"    4'6"

Concrete in Portland Cement. 7 to 1

HALF NORTH ELE

11'0"    28.0    23.4    23.4

7.0

See Hopper Sto
Drawing Nº 8

14.0    14.0

2" framed & braced door
with H butts. 4½ x 3" rebt
frame, 7" rim lock &
brass furniture and
strong Norfolk latch

7.0

rail level.

2.3

D. Drummond
21/5/06

PART LONGITUDINA

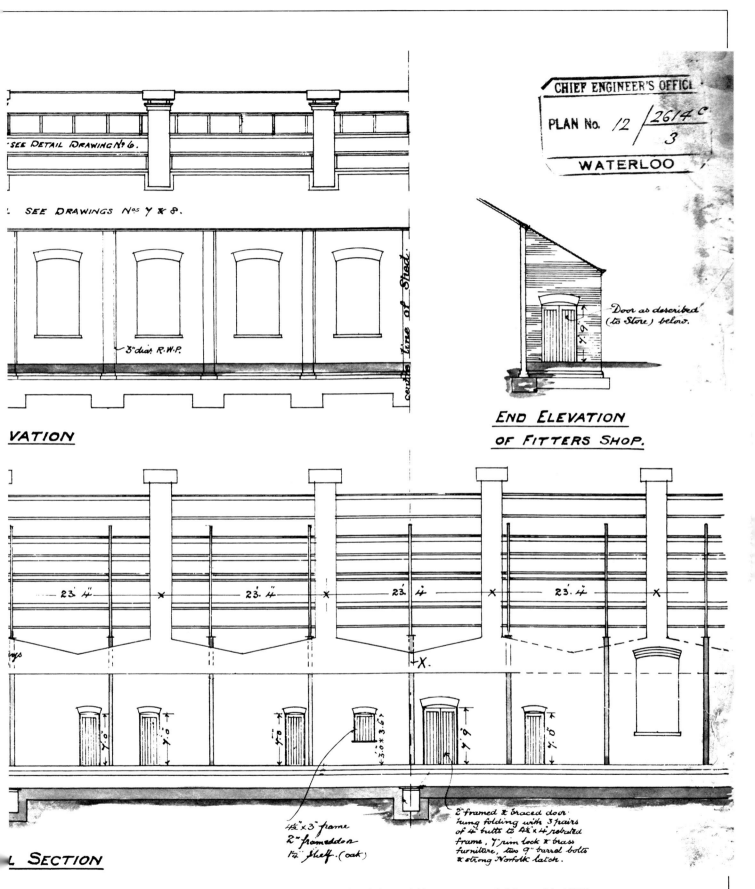

SEE DETAIL DRAWING Nº 6.

SEE DRAWINGS Nºs 7 & 8.

3" dia. R.W.P.

centre line of Shed.

VATION

Door as described
(to Store) below.

**END ELEVATION
OF FITTERS SHOP.**

23' 4"        23' 4"        23' 4"        23' 4"

4½" x 3" frame
2" framed door
1¼" Shelf (oak)

2" framed & braced door
hung folding with 3 pairs
of 4" butts to 4½" x 4" rebated
frame, 7" rim lock & brass
furniture, two 9" barrel bolts
& strong Norfolk latch.

3'.0 x 3'.6"

SECTION

*The sheer wealth of detail - materials together with the varied windows and chimneys - were a marked feature of the LSWR
sheds. Great efforts were made to bear away the smoke but most of the 'new standard sheds' eventually fell prey to the elements.
The renewals many years later inevitably rendered the buildings duller by far.*

# PLYMOUTH

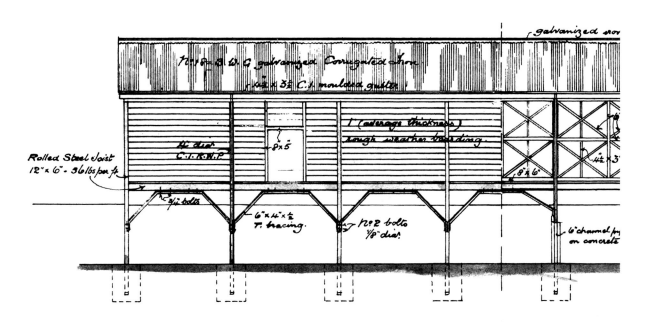

galvanized iron

No 16. B.w.g. galvanized Corrugated Iron

4½ x 3½ C.I. moulded gutter.

1 (average thickness)
rough weather boarding.

Rolled Steel Joist
12" x 6" - 36 lbs per ft.

4i dia
C.I. R.W.P.

8 x 5

4½ x 3

8 x 6

⅝ bolts

6" x 4" x ½
T. bracing.

No. 2 bolts
⅝ dia.

6" channel fy
on concrete

## HALF NORTH ELEVATION.   HAL

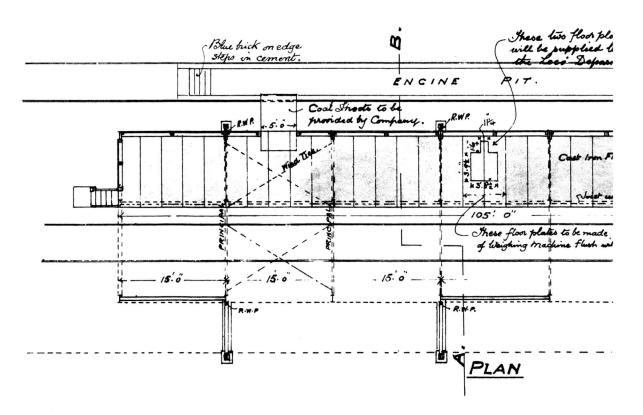

Blue brick on edge
steps in cement.

B.

These two floor pla
will be supplied b
the Loco Depar

ENGINE      PIT.

Coal Sheets to be
provided by Company.

R.W.P.

R.W.P.

Cast Iron F

Wheel Table

3.F.½"

3.F.½"

Joist en

105' 0"

These floor plates to be made
of Weighing machine flush wi

15' 0"    15' 0"    15' 0"

R.W.P.

R.W.P.

A

## PLAN

*The later LSWR coal ramps were a great improvement on the long low canopies of Exmouth Junction and others. The new stages were relatively insubstantial affairs but tubs and chutes had at last speeded up the procedures.*

# COAL STAGE.

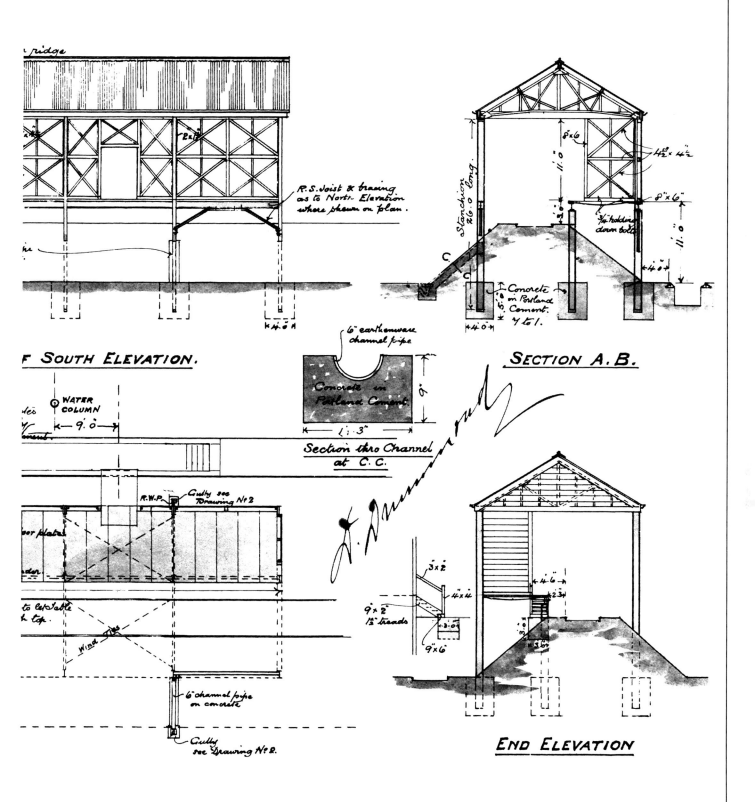

ridge

R.S. Joist & bracing
as to North Elevation
where shewn on plan.

F SOUTH ELEVATION.

8×6

Stanchion
26.0 long.

4½"×4½"

8"×6"

¾" holding
down bolts

11.0

Concrete
in Portland
Cement.
4 to 1.

4.0

SECTION A.B.

6" earthenware
channel pipe

Concrete in
Portland Cement.

9"

1' 3"

Section thro Channel
at C.C.

WATER
COLUMN

9.0

R.W.P.

Gully see
Drawing Nº 2

or Plates

Wind Ties

6" channel pipe
on concrete

Gully
see Drawing Nº 2.

3"×2"

4"×4"

4.6

2.3"

9"×2"
1½" treads

3.0"

9"×6"

3.0"

5.6"

END ELEVATION

# L. & S. W. R.
## FIFTY FEET ENGINE TURNTABLE.
## FRIARY . PLYMOUTH .
### LOCO DEPÔT

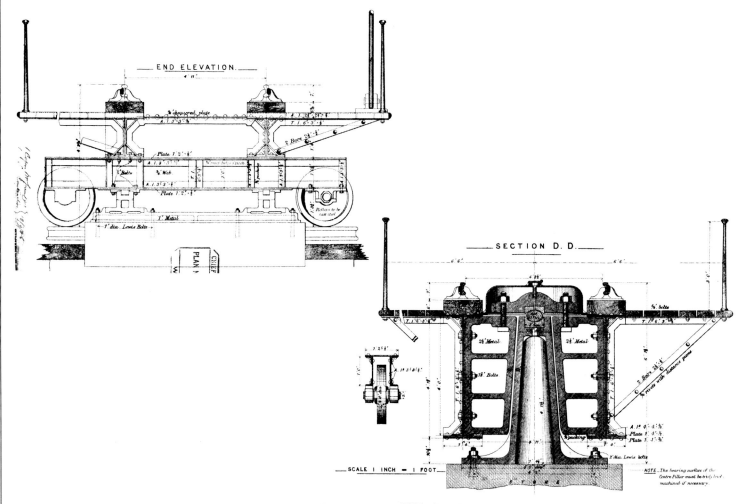

GWR Mogul No. 5321 on the turntable on 30th August 1945. The two rival systems in the West had an interplay of workings little guessed at now. Whilst a healthy mutual disregard was steadily maintained everyone was aware of the need to keep up knowledge of the 'rival route'. This kept open the Plymouth road at the worst of times, whether it be gales on the coast or snow on the moors. On another level it allowed the use of each company's resources in times of damage, repair or wartime disruption.

*H.C. Casserley*

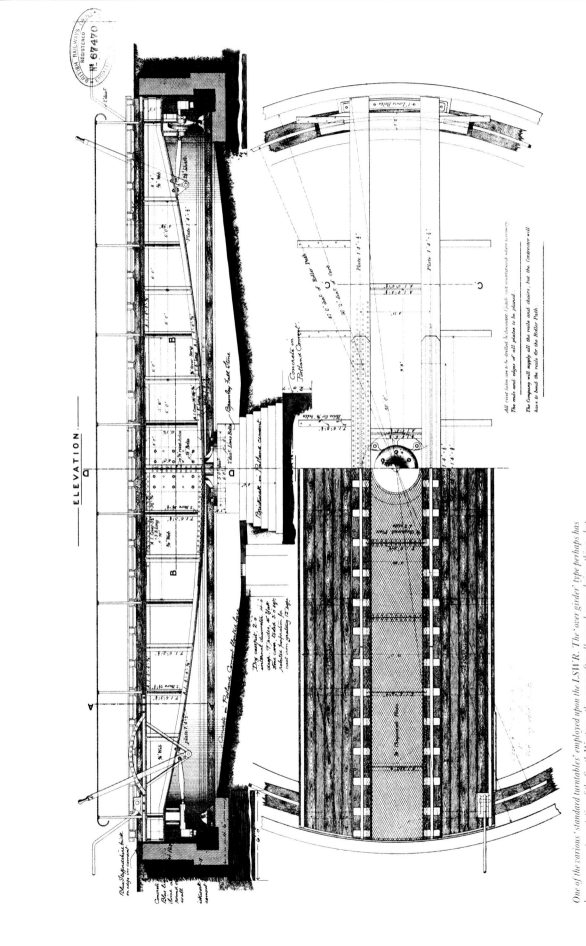

ELEVATION

One of the various 'standard turntables' employed upon the LSWR. The 'over girder' type perhaps has
become more representative of the South Western - they were after all a much more obvious thing - but
this is the sort of provision made at most LSWR sheds.

The new Salisbury shed 'excellently arranged .. as will be noticed .. to provide good and sufficient space'. A Mr. Anwell was the foreman when this vast new place opened, in charge of an assistant foreman and 'upwards of 200 hands'.

# Salisbury

### 'The Salisbury Branch': Milford

The LSWR had first approached Salisbury from Bishopstoke, on the main London-Southampton line in 1847 and had constructed a station on the outskirts at Milford. Here they assembled a small terminus with all the usual buildings, including a two road engine shed. 'The railway to Salisbury' had been floated as long ago as 1837 but the idea, of GW origin, never materialised. It was'nt until some years later that the question was mooted again, during a hectic period in which a number of projects emerged. This line from Bishopstoke was to be some twenty-two miles long and terminate 'in the town of Salisbury at Milford'. The project gained Royal Assent in 1844 but was dogged by slow work .....*17th July 1846. Progress of Salisbury branch: The Secretary produced a letter from Mr. Townsend of Salisbury relative to the slow progress of the Salisbury Branch, a copy of which is recommended to be sent to Mr. Locke and to Mr. Smith.....*

The station at Milford finally opened 'to coal traffic' on 27th January 1847, double throughout although single line had originally been planned. From the first a locomotive shed was required and this was established at the head of the yard on the northern side of the line. A commodious two road building, it was constructed entirely in brick, some 150 ft in length and 38 ft wide. Water was supplied from a cast iron tank surmounting an office with stores, messroom and workshop situated alongside. The roof was hipped and slated and a 25ft turntable lay adjacent to the building. The connecting service at Bishopstoke provided for trains to London, Gosport and Southampton and it was there that Beattie had requested another .....*shed to serve the Salisbury branch.....*

It was clear that Salisbury would not long be content with this branch line status; a direct route to London was demanded and the Milford-Bishopstoke route was regarded as a temporary measure - 'this has been established in most pointed fashion'. The line from Andover (or rather the direct route from London) arrived to the north of the city in 1857, into a new station at Fisherton Street in 1859. This was a marked improvement upon Milford and stood on spare ground just to the south of the Great Western station (the GWR had arrived in 1856). The completion of Fisherton Street also heralded the opening of the (ostensibly) independent Salisbury and Yeovil Railway, worked from the first by the LSWR.

Legal and commercial tussles had plagued the 'direct line' to Salisbury (see for instance the accounts by Sands, *The Railway Magazine, August 1961* and J.R. Fairman *Salisbury 150 Commemorative leaflet*). The line from Andover was completed to the outskirts of Salisbury in 1857, trains using Milford terminus until May of 1859 when the London line was linked at Fisherton station with the Salisbury and Yeovil, then complete as far on as Gillingham. The site at Fisherton comprised some nine acres, sandwiched between the GWR ('hostile and unco-operative' - Sands) terminus and the River Nadder.

### GILLINGHAM - an aside

It may be convenient at this point to mention a small establishment erected at Gillingham by the Salisbury and Yeovil Railway. Gillingham had acted as the temporary terminus from May 1859, the line beyond to Yeovil opening twelve months later. Accommodation was required for loco-

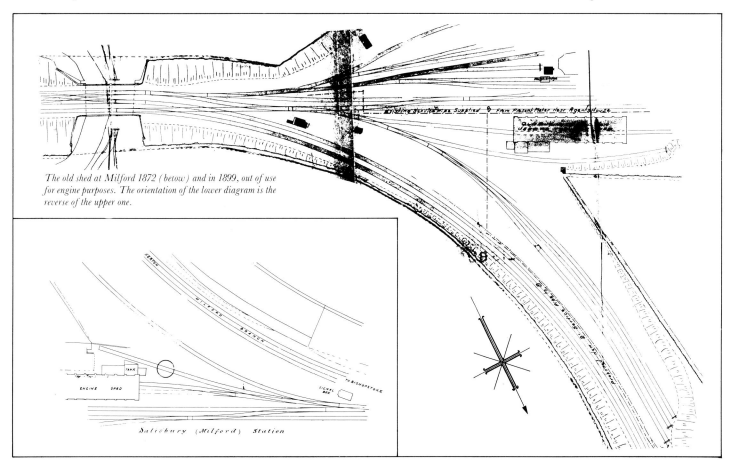

*The old shed at Milford 1872 (below) and in 1899, out of use for engine purposes. The orientation of the lower diagram is the reverse of the upper one.*

Salisbury (Milford) Station

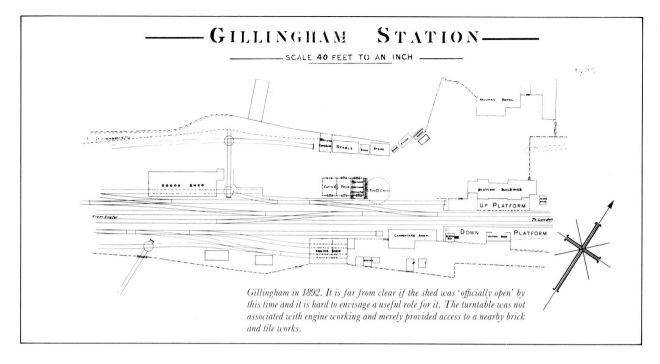

## —— GILLINGHAM STATION ——
### —— SCALE 40 FEET TO AN INCH ——

*Gillingham in 1892. It is far from clear if the shed was 'officially open' by this time and it is hard to envisage a useful role for it. The turntable was not associated with engine working and merely provided access to a nearby brick and tile works.*

motives working to and from Salisbury and a substantial two road building was erected on the down side at the country end. Of generous proportions it measured 83ft x 36ft with a gabled slated roof and central raised vent. It was louvred with roundels located at either end. The construction is described in the architects notes, accompanying a drawing of 1857 .....*Build hanging stones onto wall at top and bottom of piers; those at top to be 18ins x 10ins on the face and those at the bottom 18ins x 14ins, each stone to be of the same thickness as the wall. The Gates to be 3ins deal framed and braced gates, filled in with deal snatched and beaded boarding; the stiles and top rails 6ins wide, bottom rails 9ins wide, cross rails and brackets 4½ins wide; heavy with wrought iron strap hinges to proper carriages let into stone and run with lead. Note:- In the tracing sent to Mr. Fraser (Nov. 18th) the gates are shown to be hung on the outside.....* The drawing is labelled 'Salisbury and Yeovil Railway Engine Shed Gillingham'. The twenty-two miles of course to Salisbury were subsequently worked by the LSW.

The progress of lines was often piece meal, periods of frustrating lassitude broken by frantic pell-mell activity, *The Railway Times* 7th March 1857 .....*the cuttings have been commenced and about 120,000 cubic yards of earthwork between Wilton and Gillingham have been removed. Several bridges and culverts between the same points have been built and others are in progress.....*

By 1916 the Gillingham building of course was long given up but it had found a subsequent use, forming the premises of a private trader. Tracks remained in situ until at least 1901, conversion to the above being carried out sometime after.

### 'The Engine Shed, Salisbury'.
### Fisherton 1858

It was necessary to establish proper engine accommodation as close as maybe to the new Fisherton station and the company was mindful of this even before the new station opened .....*10th November 1858:...Read board minute referring to this Committee and the Way and Works Committee a letter from Mr. Evington as to the supply of gas and water and erection of an engine shed at the new station Salisbury. Mr. Beattie to arrange to meet Mr. Furington and to ascertain where the gas and water pipes should be laid and to the position of the Engine Shed.....* The two parties retired, as it were, to deliberate over the matter and returned in February of 1859 with the following suggestions .....*Read letter from Mr. Beattie re. water and gas supply at Fisherton Station Salisbury. Submitted plans and estimates for laying pipes, erecting a water tank and cranes, tender from Messrs Dunns accepted. 20,000 gallon tank to be erected as shown and 10,000 gallon tank at the engine shed. The Way and Works Committee to arrange to provide the engine shed, the plans of which have not yet been received.....*

The shed opened to traffic in the summer of 1859 and was located west of the station; it had three roads all terminating inside with a slated gabled roof. A 45ft turntable was laid down at the country end of the yard along with a small coal stage. The water tank was mounted above a small office and stores and pits were supplied inside and on the western approach roads. 'No. 3 road' the southernmost, was used primarily for the lifting and repair of locomotives; shear legs were provided inside the building and a small siding was available for locomotives awaiting attention.

Two small cottages were put up, Beattie recommending that they .....*be built on a piece of ground between the engine shed and turntable at Salisbury for the use of the Foremen employed there and for which they would pay a suitable rent. Recommended this to the Way and Works, but that the cottages be erected on company land.....* The two buildings can be seen in the plan of Fisherton but were not enjoyed long by the Foremen; not many years later both were being used as dormitories for enginemen.

### 'Mr. Strapp to Consult with Mr. Beattie re Cost'.
### Salisbury to 1899

Salisbury was never a mere stopping place on the main line - Gillingham or other points may have served as the 'frontier' for a time until Exeter was reached but from the first, operations were centred upon Salisbury. The sequence is a wholly familiar one, early accommodation rapidly proving inadequate, added to in unsatisfactory fashion until wholesale replacement some decades afterwards. Beattie after only ten years or so was seeking enlarged quarters .....*January 1870. Read letter from Mr. Beattie recommending that the engine shed at Salisbury be lengthened to accommodate two or four more engines. Mr. Strapp to prepare the estimates for lengthening the shed for two and four engines.....* It is tempting to imagine Beattie playing his Board in the ancient manner of things, the submission of a lesser proposal in tandem could have constituted a simple hint to the Committee, which

The two sheds at Fisherton are obscure in the photographic sense and no record seems to have survived, other than as background. At the top is *Hecla* outside the three road wooden shed of 1885 which sowed 'great agitation and concern' amidst the householders of Churchfield Road. Their constant and unwelcome surveillance was a minor factor in determining upon the move out to Cherry Orchard Lane. The lower photograph shows the earlier extended Fisherton shed, again of three roads, with 509 outside.

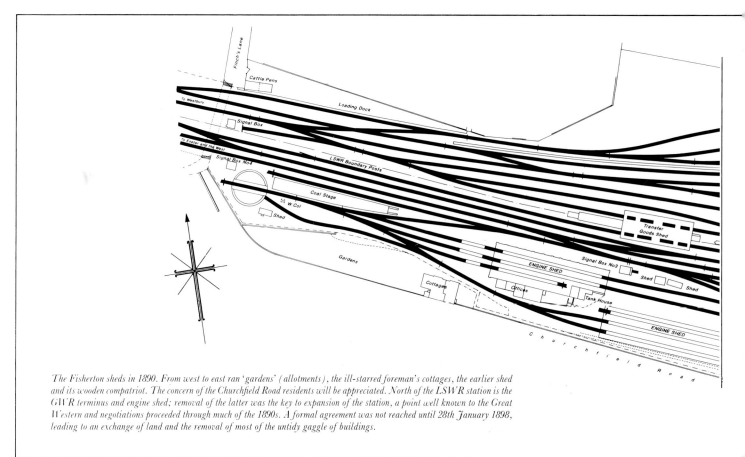

*The Fisherton sheds in 1890. From west to east ran 'gardens' (allotments), the ill-starred foreman's cottages, the earlier shed and its wooden compatriot. The concern of the Churchfield Road residents will be appreciated. North of the LSWR station is the GWR terminus and engine shed; removal of the latter was the key to expansion of the station, a point well known to the Great Western and negotiations proceeded through much of the 1890s. A formal agreement was not reached until 28th January 1898, leading to an exchange of land and the removal of most of the untidy gaggle of buildings.*

could comfort itself with turning down the more expensive proposition: A month later .....*Referring to Minute from last month re lengthening of engine shed at Salisbury, Mr. Strapp has supplied the following prices, £345 for two engines - £675 for four engines....the shed be lengthened for two engines*..... The work it can be imagined was not extensive. The brick building was lengthened by some forty feet, the most northerly of the three roads taken through the building to serve as a rearward loop. A doorway was also opened up for the middle road but was at this time not used. Having now been converted in some part at least to a through shed, better doors were required at either end .....*June 1870. Mr. Beattie requires doors to be provided at both ends of the shed at Salisbury. Mr. Strapp to consult with Mr. Beattie re cost*..... Strapp and Beattie discussed the matter fairly promptly, Strapp able to report at the following meeting .....*that doors had already been fitted to the west end and that the cost of doors for the east end would be £44.13.0d. Recommended*.....

By the late 1870s a number of further improvements had been carried out; No.2 road had been taken through the building to link via slip points to No.1 road near the station water tank, the coal stage had been lengthened from 60ft to an impressive 160ft and offices, stores, messroom, latrines and 'workroom' were added to the southern wall of the building. A larger 50ft turntable had been laid down and in 1876 £208 was approved for a new 'dropping pit' and siding accommodation and a 'soak hole' was added to the end of the coal stage. The burgeoning growth of the railway was sure to put considerable strain on the shed and although somewhat improved since opening, the accommodation was now wholly inadequate for the complement. A proposal for 'a new engine shed at Salisbury' came in the early part of 1883 - the building, in wood, was to be some 200ft in length and 50ft wide with again three through roads,

No.1 (and the most northerly) ending at stop blocks close by the offices of the first shed. It was to be adjacent to the earlier building and had pits on all roads, as well as in the yard at the eastern end, where a headshunt was provided to connect with the old shed. The roads at the western end ran onto the turntable. Churchfield Road separated the shed and Company property from the prosperous villas opposite, splendid properties backing onto the River Nadder, and a view of the industrial side of life did not commend itself to the occupants .....*25th June 1884, New Engine Shed Salisbury. Letter from Mr. W.H. Devenish and other owners of houses in close proximity to the site of the above shed asking that it may be erected so as to interfere as little as possible with their properties and that arrangements may be made to reduce the noise and carry off the smoke*..... The Committee recommended that 'all reasonable precautions be taken', which can hardly have reassured the good burghers of Salisbury.

The new shed opened in the early part of 1885 and more or less doubled the existing capacity. It was probable that engines entering did so at the west end, turning and coaling before disposal. All engines leaving would sensibly have done so at the other end of the yard clear of the coaling and watering areas. The two buildings sufficed for some ten years before the 'question of accommodation' was raised yet again; as early as 1895 the company was seeking new land and some ground to the far west of the station was selected, a total of about six acres between Cherry Orchard Lane and Churchfield Road. Churchfield Road was to be extended taking up an 'occupation road' in the process and linking with Cherry Orchard Lane, the land to the north of it reserved for the new shed and its yard. This was but part of an extensive scheme to completely rebuild the station and its approaches, the old shed and yard being swallowed up in the process. Around this time the GWR had

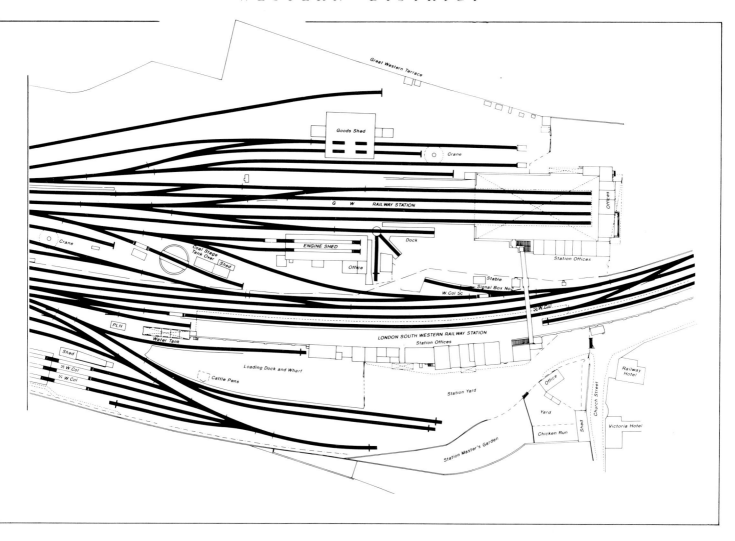

itself removed its own engine accommodation, from the (originally broad gauge) shed to a new site just off Finches Road. A smart new 'Dean' shed, with three roads and elevated coalstage, it opened about 1899.*

Progress on the LSW could be painfully slow and by the latter part of 1899 (even though all the necessary land had been purchased some years earlier) plans were still not complete. March of the following year finally saw the submission of structural drawings to the Committee and 'copies to Eastwood Swingler, the contractor'. (The latter are likely to have been concerned with ironwork only).

## THE NEW SHED - SALISBURY
### 'Thoroughly up to date and a model of modern requirements and management'

The new shed at Salisbury was a thoroughly 'standard' example of LSWR practice - a grand straight shed, high gabled with great strength and not a little elegance. By comparison with its predecessor(s) it was immense. There were ten roads, the northernmost reserved for lifting and repairing of locomotives, an overhead crane running the full length of the repair bay. The two roads on the south side were used for washing out and a number of hydrants were installed for this purpose. The

*Lyons - An Historical Survey of Great Western Engines Sheds - OPC 1972.

shed stood on slightly raised ground and access to the building came in the form of steps from Cherry Orchard Lane. Along this rear wall lay the staff accommodation - foreman and clerks offices, drivers lobby, cleaners room and beyond, stores, fitters shop and sand drying furnace. The building was constructed entirely in red brick with blue Staffordshire brick dressings. Deal had been used extensively in the construction of the roof with 'steel tie-bars and steel joists traversing the whole width of the shed'. A huge 100,000 gallon wrought iron tank stood adjacent, the rooms below it serving as a dormitory. This was far from idyllic, close in the shed yard but was standard practice and 'kept the men from straying'. 'All the modern conveniences' were supplied nonetheless; comfortable beds, washrooms, latrines and mess arrangements. The question of water supply to the new tank had been the subject of discussion at a Committee meeting in March 1901 .....*Water at Salisbury presently supplied (at 3d per 1,000 gallons) by the Fisherton Onger and Bemerton Water Co. and by the Salisbury Urban Sanitary Authority. These will be continued but in order to reach the new Engine Shed the Fisherton Co. will need to lay down a new 6ins main, cost about £600, in return for which they ask the company to take water for a period of ten years. Approved.....* A large 'standard' elevated coal stage was built, four engines able to coal simultaneously under the high, slated gables. Water columns were strategically placed throughout the yard and a 'standard' 55ft diameter turntable was put down between stage and water tank. The shed opened its doors to traffic in 1901 and *The Railway Magazine* was invited to comment in 1904:

Salisbury new shed, open and uncluttered on 18th April 1914. The locomotives include 122, 703, 549, 646, 452, 455 and 487. 'A branch of the Enginemen's and Firemen's Mutual Improvement Class is held at Salisbury,' according to *The Railway Magazine*, 'in a room provided for that purpose under the supervision and direction of Mr. D. Drummond, the railway's Locomotive Superintendent, who instituted these classes on the London and South Western Railway as a means of improving and perfecting the knowledge of the men in the mysteries of the steam engine and the ways and means of providing against or dealing with cases of failure etc.'

*J. Scrace Collection*

4-4-0 No. 115 and 0-4-2 No. 597 inside Salisbury on 30th July 1925. The mix of iron and timber in the construction of the shed will be apparent.

*H.C. Casserley*

**Salisbury on 18th September 1938. There were over sixty engines at the shed that day; Nos. 10, 16, 41, 118, 122, 237, 279, 288, 315, 317, 327, 330, 332, 333, 334, 335, 351, 361, 382, 389, 417, 437, 449, 451, 452, 453, 457, 475, 514, 531, 652, 654, 675, 691, 717, 737, 739, 746, 747, 748, 792, 824, 826, 829, 830, 831, 832, 930, 957, 1625, 1809, 1827, 1843, 1860, 1891, 2084, 2087, 2088, 2089, 2333, 3441.**

*W. A. Camwell*

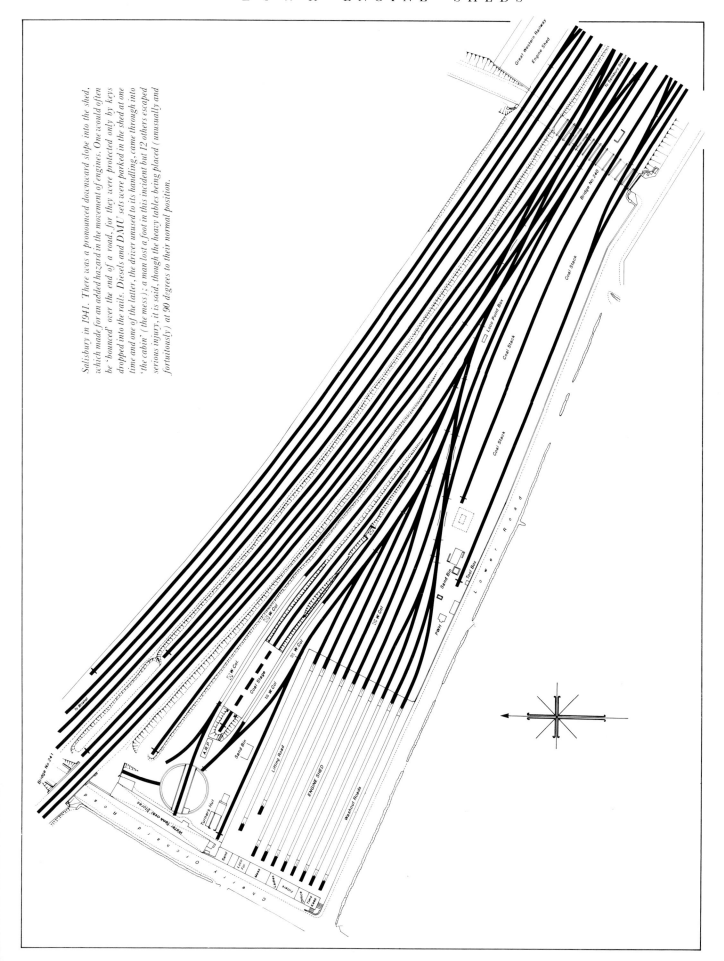

Salisbury in 1941. There was a pronounced downward slope into the shed, which made for an added hazard in the movement of engines. One would often be 'bounced' over the end of a road, for they were protected only by keys dropped into the rails. Diesels and DMU sets were parked in the shed at one time and one of the latter, the driver unused to its handling, came through into 'the cabin' (the mess); a man lost a foot in this incident but 12 others escaped serious injury, it is said, though the heavy tables being placed (unusually and fortuitously) at 90 degrees to their normal position.

Salisbury at the present day is one of the most important locomotive depots on the line, no less than forty-two engines being stabled there. All the regular main line trains between London and the West of England change engines in each direction at Salisbury, so that a large staff of modern express locomotives is necessary to cope with the traffic, and in addition power had to be provided for many 'local' services such as the trains to and from Southampton, Portsmouth, Wimborne and Bournemouth etc. together with short journey goods trains to those points and Andover and Basingstoke. Some of the latest and largest express locomotives designed by Mr. Dugald Drummond, the railway's chief mechanical engineer, are now stabled at Salisbury, and work between that station and Exeter or London.

Consequent on the large increase in the traffic and number of trains run, combined with the rebuilding of the passenger station etc. the shed at Salisbury was found quite insufficient to provide accommodation for the large number of engines required to be stationed there, and in February 1900 the directors of the railway decided to erect a new running shed to accommodate fifty engines, which was brought into use in December 1901, the site occupied by the old building being also required in connection with the station improvement scheme.....the building, as will be noticed, consists of five spans, excellently arranged to provide good and sufficient space and light for all purposes connected with the washing out and preparing of engines for duty etc. The walls are of brick and the pits bricked at the sides, with concrete floors and all are drained. Only two of these pits are utilised for washing out, eight hydrants being provided for that purpose, and these are specifically drained for rapidly carrying away the large quantity of water used in this operation. Each pit is provided with six electric light connections, and lamps are fitted with flexible tubes, so that light can be thrown on an engine standing in any position in the shed. The building itself is lighted by means of twenty large arc lamps with incandescent burners round the walls.

The crane or hoist, worked by hand power, for lifting and repairing engines, changing wheels etc. is of modern type and can be easily moved from one end of the shed to the other. At one end of the building are situated the offices, cabins, stores and fitting shop. All necessary running repairs to the engines stationed at Salisbury, as well as to those working to the station, are carried out by the mechanical staff attached to this depot comprising about fifty four men and boys.

In all respects the locomotive depot at Salisbury may be considered as thoroughly up to date and a model of modern requirements and management. The London and South Western Railway had recently erected a new shed at Eastleigh, Hants. of similar design but of bigger dimensions, and new engine sheds at Basingstoke and Andover etc. have been or are being completed. The shed was thus a splendid addition to the London South Western Locomotive Running Department and remains one of the company's most important and strategic depots.

By 1912 the 55ft turntable was the subject of debate at an engineer's meeting, in August of that year ......As to the turntable required at Waterloo (north side) - recommend the one at Salisbury, 55ft be transferred there and a new 65ft unit be purchased for use at Salisbury locomotive shed. Cowans Sheldon have agreed to supply one for £870, a duplicate of the table recently ordered from them..... It is not quite clear when this new 'table was put in and it next turns up in the Southern Railway Magazine around 1925 .....Modern Turntables - An engine of 180 tons turned by hand... The turntable .. is situated at Salisbury Locomotive Shed and is capable of turning the largest and heaviest engine which including table, weigh upwards of 180 tons.

The length of it is 65ft, the centre is mounted on roller bearings and the table is actuated by hand power; two other tables of the same dimensions at Nine Elms and Feltham are operated respectively by hydraulic and electric power. When an engine is about to be turned, the track on the turntable is made to coincide with the track on which the engine is standing. Locking bars, to prevent movement, are brought into operation, and the engine is then run on to the table until it is balanced and the whole weight is resting on the centre bearings.

The locking bars are now withdrawn and the table is rotated to the extent required.....

**0-4-2 No. 617 on the 'lifting road' (at the north side of the shed) on 19th July 1924.**

*H.C. Casserley*

Little rebuilding was necessary at Salisbury until National-isation. The iron water tank was 'renewed' and repairs effected to the coal stage in late LSWR days, amounting to £705. British Railways replaced the crumbling roof, at first the front portion only, in the asbestos sheeting and steel girders familiar through-out the 1950s (see in particular *BR Engine Sheds No.2 - A Southern Style, Irwell Press, 1989*)

The GWR shed located almost opposite, across the running tracks, had closed in 1950, the locos being 'disposed elsewhere over the system'. Western Region locomotives working in from Westbury were then serviced and stabled at the Southern Region shed. Yet a third, 70ft, turntable had been installed in 1956, probably the last major improvement carried out at the depot; locomotives were necessarily diverted, in some cases to the old GWR yard, *The Railway Magazine* reporting that with the turntable removed the pit was being enlarged by a bulldozer/crane. This recalled earlier days when engines from both sheds readily made use of either Company's 'tables in the event of maintenance or mishap.

Salisbury finally closed at the end of steam on the Southern Region, at midnight 9th July 1967, along with Nine Elms and Guildford. The shed stood decaying and empty for a number of years but was later demolished, the site marked by straight rows of *buddleia*, ideally suited to the well drained, rubble-filled pits.

### 'Shuntin'? We never stopped'

Salisbury had proved a convenient staging-point in the early years of the LSWR, neatly dividing the main line so that engines and crews either from Salisbury or from the London or Exeter ends were not (in theory) over extended in hours or effort. In its essentials this was the system worked by the shed until the end of steam. This constant engine (and later crew)

changing characterised the work to a degree possibly unique, at least for the rigid absolutism of the practice and the way in which it survived with so little change even into the 1960s. The Southern in fact compromised; through running enabled no better use of engines between London and Exeter in the absence of enough up and down trains to balance the engine workings each day. This problem was to lead to the withdrawal, in fact, of the early SR main line diesels, following disappointing daily mileages. There was thus an endless to and fro of engines from the shed to the station and yards, in response to the daily round of train working. Summers at Salisbury mirrored those at Exmouth Junction - hectic, frantic, crowded and improvised.

Engines due to relieve down trains stood behind Salisbury West Box on the south side of the main line between the shed and the station. Standing in the shed yard the driver would give a whistle signal to indicate the destination of his engine (2 crows for up, one for down) and it would be drawn forward to its holding point behind West Box, on the instructions of a man in the 'Point Box' by the shed exit roads. These were delivered magisterially and incoherently, unless one was familiar with everything that was going on, through an army-style tannoy mounted on poles in the shed yard. Throughout 24 hours obscure commands 'right ll o'clock Exeter' or whatever would crackle out, drifting sometimes with peculiar clarity across to the houses beyond Lower Road. The engine off a down train would come forward past the West Box, reversing into the position occupied seconds before by the replacement engine, already 'away' and coupling up for the onward journey on the Exeter line. As the replacement engine made off with its train past the shed, the engine which had worked it down from London was hurrying to the yard to coal and turn.

The Salisbury tannoy would call out an engine destined for an up working with the command 'xxxx (usually garbled but

**No.181 outside the shed on 19th June 1926. Behind the tank engine is the western extremity of the West Yard, at times given over as a coal stacking ground. Distantly beyond, to the north across the main line, is the westernlight roof of the Great Western engine shed.**

*H.C. Casserley*

The south side of the coal stage, later equipped with a belt (the 'opper) with E411 and E083 on 28th April 1928. By the north wall of the shed was a sort of stores road, wagons of spares, oil drums and other bits and off it (disappearing here behind the men and water column) runs the line known as the 'corner'. Engines would be left here after leaving the turntable ready to be grouped for stabling.

*H.C. Casserley*

No.17 on the north side disposal road, 20th May 1935, the 'Windsor Side' named after a pub actually some distance off. It was, as the crow flies the nearest to the coal stage.

*H.C. Casserley*

**The coal stage amidst a wasteland of ash and clinker.**

known to the crew) - Waterloo' - this was the signal to proceed to a holding place at the east, up, end of the station opposite East Box and the Salisbury Market branch. The spur here could hold up to three locos, the train engine coming forward and reversing back through the station to the shed whilst the replacement engine promptly backed out onto the train and took it forward to London or wherever.

Between the station and the shed then, a stream of light engines clattered by, a bewildering succession serving only to further complicate matters on a summer Saturday. Salisbury on such occasions played a great part in traffic to and from the West, but there was also a considerable freight business to be dealt with. Trains came with great regularity, more or less to booked times, with many by convention afforded names. Household coal alone might be worked through Salisbury in several trains in a single day, *the Bassaleg*, *the Radyr*, *the Aberdare*, and so on. *The Avonmouth* was a regular mixed train, often including tobacco. These and other long vanished traffics sustained a considerable body of shunting and pilot work at Salisbury, divided and sorted in the East and West yards. Mixed loads from Exeter - rails, loco coal (from South Wales by sea, through Fremington Dock), tar, petrol, went principally to the East Yard and required two pilots. The yard lay to the east of the station on the up side of the line and became so busy in the Second World War that two separate parts had to be designated, A and B. B sidings comprised the northernmost set of tracks by 'Dunns Farm Seeds ', with a lengthy headshunt alongside the main line, out across the River Avon. A G6 0-6-0T No. 279 was on this job in the war years, through until about 1948. The A side lay between B and the running lines; the work was rather less onerous but both shunts were booked for 24 hours, remanned through the day as shift changes demanded. At busy times the new crew would walk down to the yard, along

Lower Street and across the station, or the engine might be recrewed at the shed, when a necessary run back for coal could be arranged to coincide with a crew change. A Z 0-8-OT later served at the East Yard, No 957 handling any shunting duty that might arise.

The West Yard was a more drawn out affair on the (down) side. Its western extremity brought it within the confines of the shed yard (the three tracks serving the coal stack) and it extended eastward past West Box to the southern edges of the station. All manner of freight came in here to and from Feltham, Eastleigh and Exeter 'and almost anywhere else'; there were two stopping goods every day for Templecombe alone at the time of Nationalisation and the incessant shunting was the work of the West Yard Gang, manning a shunting tank through three shifts a day. It was no trouble simply to roll down to the shed in a spare moment and take whatever supplies of coal, water or tea might be necessary. The East and West Yards were mirrored by East and West Carriage Sidings, worked by M7 0-4-4Ts largely during the day only. The sidings to the west, where Bournemouth trains were generally got ready ran more or less opposite the engine shed, alongside the Great Western running lines whilst the East carriage sidings were on the down side, opposite A and B. The M7s worked between the station and these two yards to east and west and shunted the station as necessary. Coal would probably last the entire shift and water was taken from the station columns; these and the examples in the shed were charged with an enormous pressure, far beyond that normally encountered elsewhere. They were justly renowned for this singular feature and were accordingly worked with some considerable circumspection. This peculiar force was no accident and derived from the need to water two tenders simultaneously at either end of the station.

4-4-0 at the stage. Coal at Salisbury came from the west, good South Wales steam coal brought in through Fremington Dock. In times of shortage it was usual to get Kent coal, Betshanger or Tilmanstone, said to stick like toffee (or worse) to the firebars, and its arrival was generally greeted with dismay. Welsh coal also came via Bristol and later on the various briquettes were tried, to the usual scorn.

'The 'Opper' on 12th September 1965, with BR Standard 4-6-0 No. 75077. Pacifics had arrived at Salisbury in the war and a mechanical belt feed apparatus was put in for them. Their tenders were too high for the Salisbury stage but the north, 'Windsor' side was not similarly equipped and the less straightforward expedient of lowering the coaling road was employed instead.

*W. Potter*

The Great Western shed on 18th September 1938 with Moguls, a 2-8-2T, a Castle *Earl of Shaftesbury*, a Manor *Childrey Manor*, a Star *Princess Alice*, 2-8-0s and pannier tanks. It was put up at LSWR expense closing apparently at the end of 1950 and though engines and men were officially transferred across to the Southern shed, it continued in use for stabling. The transfer took effect on a Saturday night and the Western Region men were merged into the old Southern links, to some unpleasantness, for a few SR drivers lacking seniority were reduced to firing duties. Three GW drivers - 'the Gang of Three' inevitably - chose to keep to familiar workings and for three years until retirement, worked only (with SR firemen) the 7.44 a.m. Temple Meads and return, the 1.40 p.m. Bristol Stapleton Road, returning from Temple Meads, the 11.17 a.m. Cardiff return 4.45 p.m. to Salisbury .'and two Sundays in three'. There was no nights and no preparation/disposal all this being done at Cardiff and Bristol .. 'an 'oliday'.

*W.A. Camwell*

**Drummond 0-4-4T No. E25 on the over girder 'table, 28th April 1928.**

The 'Fisherton Shunt' was an inheritance from the Great Western shed, coming across with the transfer of the Western Region men. With classic railway devotion to continuity, it was contrived to put a pannier tank on this job for as long as possible. A Drummond tank was normally on the Market House branch pilot turn; the short line was steep and could be treacherous even with light loads. There was Main & Sons agricultural seedsmen at the top, a builders yard in the middle and the coal yard at the bottom (the connection to the Market House itself had been severed by 1929) serving 'the Electric Light Place' - the Electricity Board. All might be shunted daily, the tank engine like most of these jobs crewed by 'not to go' or 'cripple' link men, cleaners on their early firing turns and so on. The Milford shunt was probably the furthest flung such job, the Milford yard a busy one with a shed for box wagon traffic, the working demanding a 24 hour shunt and three or four trips a day to Salisbury. Relief crews were allowed an hour on a shift to cross the city from the main shed.

### East and West - 'City Breeds and Shorthorns'

There were many parallels in the working arrangements with those at Exmouth Junction - big links of 12 'doubled up' to 24, a highly specialised top passenger link, stone trains, a large and highly flexible spare link and similar goods links. This was hardly surprising in that the two depots worked closely similar trains, the very same for much of the time. The nature and amount of traffic and its patterns have wholly changed since those days, when trains worked doggedly in stages, from one yard or junction to the next.

The Salisbury men naturally considered themselves the elite of the line and viewed others, not all-together lightheartedly,

with a mix of pity and suspicion; *City Breeds* was a pejorative term originally applied to certain locos transferd down from the London area, though it is difficult to dissociate the twin notions - were they lousy engines and therefore a London conspiracy or were the London blokes simply incompetent? It was good fun either way. Scorn for 'the puds' grew strictly in ratio to distance from London and in time honoured cliche, if the Londoners were spivs the Exeter lot were dullards - *shorthorns*. At the bottom of the Salisbury links were the usual 'cripples' or 'not to go' men barred through eyesight deficiencies or injury or convicted of various transgressions; 'shed men' or 'p & d blokes' (preparation and disposal) and cleaners having a go. There were two links of twelve mostly confined to Salisbury shed and the various pilots round about but a 'Bulford Gang' worked a passenger train there from Salisbury No.6 bay - three return trips with an M7 taking water by the East Box. There was also an Amesbury job, double heading a goods with an M7 and a Jubilee 0-4-2. The tender engine would proceed to shunt at Amesbury, the tank coming back to Salisbury with a passenger train.

Preparation and disposal of engines by the crew was not rigidly enforced nor was it regarded as inconceivable, as on the Great Western. Gangs existed for 'p & d' and to manoeuvre engines around the shed but crews, depending often on the particular link or turn within it and of course the time (booked or available) frequently took some part in disposal. The crew would in any event ensure that the fire had been run down to the minimum before reaching the shed and at Salisbury engines conventionally ran first of all onto one of the two coal stage roads. Scurrying around the stage, in and out of its pits and glimpsed only briefly (by the whites of their eyes) through the various openings were a succession of coalmen and 'not to gos'

Turning at Salisbury. The base of the immense water tank was designed (it doesn't look it) as a dormitory, according to the original *Railway Magazine* account. Certainly such provision was in mind however; in March 1898 the Locomotive Superintendent is recommending 'Dormitories for 10 men at Nine Elms and Exmouth Junction .. question of dormitories for Yeovil and Salisbury .. can remain over for the present'.

The 'standard' 'table on 18th November 1954, a year or so before its replacement by an undergirder unit. Odd stores were placed round about, unloaded and loaded from open wagons using the gantry over the turntable road. With it such items as axles etc., could be hoisted up and set down; it was moreover handy for the odd coal stage tub, hurled out by younger firemen in misplaced enthusiasm.

arranged in shifts. There were two coalmen each side of the stage, that is, four per shift. Two shovelled the traditional wheeled tubs provided when the shed was originally constructed; these remained in use on the north (or 'Windsor' side - it was closest, by a certain convoluted logic to the *Windsor* pub), whilst on the south side closest to the shed an elevator or conveyor belt christened the 'Opper (Hopper) was provided. The belt seems to have been introduced for the Merchant Navy Pacifics, their tender sides too high for the original tubs. This led to complications as more and more Pacifics came into use and the north road was eventually lowered by a foot or two, putting the 'Windsor side' out of action for a number of weeks. There was a shedman on each of the pits either side of the stage through 24 hours, though crews played their part and both men arranged matters to best advantage. Cleaners were pressed into service at peak times and it was hot and dreadful work - the ash and char in a King Arthur smokebox might be heaped half way up the door, a terrible dry gasp of heat and dust as the stuff tumbled out over the buffers.

The turners knew the shed and its yard intimately, every nuance of slope and bump, the precise capacity of any road whatever the combination of locomotives, the quickest way of reorganising a queue of engines for the off next morning and the exact capabilities and characteristics of engines almost devoid of steam. An engine was moved forward from whatever coal stage road it occupied and turned (if the next duty so demanded) on the vacuum operated 'table. It was then moved off on the road between the coal stage and shed yard. It was usually then dumped on 'the corner' a useful point where an engine could be left clear of all roads for the turner and his mate (three sets covering 24 hours) to determine its ultimate position. They were armed with the usual list which revealed what engine might be doing next but on a rainy afternoon with night coming on, instinct, brute force and strong nerves were demanded.

The turners sensibly declined Sunday work - by 1 a.m. on a Monday the yard was more or less swamped with four or five engines on every outside road. Spare men, 'strappers' in some arcane usage, were drafted in for the 10 o'clock Sunday night shift. It was the worst time of the week and it was advisable to use one engine properly fired up to move the rakes of engines. On an ordinary day it was customary to make use of whatever loco might be handy, putting it aside for another as it became bereft of steam. In the early 1950s one of the pannier tanks inherited from the Western was found suited to this task whilst later on a BR standard tank found favour.

Moving up from cleaning, shed and pilot duties meant firing in the Goods Link. This in turn appears to have been divided into two, notionally at least; the Stone Train Link and the Goods proper. Top Link firemen generally entered the Stone Link as drivers and the work included much that was not strictly 'stone'. Salisbury men at one time worked through to Meldon on the trains, for years an unpopular turn through the necessity to lodge in dilapidated and unsavoury cottages near the station - Such 'Double Homes' had long become alien to Southern men. Most of these trains in the period of the Second World War and after seem to have been worked by H15 4-6-0s in the 330-335 series. They were unloved at Salisbury and the story went that other sheds had a similar ill regard; the H15s were sent away at intervals to Feltham and Exmouth Junction 'but they always seemed to come back'. These were the 'city breeds' proper, a mocking reference to their days at Nine Elms where the crews it was said were unable to adapt to the long flat box. Exeter men, the 'shorthorns' on account of the cattle trains worked in from the west were adjudged a fair second to Salisbury men but the London blokes would scarcely be charged with Salisbury junior work .. ...most of the Meldon loads were ballast, invariably destined for railway use and also fine chippings for concrete, known as 'Meldon dust.' The rest of Salisbury goods workings took men and engines everywhere, to

**The endless 'prep & disposal' at Salisbury, 31st May 1929. Engines are 162, 148, 755, 579 and 512.**

*H.C. Casserley*

Nine Elms, Exeter and Southampton, varied work, often very hard and frequently at night. One engine with forty or more on meant repeated buffering up and tying down. About the only fitted trains were the 'Tavy goods' most of it perishables and originating west of Exeter - the 'Tavies' of Plymouth Friary and Exmouth Junction.

The Spare Gang as at Exeter was the largest link, a versatile 'go anywhere' group with an astoundingly comprehensive route knowledge. A reflection again both of the great variety and seasonal peaks experienced at Salisbury, the spares covered all sickness and holidays and specials, passenger and goods on all routes. Spare gang men could find themselves on all manner of turns and locomotives from day to day. 'Black Motor' 0-6-0s on the Bournemouth goods, Saturday expresses with Merchant Navy Pacifics, or local passenger work. This was available in almost any variety, relieving Schools 4-4-0s on London - Yeovil jobs and T9s on paper trains to Yeovil Town, turning at Junction and coming back with a stopping passenger.

No. 2 Link was frequently regarded as the best with a good mix of work, stopping and fast and a few turns which were comparable to Top Link jobs (the Top Link wouldn't work nights). No. 2 even had the *Devon Belle* trundling off to the siding at Wilton to change engines there. The Top Link was envied by many depots, twelve turns with nine attracting mileage payments. All the jobs were to Exeter or London, Salisbury having the best of the Southern main line work. The three non-mileage turns were one each to Portsmouth, Yeovil and Basingstoke; relaxed workings which were far from unwelcome, they leavened the main line work and really the crew needed the rest. As a rule all engines were changed at Salisbury and a day's work took one either to Waterloo, turning at Nine Elms or to Exeter Central (not to St. Davids) retiring to the 'Junction' for servicing. At Waterloo the engine simply backed out of the terminus for the shed and returned a couple of hours later. At Exeter Central the procedure was rather different and entirely in keeping with the propensity in the west for dividing and joining trains. An up working with a Salisbury Pacific or 4-6-0 would mean backing down from Exmouth Junction; with an expected load of thirteen coaches made up often 'in six and seven,' seven from Ilfracombe maybe and six from Plymouth. The first portion came in, the engine immediately uncoupling and running forward across the scissors to allow the Salisbury engine to back down. This portion would be drawn forward for the second train to come in, the whole backing down to form the thirteen coach train. Down engines to replace those off trains for the west waited at the down end of Central station in sidings known as 'the field'. Exeter Central was yet one more hectic bottleneck on the road to the west, where even the station pilot could be booked for losing time.

**The shed in re-roofed style, 6th September 1959. Western Region engines could usually be found throughout the 1950s, though it reflected a tradition of co-operation between the two neighbouring sheds. In particular either company would make use of the other's turntable in time of trouble. There was no standby engines as such at Salisbury, despite its strategic position - 'one had to be dug out and got ready quick' in emergency.**

*W. Potter*

**The shed achieved the status almost of a hallow in the last years and was notable for the lines of dead locomotives (en-route to South Wales scrapyards) months after closure.**

*E. Wilmshurst*

*Shaw Savill* **in brighter times. The Pacifics were well liked, despite early problems. The valves, it was rumoured were very finicky and the Merchant Navy 4-6-2s were christened 'homebirds' such was the early failure rate. The trailing truck 'shook the fire out' when advanced in wear but firebox cleaning was easier - 'they used to chuck most of it through the chimney'.**

*P. J. Kelley*

The best and classic views of the shed at Yeovil were to be obtained from the footpath climbing the hill opposite. From there the strange cluster of high roofs , two of the station and one the shed could be observed. 12th April 1925.

# Yeovil, Chard and Templecombe

**Town or Junction?**

Gillingham had acted as temporary terminus to the Salisbury and Yeovil Railway since its opening in May 1859 and a small two road shed had been provided (see elsewhere). Early on Joseph Beattie, the Locomotive Superintendent, was aware that some form of accommodation would next be required at Yeovil: 'May 1860. Read letter from Mr Beattie and Mr Scott as to providing a temporary engine shed at Yeovil *Junction* station. Referred to The Board' (author's italics). The Junction station of the nominally independent Salisbury and Yeovil Railway opened on 1st June 1860 (plans were already advanced for a branch from here to the town) and the link with Exeter was complete on 19th July. There is little evidence as to what Beattie had in mind for the Junction station; engines quite clearly were being dealt with from the first and some form of shed seems to have been in course of erection, or at least contemplated, towards the end of 1860: *Read letter from Mr Beattie with report from the Locomotive Foreman at Exeter Queen Street as to the necessity for the early completion of the engine shed at Yeovil Junction Station. Mr Tite to be written to, urging the immediate completion of the work.....*

Details for this period are hard to come by, save a 'deposited plan' showing only the barest of detail. The turntable is observed to be on the up side (latterly the engine servicing area was located on the down side, Exeter end) but the goods transfer shed is marked, as is the water tank. What appears to have been a coal stage lay adjacent to the turntable whilst an unmarked building stood opposite. This may or may not have been the engine shed and no clear conclusion is possible as to whether the drawing depicts existing or proposed arrangements.

The branch to Yeovil Town was opened on 1st June 1861, a long curving line running (for a stretch) parallel with the Great Western Weymouth route from Pen Mill. Just before the South Western line swung westward into the joint station at Yeovil Town a loop from the GWR station was laid, to facilitate through running to Town and on to Taunton. The station at Town was 'joint' property and a plan details the buildings and land either owned solely or jointly by either company. The Officers Committee recommended 'the enlargement of the engine shed at Yeovil for the accommodation of three more engines' in July 1866 though it is impossible to divine this reference; whether it relates to a building at the Junction or to a shed at Town station. An Officers Committee Minute of December 1868 is similarly unenlightening .....*Recommended-....that the coal stage at Yeovil station be lengthened....at a cost not exceeding £55.....*

Only by 1880 can the Town shed be absolutely 'fixed' from documents but an origin in the 1860s must remain probable. A 'Junction' engine shed with increasing confidence, can be seen as its 'predecessor'.

## YEOVIL TOWN

The shed at Yeovil Town was high and lofty and well laid out, the earliest and eccentric arrangements of the 1830s and 1840s abandoned for something recognisably akin to subsequent conventional practice. The site at Yeovil laboured under cramped conditions after a few years. It was constrained by Newton Road, a stream and the station itself; there was a turntable for many years, 'two coal stages' for a time and an

**Yeovil in the early days, long before its turntable was removed. The lines to Pen Mill and Yeovil Junction hurried out of sight under a low bridge, creating the illusion of a terminus.**

office building serving in the first years as enginemens dormitory. Three roads ran the entire length of the brick building, the whole covered by a pitched roof in 'Countess Slate'. Pits were supplied throughout with another two outside. Lifting was carried out on No.1 road, using a hand operated crane. Stores ran alongside the south wall of the building with adjacent workshops and boiler house. It remained much in this original condition over many years, its solid construction and high beams proof against the long onslaught of time. Upon removal of the turntable the ground formerly occupied became a siding, requiring the foreman to book his engine duties according to how they stood for up or down trains, avoiding as far as possible a light run to the Yeovil Junction 'table. In December 1917 it was decided that an old van body should be fitted up .....*for the accommodation of Engine Cleaners employed at that place. The total cost including foundations, fittings and lighting will be about £31.... Approved.....* Modest in the extreme, the new accommodation was nevertheless a considerable improvement; it was still there, in a state of advanced dilapidation, until the last years, when it was rebuilt in brick.

Although two coal stages existed at Yeovil the larger and southernmost served principally as coal stack. The smaller, and more conveniently sited, underwent some renovation work in 1920 .....*as a protection against the weather it is proposed that a covering should be provided at the locomotive coal stage at Yeovil. The estimated cost of the work is £176 plus a sum of £6/10s for lighting. The Engineers Committee by their Minute of today have ordered the work to be proceeded with subject to approval of this committee. Approved.....* One of the last acts of the LSWR was to approve the installation of a new sand bin in 1921 at Yeovil Junction. For many years previously engines had either travelled to Town shed or made use of a limited supply placed under the water tank. This had proved 'most unsatisfactory' and 'prey to damp'.

Yeovil was always a cramped and awkward shed to operate, over two miles from the main line which was its principal concern, with frequent light engine movements. Stabling space was extremely limited and at weekends in particular little spare room was available. The basilisk stare of the General Manager was apt to turn itself upon country places, particularly in the summertime and the great man descended on Yeovil in a grand tour of the west in August 1935. Sir Herbert Walker as a consequence moved the Traffic Manager, E C Cox, .....*to undertake to arrange for the Investigation Committee to overhaul the services at Yeovil Town and Sidmouth Junction with a view to seeing how the timetable could be improved in this respect.....* Turning to the problems suffered at the shed it was noted under the heading 'Engine Workings'.....*when visiting Yeovil Town it was mentioned that this Depot has 14 Engines, many of which are used for passenger services. From an examination of the timetable it would appear that the local services between Salisbury and Exeter are broken up into too many sections, which include change of engine en route....*

The Traffic Manager was requested to review the whole of the workings but little change in the circumstances was warranted; the question was whether services could be 'overhauled with a view to seeing if they can be revised in such a manner so to effect economy in engine power without detriment to the travelling facilities'. Local trains out of Yeovil Junction however were timed to make connections with, and act as feeders to, the Waterloo fasts, without getting in the way ....*It becomes a question whether Yeovil Town is the most convenient place for stabling the engines, many of which have to run light for considerable distances......the Investigation Committee are to examine the workings and see whether by redistribution, the number or engines employed could be reduced, or whether there are other places, such as Templecombe, where it could be more convenient to stable some of the engines with a view to avoiding light running.....* Indeed some considerable effort was

**Yeovil turntable about 1908. The yard never seemed less than crowded and the 'table was ordered 'removed' in a Minute of 1917: 'Recommended .. that the 43ft Turn Table .. be dispensed with as it is out of repair and no longer required.' The track was ever afterwards 'The Turntable Road'.**

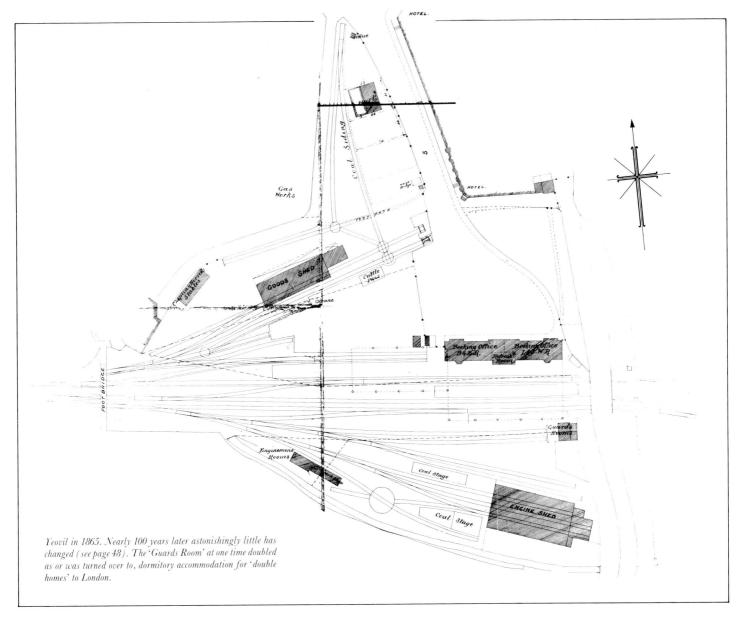

*Yeovil in 1865. Nearly 100 years later astonishingly little has changed (see page 48). The 'Guards Room' at one time doubled as or was turned over to, dormitory accommodation for 'double homes' to London.*

expended by the Land Agent at Waterloo to find space at Templecombe. The cost of infilling made the project questionable from the first and it was in any case impossible to envisage the likelihood of the Yeovil workforce (over 100 men) willingly transferring to so small a village.

The original shed roof was replaced after the Second World War, the central ridge vent supplanted by simple asbestos sheeting and the arched doorways were cut back to ease a dangerous lack of clearance. The old water tank installed in the roof had long proved of insufficient capacity and with the transfer of Western Region stock to the shed the SR constructed a tall metal tower with tank.

Rejuvenation of 'Town's' allocation took place in 1959 due to the demise of the former GW shed at Pen Mill. 'All stock', which numbered some ten locomotives, 2-6-2Ts and some pannier tanks, was transferred to Yeovil Town. The Southern shed could accommodate something like eighteen small locomotives; it had long been an engine changing point and in the 1950s through workings were set up as far afield as Portsmouth. Transfer along with Exmouth Junction, Barnstaple and Wadebridge to the Western Region took place in 1963, the shed closing completely in June 1965. A number of locomotives continued to use the shed, notably those working in off the former GWR routes; however, demolition soon followed and the site was converted by the local authority to a car park.

## CHARD

Two other sheds were associated with Yeovil - Chard and Templecombe, the parent shed supplying locomotives to both. Chard Road (latterly Junction) had opened with the Yeovil and Exeter line on 18th July 1860, along with a number of other stations on the route to Exeter Queen Street. A branch was later proposed from here 'three miles distant' to a station at Chard Town. The line opened in May 1863 and the London and South Western took control in 1864. The company had come under serious criticism from some residents of Chard, for initially passing their town by, 'noted as it was for its production of lace and cloth'. The branch was ostensibly privately sponsored but with the GW broad gauge winding its way ominously down to the town from the north the South Western took fright. It was a potential infiltration conduit and purchase was accordingly swift. The Great Western line was complete by 1866, trains running through from Taunton to a joint station located just north of the LSWR premises at Chard Town. The journey between the two was by way of a converted tramway and carried passengers for the first time on 26th November 1866. *(For most of this detail see Williams' LSWR History, David & Charles)*

A small shed had been erected at Chard Town for the independent company and had opened with the line. Built on the down side it measured approximately 50ft by 20ft with a

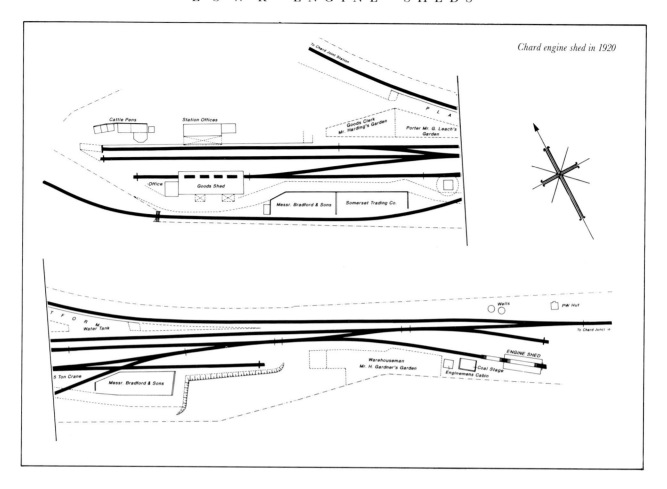

*Chard engine shed in 1920*

small coal stage and enginemens cabin erected outside. It was a through building and from the only photograph thus far uncovered *(see the forthcoming history of Chard by Ian Harrison, to be published by Wild Swan)* it would appear to have been clad in corrugated iron. The roof had a curved habit, something after a 'Dutch barn'. No turntable was ever installed at Chard Town but following the arrival of the Great Western a 43ft 3ins example was put in for the use of both companies, at the joint station. This was necessarily of mixed gauge and a plan examined shows the work involved and the areas of the layout which allowed for mixed running. Almost no documentary evidence has been unearthed but in 1899 it is recorded that one engine was outstationed from Yeovil for the shuttle service between Junction and Joint stations. A small amount of shunting would also have been carried out, mainly local commodities and livestock. By Grouping the shed had lost its 'allocation', the engine returning to Yeovil nightly. The station had been given over to industrial use as early as 1920, all trains running into Joint station thereafter. The shed was removed in December 1929 only the site, covered in rubble and overgrown, remaining by 1935.

## TEMPLECOMBE

Templecombe, a centuries-old Somerset village, had long been only a collection of dwellings, huddled close to, but little changed by, the invading West of England main line of the LSWR. The Somerset and Dorset Railway from Wincanton created a busy junction but the village slumbered much as before, passengers awaiting connections finding little diversion other than *The Royal Oak*.

Whatever its shortcomings for passengers, better accommodation was soon necessary for locomotives off the growing transfer freights; to this end a small wooden shed opened in 1863 at the S&D 'Templecombe Lower', housing engines of both companies.

Relations between the two were not entirely harmonious and a rather indignant Beattie read a letter to the Locomotive Committee on 8th December 1867, stating that .....*at the request of the Somerset and Dorset Company, this Company's engine has been removed from the above accommodation ( Templecombe) and asking for instructions as to the water pipes and washing valve which remain at the shed.....* The only recorded response is a concern for LSWR property .....*The articles to be removed if the Somerset and Dorset do not pay value, viz £7/13s/9d.....* Thus ejected without ceremony the LSWR shunting tank must needs have stood outside thereafter, or come daily from Yeovil.

The completion of the western connecting spur in 1871 allowed for the through running of trains from the LSW onto the S&D and *vice versa*. On the up side extensive yards were put in to allow for the reforming of trains, with a need for a shunting engine available more or less continuously. In January of 1871 the LSWR Officers Committee accordingly recommended 'an engine pit at Templecombe Station. Work to be done and charged to revenue'. The minutes from this time maintain a dogged silence and it is only possible to speculate on how the recommendation eventually transmuted itself into a shed building. A new shunter arrived in 1877 - 'Approved, the purchase of 12 shunting engines, one for Templecombe.....'

By 1885 an official plan shows the shed, at the head of an extensive headshunt. The line ran over the Somerset & Dorset, hence the epithet 'Templecombe Upper' but the description was probably not used by the LSWR. Of modest proportions

**Templecombe shed around 1934, with K10 4-4-0 No 145. The place was a strange one with an evil reputation - Yeovil administered it and drivers who made application to serve there or were sent for disciplinary reasons,** *never came back ..*
*W.A. Camwell*

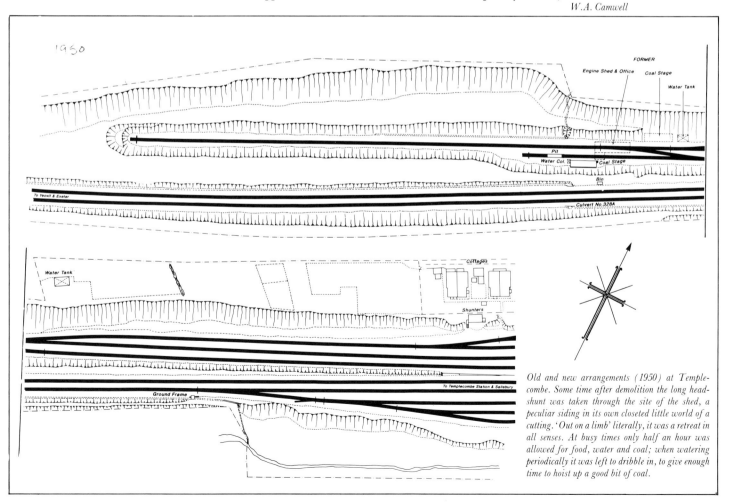

*Old and new arrangements (1950) at Temple-combe. Some time after demolition the long head-shunt was taken through the site of the shed, a peculiar siding in its own closeted little world of a cutting. 'Out on a limb' literally, it was a retreat in all senses. At busy times only half an hour was allowed for food, water and coal; when watering periodically it was left to dribble in, to give enough time to hoist up a good bit of coal.*

(32ft x 15ft) it was a solid timber construction with 'a blue tiled floor'. The walls stood on firm foundations of brick and a small mess room with stove made up the very limited accommodation. A pit ran the length of the building and louvres on the front gable ushered smoke away. Outside, coal was tossed by hand from a sleeper coal stage whilst water was supplied (although this was a much later addition) from a small tank perched atop a tower of local stone. Water had been a considerable problem for the railway here for many years and the literature is punctuated with references to the difficulties. The tank at the station held 25,000 gallons which 'during the summer months is greatly diminished'. Considerable correspondence was raised on the matter over the years, too lengthy to detail here but by the latter part of the century the matter still required resolution .....*15th January 1890.....yet again there is deficient water supply at Templecombe; propose 4 miles of pipe from Buckhorn Weston Tunnel where there is an abundant water supply.... with reservoir the total cost would be £2,020. The supply would only be used for locomotive purposes by the application of Seales patent water purifying apparatus to the engine boilers.....* This it seems would have complicated matters unduly and the simple expedient was adopted instead, to 'minimise the water consumption'. Nevertheless more references in 1890 seem to indicate further work and £1600 was ordered .....*for the improvement of the water supply at Templecombe.....*

A set of enginemen resided at Templecombe, and Yeovil normally supplied a G6 shunting tank, changed fortnightly. Train engines were also used for shunting and by about 1950 the work was heavy enough to warrant a Z 0-8-0T. Some disaster had struck the building in the middle part of the 1930s - it was in good condition in 1935 but wholly demolished by the following year. The cause could be attributed to fire although gales may have put paid to the tiny building. Locos continued to stable at the site, making use of the pit, coal stage and water supply. During rearrangements of the yards in the Second

World War it was found necessary to remove what remained to a new site, a little nearer the main line (see plan). The coal stage was dismantled and re-erected on a spur off the headshunt whilst 'the shed' was reincarnated through a pit and water column, a coach body serving as a mess/store.

Yeovil and both the Templecombe establishments, the LSWR at Upper and the Somerset & Dorset at Lower, came under Southern Region management upon Nationalisation and the Z 0-8-0 shunter was sent to the former S&D shed. There was now little need for separate pit and coal stage though it is quite probable that these saw further use right up to the latter part of the 1950s. By 1963 rearrangement of the sidings had seen all trace swept away.

**Nippers**

Yeovil was a place of great contrast; its position astride the west of England main line meant it played a considerable part in the passenger and goods working thereof, yet the shed itself lay two miles away in a seemingly sleepy backwater. A characteristic feature of work was the constant to and fro between the Town station and 'the Junction' on the main line. It had several aspects - it was useful for crews on the Junction - Town workings to include passed men, instantly available in emergency, whilst simultaneously proving an agreeable last resting place for a variety of old boys. Certain disposal jobs were usefully carried out down at the Junction but an extra complication was added to the turning of engines.

The shed played an essential role in the operation of the 88 miles between Salisbury and Exeter; besides train working it provided emergency locos and a breakdown gang. For the man in charge it was 'generally regarded as a stepping stone', an experience for those destined for further promotion. By the mid 1930s things had hardly changed since the earliest days though the Southern was an increasingly recognised institution,

**G6 No 238, 13th September 1936, on the site of the shed, before removal of the coalstage and extension of the headshunt. With any number of wagons at Templecombe on a night shift the Upper Yard tank could be hard pressed. It was 'three-shifted' at the 'Top End'; 6 p.m. - 2 a.m, 2 -10 a.m. 10 a.m.- 6 p.m, changed every Saturday night for washout/repairs at Yeovil (there would be trouble on its return if it wasn't clean enough underneath..)** *W.A. Camwell*

**Apart from odd engines off trains there was a second pilot at Templecombe, a small 4-4-0 which came on at about 10.30 in the evening at the station end, its purpose to assist Somerset and Dorset trains from Templecombe lower to the Southern yard or from the station to the yard. This practice thus made for two engines at Templecombe at night and only one throughout the main part of the day. 9th July 1949, engine No. 30134.**

*H.C. Casserley*

especially in the person of the guv'nor, a man whose youth could seem out of kilter with the power he wielded. There was a body of older drivers at Yeovil entrenched by tradition, who would report a cleaner if he so much as ventured on a footplate yet they, to the young men, could seem further remote in years from the guv'nor than themselves. In the 1930s this could be confusing. Yeovil cleaners in 1935 were organised into three gangs, the oldest and thereby most privileged coming on at noon on a Sunday. The three gangs covered 6 a.m. - 2 p.m., 2 p.m. - 10 p.m. and the 'Nippers' or junior lot 10 p.m. - 6 a.m. Nippers as a term also served for those legally too young for nightwork and these sub-juniors worked 'in between', 8 a.m. - 4 p.m. A verminous coach body for messing was replaced during the war by a brick hut on the same site but it nevertheless continued an unsettlingly close association with a variety of wild invaders. It was particularly noted (the warmth drew them at night) for the startlingly sudden call of crickets - 'big as 'orses comin out a' the wall'.

'A gang' at Yeovil meant only a handful of lads, generally given one engine for a shift and engaged in every time-honoured device both to evade the worst of the labour and to grasp whatever free time or odd perquisites that might be going. Such contrivances however cunning and original they might seem to their practitioners were seldom new, and were usually safely crushed by the shed regime. It depended often on the foreman - some would declare themselves content with a relatively perfunctory clean - 'a bit of grease to catch the light just right' - but not so the guv'nor. The Running Shed foreman at Yeovil inhabited the top floor of the dwellinghouse, converted into offices above with a signing-on room for enginemen below. He

could observe the tops of boilers as engines left the shed and if inadequately attended one incumbent was said to have dispatched the guilty cleaner to the station with a bucket of grease. The public he was rumoured to affirm, were fond of observing the company's engines from the various bridges along the way. Cleaners at Yeovil were barred from smoking in the shed and for social and other reasons.

**Senior Work; The Clinker Gang and others**

The most senior work at Yeovil was placed with the passenger link, eight sets of men working trains to Exeter and Salisbury (and beyond at times with a pilotman) relieving crews from either shed at Yeovil Junction. Specials to the S&D were occasionally worked with Midland (LMS) pilotmen.

The links at Yeovil were necessarily a bit diffuse and varied widely in size; some were tiny and highly specific. The 'spare' was accordingly prominent as at Exeter and Salisbury, but of course greatly smaller in size - twelve sets to cover any job. This principally concerned the top passenger link and the one immediately below - the vaguely termed 'pilot link', intermediate in seniority (more or less) between passenger and spare. The pilot link covered all manner of goods in any direction out of Yeovil and often involved shunting, reforming or getting a train ready at some point. The up 'milk & horsebox' all stations to Salisbury was more or less typical of the Yeovil jobs - it might include a spell of shunting at the Junction and others might also involve a short trip up to Templecombe. Milk and a network of trips kept six sets busy through twenty four hours.

47

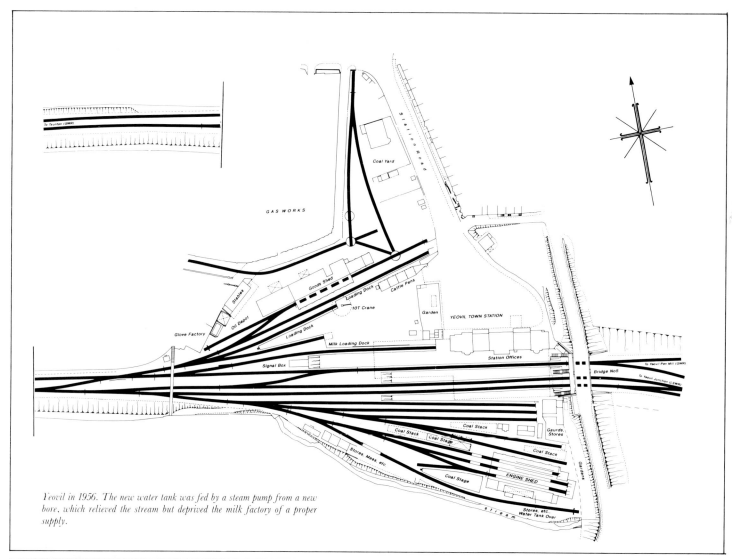

*Yeovil in 1956. The new water tank was fed by a steam pump from a new bore, which relieved the stream but deprived the milk factory of a proper supply.*

Map labels: To Taunton (GWR); GAS WORKS; Coal Yard; Station Road; Stables; Goods Shed; Loading Dock; Cattle Pens; 10T Crane; Garden; YEOVIL TOWN STATION; Glove Factory; Oil Depot; Loading Dock; Milk Loading Dock; Station Offices; Signal Box; Bridge No5; To Yeovil Pen Mill (GWR); To Yeovil Junction (LSWR); Coal Stack; Coal Stage; Coal Stack; Gaurds, Stores; Coal Stack; Stores, Mess, etc.; Coal Stage; ENGINE SHED; Gardens; Stores, etc.; Water Tank Over; Stream

4-4-0s Nos. 380 and 439 inside the shed on 12th June 1926. This picture shows the peculiar 'lobby' at the rear, which could just about accommodate a pair of tank locos. The third road, off to the left, was the old crane road, used for repairs; it too had a sort of extension at the rear, which boasted wooden doors until their removal by an errant engine.

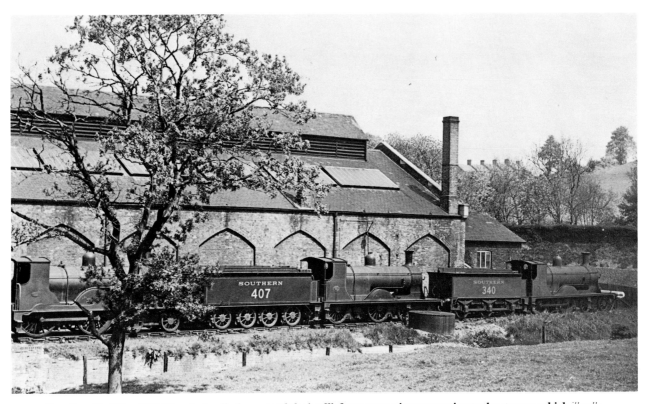

**Yeovil on 21st May 1935. The steel cylinder capped the 'well', for years a pipe connection to the stream, which** *illegally* **abstracted the water.**

*H.C. Casserley*

Much of the rest of the work at Yeovil seems to have devolved onto an amorphous grouping, termed 'the clinker gang'. It apparently embraced everything from the 'not to go' cripples and miscreants through 'p & d' turns (preparation and disposal - 'squaring up' engines either throughout or as part of a shift) and various local goods and shunting work, including the Junction - Town local service. There was for instance a Chard - Axminster goods which dropped off drinking water at Axminster Gates - a booked stop which involved the exchange of various items, principally cider for the crew. Such work offered endless opportunity for trade and barter along with official deliveries of heating coal to a succession of signal boxes, such as Broom Gates.

A career at Yeovil inevitably included a lengthy spell on the local service. At various points in the links a day's work might involve a couple of hours on the push/pull from Yeovil Town to Yeovil Junction, returning to the shed and 'squaring up' four or five engines for the rest of the shift. Adams tanks were usually on these jobs - 182, 204, 207 or 220 for a number of years, the first train an empty working with the two-coach push/pull set, to Templecombe, returning with the workman's train. The rest of the day was spent 'up and down' pushing to Junction and pulling back. It was regarded as dull and monotonous work and complaints were loud and long if a push/pull engine was unavailable. It was hard to repeatedly run round within the smarter timings allowed to the usual workings, the hapless fireman leaping from the cab in increasing agitation every time the engine came to one of its frequent halts. As the day wore on muttered curses against the Yeovil fitter, the guv'nor and eventually most of the railway grew in vehemence; crouched on filthy ballast as yet another discarded cigarette sailed down from the platform above, it could be hard not to regard the absent push/pull engine in some personal light

Members of the clinker gang worked the push/pull trains regularly but the bulk of the work was the preserve of a 'No. 5 link' of two sets only. Each comprised a junior passed fireman, handy for any emergency 'out on the line proper' which might ensue and a driver appointed on application, generally an elderly and curmudgeonly figure with no desire to work anywhere else. Shunting was carried out by various crews on all sorts of turns but there was a specific shunting engine engaged at Yeovil Town for much of the day. Market was particularly busy and saw hundreds of cattle handled in the yard, the engine in the 1930s customarily a 'Jubilee,' No. 606 or 612 manned by the two sets of 'No. 6 link'.

A 'not to go' man served as shed turner at Yeovil, one on each shift throughout 24 hours. For years they never turned engines of course, but moved them about the yard and attended to a variety of sundry tasks. Washouts took place on Nos 2 and 3 roads. Coalmen came on duty at intervals, the early turn men at 6 a.m; they cleared most of the ash and clinker in the slack periods, when most of the engines were out at work. There followed something of a hiatus in the afternoon, the early coalman took off for home and the next man came on at 6 o'clock ('teatime') to clear whatever debris had built up and to begin anew the coaling of engines. The night man arrived at 10 o'clock so that from 10 p.m. - 2 p.m. 'when all the locos had crawled in' there was a pair of men available. Wielding great No. 6 shovels, 12ins by 18ins, they slung the coal up onto tenders from wagons. The yard at Yeovil was cramped and awkward and really only the branch push/pull and the Town shunter were coaled from the stage. A crane arrived after the Second World War; many of these improvements came only *after* the war, when the worst of the work was finished with, but it allowed much of the punishing No. 6 shovelling to be consigned to legend. Half a dozen tubs of 10cwt capacity were provided with the crane. Coal could thus be transferred from wagon to tender with great expedience and, running independently on rail in the time gained, it could whizz about the shed yard clearing the ash and clinker.

**Crowded yard at Yeovil on 22nd April 1962, with 34024** *Tamar Valley,* **5548 and 31614. Larger engines prevailed in the latter years though the loss of much passenger work to DMUs meant that space was not at too much of a premium. 'You could'nt move in that shed' however remained a fair comment.**

*P.J. Kelley*

Lifting of engines took place in the open air alongside No.l, the appropriately christened 'crane road' although lifting was originally carried out inside on No.1 road, the shearlegs having been removed before grouping. As at many of these smaller depots the level of work demanded of fitters 'was somewhat agricultural' Coppersmithing jobs, white metalling, lathe work and suchlike were sent to Exmouth Junction loaded on engine tenders. There were three fitters and one boilersmith, all trained at Eastleigh Works.

**'Amalgamation'**

Greatest event to affect the shed in BR days was 'The Amalgamation', consequent upon the closure of the former Great Western shed at Pen Mill. A short distance away it was nevertheless wholly foreign and poorly comprehended. The Western Region men and engines came over to mutual suspicion and anxiety regarding the rearrangement of links and division of the work. At first the Western jobs were carried on precisely as before but slowly crews, particularly the younger men with most to gain, and engines were mixed together across the duties. Much of the local work in any event began to decline around this time with the introduction of DMU sets, working

out of Bristol and elsewhere and only remanned at Yeovil. After such a long tradition of, if not enmity, then a certain mutual coolness, first contact with 'the Western blokes' wherever it occurred on the Southern brought a startled reaction from the natives. It is strongly recalled even today - see elsewhere in this book, notably at Salisbury and Exeter. Yeovil men soon found themselves on the WR routes and stood blankly amazed that a Western driver could pull in at Westbury and demand that the tubes be cleared or fire cleaned. Western devices to confound timekeeping and wrestle extra overtime are recalled with indignation and something not a little unlike envy.

The Western Region had decided that all fire cleaning and smokebox emptying should be done by shed workers and not by enginemen. The purpose of this was to make better use of footplate staff, eliminating such unskilled work from their roster, allowing more driving time. A weakness of the agreement was that in the event of an engine developing an excess of clinker in the firebox, the enginemen could decline to clean it and would stop for a relief engine. Southern men looked somewhat down their noses at this, confirmed in their belief that GWR stood for *Go When Ready.*

**4-6-0 No.30846 on 6th July 1959.**

*H.C. Casserley*

'Yeovil Junction looking towards London 17th February 1911'. The Yeovil Town platform is on the left, the line curving away beyond it. Alongside was 'The Neck', where engines were stabled in the Second World War (in the event of a direct hit on the shed).

## LOCOMOTIVES

Yeovil, sitting as it were on the main line between Salisbury and Exeter, attracted a variety of mixed traffic work over the years with the men requiring a considerable route knowledge. Exeter, Salisbury and Weymouth on the Southern and over Great Western metals to Taunton and Westbury were all part of the everyday work at the shed. The locomotive stock likewise was varied; Town station and shed were set aside from the main line at Yeovil Junction with much light running required. O2 0-4-4Ts were used on the Yeovil Town - Pen Mill and Junction shuttle Motor Train services with M7 0-4-4Ts taking over some time after grouping. O2s performed admirably on these turns with the occasional early morning return passenger work to Templecombe and late evening visits to Pen Mill.

Jubilee 0-4-2s were evident in the early days on transfer goods work to Junction and Pen Mill, interspersed with shunting at the Junction. G6 0-6-0s were used extensively on local shunting with one of the class outstationed at Templecombe to handle the heavy duties in the yards. K10s were powerful mixed traffic engines used mainly on the goods turns to Salisbury and Templecombe with the odd spell of shunting at Chard, Yeovil and Templecombe. They were occasionally used on local

passenger work to Pen Mill but tended to be selected mainly for goods.

L11s and S11s were regular engines on the Sidmouth Junction pick up goods, and were put to milk van shunting at Chard. Either of the class could be called upon as 'spare engine' in the day which normally required them to be available for piloting the 'Stone' destined for Salisbury and Woking.

The allocation at Yeovil never normally exceeded more than a dozen or so locomotives. It is somewhat confusing therefore to see many photographs of the shed and yard, taken over the years, full to bursting point. Because of the sheds strategic location many services would terminate at Yeovil allowing engines to run from the Junction for servicing. The shed also acted as a welcome refuge for crippled engines off the main line, the shed fitters able to cope with many of the problems encountered. S15 4-6-0s were later drafted to the shed to cope with the increasing weight of goods trains with Moguls dominating much of the latter mixed traffic work to Salisbury, Portsmouth and Exeter.

Standard locomotives arrived in the late 1950s and early '60s, class 4 4-6-0s and 2-6-4Ts amongst a variety of other types (including West Country Pacifics and Ex-Great Western locomotives from Pen Mill).

**The Yeovil Junction turntable. It was hand operated for a long time but was eventually fitted with a vacuum tractor. There was also, often, a shunting engine at the Junction, though one was not** *booked* **as such. It would 'square up' at the turntable siding, or in 'The Neck' at the end of the day, crawling back to the shed with the fire (against regulations) pushed to one side, ready for a quick 'off'.**

*D. Clayton*

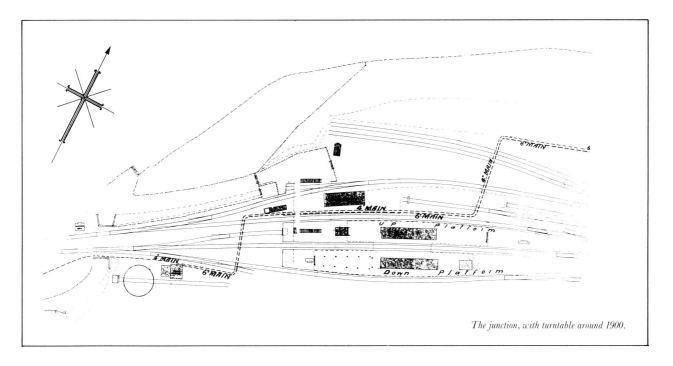

*The junction, with turntable around 1900.*

**The Junction goods shed and 'table. The latters' use was determined by the duties. A No.1 Link job might involve a trip to Salisbury for instance, returning to the shed at the end of the job. It would'nt turn, for the next day it might be booked for an Exeter working. Other than this, an engine might be sent down light in steam to the Junction to turn in readiness for the next days work.**

*D. Clayton*

The corrugated iron shed at Exmouth Junction. Apart from the lamentable state the fabric of the building had been brought to, manpower shortage by 1919 had reduced its whole operation to a low: 'they're in trouble down there' (the Exmouth Junction boilermakers were Great Western trained and fair game) it was declared at Eastleigh. A boilermaker sent down to help out found the building an appalling mess – 'might as well have done your work in the River Exe' – water built up cunningly depending upon the wind and could channel through particular holes in unpredictable fashion. It was common to be soaked before a job finished even though it might have began in dry weather. A forge existed to manufacture tools from bar steel and the lodge was long out of use even by 1919. By that time it was a store for drivers clothing and other *nickable* items. Part of a boilermakers' job was to fashion an extension for

# Exeter

## QUEEN STREET AND EXMOUTH JUNCTION

The London and South Western Railway had eyed keenly the City of Exeter in Devon for many years. It occupied the principal approaches to the South West and was favoured also by the Bristol and Exeter (GWR), Plymouth and North Cornwall being the inevitable goal.

An 'independent' line, the Exeter and Crediton, had been opened on 12th May 1851, worked from the first by the Bristol and Exeter using the broad gauge. This line was later to form the LSWR route to North Devon and Cornwall. The South Western's extension to Exeter had come under the auspices of the Salisbury and Yeovil and latterly the Yeovil and Exeter companies, to reach 'Queen Street', in the east of the city, in July 1860. A line to the Bristol and Exeter station at St. David's through St. David's tunnel and down the steep bank was laid in 1862. This allowed trains to run via Cowley Bridge Junction and over LSW metals to Bideford in the far north of Devon.

It was a period of manoeuvre and intrigue with the LSWR narrow gauge taking the victory. The line up to Barnstaple and beyond had begun a conversion to narrow gauge and Beattie was left to sort matters out .....*April 1863. Read letter from Mr. Beattie as to the provision which will have to be made at Exeter for the repair of the company's narrow gauge engines running between Exeter and Bideford, the present workshops at Barnstaple being no longer available for the purpose. Referred back to Beattie and Strapp for estimates.....* An engine shed had opened when the LSW reached Queen Street in 1860 and here the small workshop was also erected. The shed was located at the London end of the station on a somewhat restricted site, sandwiched between New North Road and Howell Road. It replicated in most details the Company's shed

at Yeovil. It had three through lines some 170 ft. in length and was constructed entirely of brick with a gabled roof, a large water tank surmounting the accompanying offices. A 42 ft. turntable and coalstage stood alongside the building and on the far side of the yard was a large store.

Exeter, it was not hard to divine, was destined rapidly to become a major operational centre, a changing point for trains bound for west and north. The line to Okehampton opened in 1871, plans were being floated to connect up with the Bodmin and Wadebridge railway (although this was not finally accomplished until 1895), whilst numerous projects were in hand - lines to Bude in the north of Cornwall and Lydford on the road to Plymouth. Traffic in these periods of expansion invariably forged far ahead of whatever engine shed accommodation could be provided, however generous in contemporary terms, and Beattie soon felt compelled to make one of his many (usually unsuccessful) approaches to London .....*October 1872, Mr. Beattie reported that it was necessary to lengthen the Engine Shed at Exeter as several engines now stand outside in all weathers during the night.....* A recommendation that 'the shed be lengthened by 64 ft.' was forwarded but this was to prove only a temporary respite. Less than two years were to pass before Beattie returned to the committee, with the familiar entreaties, the precise details lost in the obscurantist 'Minutes' ..... '*New Steam Shed at Exeter'. Mr. Beattie reported as to the additional Engine Shed accommodation required at Exeter station. Consideration postponed. The matter referred to the Officers Committee for report.....* By September of 1876 Beattie submitted a modified plan .....*Exeter Engine House. Referring to the minute of 13th July, Mr. Beattie submitted the plans, as discussed between himself and Mr. Scott and Mr. Jacomb for additional Engine Shed accommodation at Exeter Station and upon their recommendation it*

*Mazeppa* **outside the old Queen Street shed, Exeter. An ancient building itself, it nevertheless came to outlast its successor opposite.**

was agreed to adopt the reduced plan at a cost of about £1500 as to which Mr. Jacomb will prepare further particulars..... Work was complete by the following summer, a new coal stage, engine pit traverser sidings and new water supply coming into use in August 1877.

By the late 1870s lines had opened to Holsworthy, Torrington and to Lydford; Exeter was responsible for several outstations, locos being supplied to Sidmouth, Seaton, Axminster, Holsworthy and Exmouth (opened 1897). Congestion at the shed was quite chronic and the complaints of Adams, latest incumbent of the Loco Superintendent's office, were sufficient to move the directors to inspect the premises in July 1879 .....*'Exeter Engine Shed'. Read extract from the Directors' inspection notes of 21st June as to the Engine Shed accommodation at Exeter and question removing the locomotive repairing shops from Queen Street to the land recently purchased at Exmouth Junction. Mr. Adams to confer with Mr. Jacomb and report what is actually necessary at present to be done and a plan to be made of what will probably be ultimately required*

The site to which the Directors referred was a large piece of ground on the north side of the line by Polsloe Priory, adjacent to the Exmouth branch. Here land was available for a spacious well laid out depot, of mighty proportions in comparison to the Queen Street premises. These projects rarely advanced rapidly and 'Exmouth Junction' was largely put aside for the next two or three years. Some desultory steps had been taken by the early part of 1883 and a turntable at least had been delivered .....*Mr. Adams recommended that a new turntable, 50 ft. now lying at Exmouth Junction be put in at Exeter Station in lieu of the 42 ft. turntable at that place which has been condemned as useless.....* By 6th June instructions were given that .....*the turntable lying at Exmouth Junction.....be installed at Exeter and another suitable turntable of similar dimensions will be obtained for fixing at Exmouth Junction....when required.* Plans were being passed backwards and forwards between committees, with the inevitable wrangling over costs. Congestion at Queen Street was now barely tolerable, with frequent recourse to engine stabling in the goods yard. The Company still flinched at the costs involved in the new scheme and suggestions continued to be made regarding the possibilities of a simple rearrangement at Queen Street. The first hint of something approximating to alarm can almost be detected in Adams' response, remarkable given the essentially dull nature of much of these committee records: August 1883 .....*Exeter Station Engine Shed. I cannot recommend the extension of the Engine Shed at the above*

station but suggest that the proposed new shed at Exmouth Junction be pushed forward as rapidly as possible..... It was only now that 'the Great Scheme' received final sanction; it was recognised that some time would still be required and a solution was arranged for the 'useless' turntable at Queen Street to be put to use: 'a 50 ft. turntable, temporarily put down at Exeter and a road laid in to connect it with the shed there'.

Construction of the new engine shed was destined to be a costly affair. Adequate space was available but the site needed raising and levelling quite considerably - Mr. Jacomb noted the alarming cost in January 1884: 'Progress reported.....of the Exmouth Junction Locomotive Depot...detailed the earthwork and ballasting required for forming the site of the Locomotive Department at an estimated cost of £6,000'. For reasons that are lost to us there was a further delay in work, for almost a year. On 21st January 1885 it was recommended that ...'Mr. Brady be allowed to carry out these works under his new General Contract with the Company'.

Little obvious progress took place and by November 1885 'Lord Morley' had complained at the unsightly work going on opposite his property, requesting that the company erect trees to screen the offending work from his noble view. The company, anxious not to upset such an influential neighbour sanctioned £5 for the planting of 'Quickset hedges'.

The whole programme seemed to progress on a rather desultory basis and by 14th April 1886 Jacomb had written again, asking for instructions .....*as to the following work at Exmouth Junction:*

| | |
|---|---:|
| Tank House | £1750 |
| Extra Mains | £570 |
| Wagon Repairing and Lifting Shops | £750 |
| Coal Shed and Stages | £2320 |
| Coal Pits | £296 |
| Men's Sleeping Accommodation | £750 |
| Ash Bin | £310 |
| Engine Pit 500' long on incoming road | £500 |
| Boiler Shed | £20 |
| Latrine | £58 |
| Additional Road to turntable | £100 |
| | £7424 |

.....*decision... postponed.*(!)

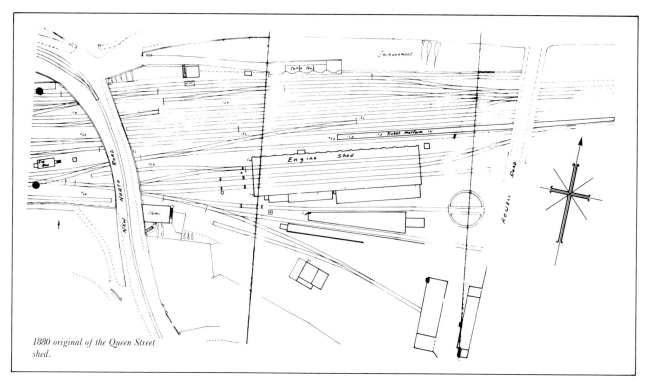

*1880 original of the Queen Street shed.*

0-4-2 at Queen Street. The building it can be seen, was closely akin to the one at Yeovil.

LSWR high stepping elegance on the Queen Street turntable.

*Coll R.C. Riley*

By the following month, however, things were again on the move; an engine hoist was approved at a cost of £220 and later in December .....'Approved, £2420, to be expended on the water supply and coal stage at Exmouth Junction'..... By April of 1887 work was far enough advanced for consideration to be given to moving plant over from Queen Street Engine Shed and £150 was sanctioned for tools and lathes to be transferred to Exmouth Junction. Various orders and instructions followed.... *Enginemen's dormitory will need to be complete before occupying the new locomotive shed at Exmouth Junction, £750*..... Some of the items and buildings deferred.....now approved, at a total cost of £2,970.17.0. viz:

| | |
|---|---|
| Dormitory | £750 |
| Lifting Shed | £750 |
| Long Engine Pit | £430 |
| Ash bin | £310 |
| Coppersmiths Boiler and Engine House | £600 |
| Latrines | £70 |
| Retaining Wall | £60 |

In July of 1887 Adams advised the committee of the 'state of work' and reported that 'work still to do before Exmouth Junction is complete includes the Dormitory for Enginemen, pit and roofing over the coal stage'.

A doubtless relieved Adams was by 3rd November 1887 able to write to the committee with the good news that .....*Exmouth Junction Loco Depot was brought into use that day and recommending that Drivers Sharland and Storey be appointed foremen there at 50/- per week wages*......

The depot was vast in comparison with its Queen Street neighbour, contemporaneous with the 'old' shed at Nine Elms. (see *London District*). Four large gables covered eleven roads, which ran through the building onto a 55 ft. turntable. Both ends of the shed were furnished with doors and the glazing, to become a familiar feature of these sheds, set off the gable ends. Exmouth Junction was constructed, extraordinarily, entirely of corrugated iron, supported on an intricate metal framework. Although an everyday material, use on such a scale was to cause many problems. A specially erected washing out shed was supplied on the north side of the building and adjacent were offices, stores, messrooms and repair bays. A huge elevated coal

stage also ran down this part of the yard, the surrounding sidings intended for the storage of coal. At the far end of the yard were the water tank and a large dormitory.

The LSWR by this period found itself at the forefront of many developments - not the least of these were dormitories for enginemen on lodging - 'double home' - turns. 'Barracks' were unusual, at least in some parts of the country in the 1880s, their development determined by a combination of social attitudes. Their establishment was resisted on some railways as a dangerous manifestation of radicalism, though the companies embodied paternalism in nineteenth century Britain - it was not *proper* to provide for the workforce in this way. The more liberally - inclined erected dormitories of a size, comfort and degree of supervision such to nurture and encourage suitable conduct and demeanour. There were few places of course less suited to a good night's sleep than a busy engine shed but to site a dormitory remote from the shed was considered inadvisable. To build as close as possible within the confines of the depot, it was thought, could discourage beer (and worse things). In those years smoking on duty or even to be caught in a pub could bring dismissal. There were actually relatively few 'double homes' on the LSWR and all but a handful seem to have disappeared by the late 1920s.

Queen Street shed was not immediately abandoned but survived as a convenient turning, servicing and stabling area for years. The old 42ft turntable, long condemned, had been replaced in 1887 (the plans for the transfer of one 'lying at Exmouth Junction' seem never to have materialised) by a 50ft unit the former going to Exmouth for use there. By 1891 the ageing building was considered in a report on the remodelling of the station and its functions; it was now regarded as something of a surplus nuisance and .....*its site would be more profitably used for the laying down of sidings ..... 30th September 1891 'Engine Shed at Exeter Station'. Read report from the Locomotive Superintendent of the 18th September, as to the question of removing the engines from the old shed on the down side of Exeter Station to the new sheds at Exmouth Junction, leaving the old shed available for traffic purposes, as suggested in the Directors' inspection note of 24th July. To come up again with a further report from the Locomotive Superintendent after conference with the General Manager and Engineer on the subject*.....

**Exmouth Junction deep in its dotage, 18th July 1925; complaints regarding its general condition are seen to be more or less justified.**

*H.C. Casserley*

The Exmouth Junction 'back yard' before the sheds' sad decline. Whilst houses now carpet the slopes round about and the site is given over to a monstrous modern retailing venture, at this period the depot lay amidst fields and trees. Across the lane from this turntable stood a farmhouse with glowering bull.

**4-4-0 at Exmouth Junction in sparkling condition. Contrast the shed gables with the dismal edifice below, far page.**

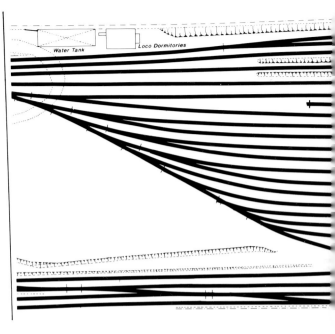

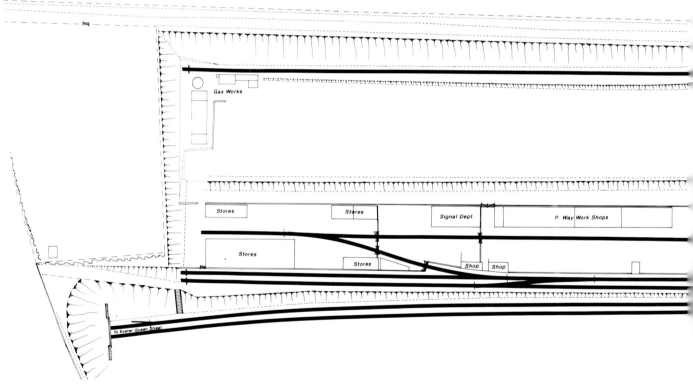

*The first Exmouth Junction shed, in 1905. Apart from a disastrously wrong choice of building material it is seen to have been laid out generously with regard to space. Engines could more easily and readily move either side of the shed, perpetuating an LSW fondness for such 'turntable-orientated' layouts. It suffered an obvious drawback however in that the natural 'flow' of engines, to and from the west, was not properly realised. There was consequently undue movement of light engines up and down the yards, both 'back' and 'front'.*

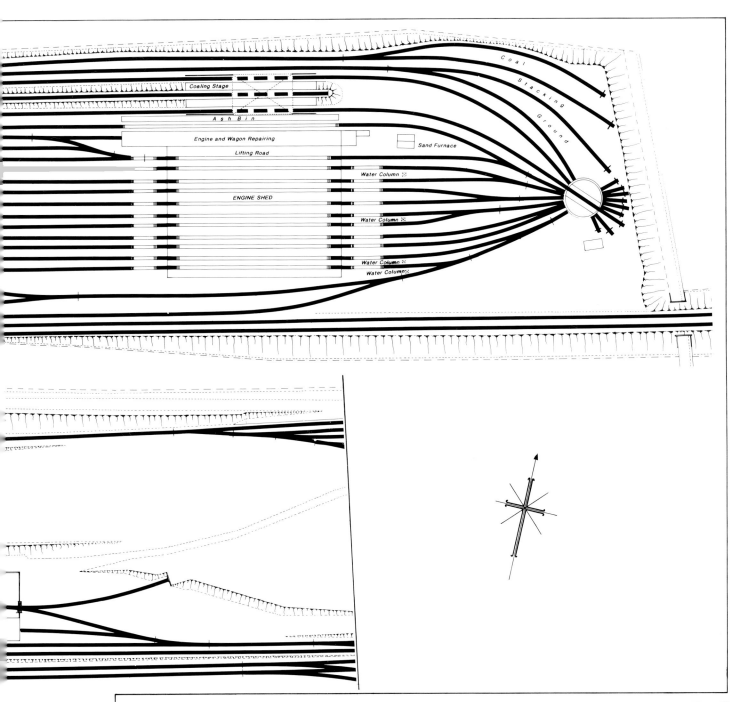

Coaling Stage

A s h B i n

Engine and Wagon Repairing

Lifting Road

Sand Furnace

ENGINE SHED

Water Column

Water Column

Water Column

Water Column

Coal Stacking Ground

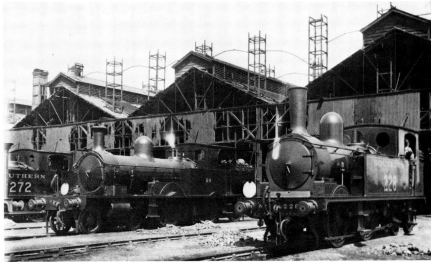

**Engines in Southern and LSWR garb on 18th July 1925. 'The Junction' appeared able to keep its charges in excellent fettle, despite the obvious disadvantages under which it laboured.**
*H.C.Casserley*

The 'old' shed in the early part of the 1920s. 'Parts of the covering are now somewhat dilapidated', a contemporary report mentions blithely.

The old coal stage. The LSWR possessed a number of such rickety structures owing nothing obviously to contemporary practice elsewhere. Built mainly in wood it settled and sagged over the weight of years to become hardly less ruinous than the shed itself. 19th July 1924.

*H.C. Casserley*

M7 0-4-4T under repair in 1926. The new repair shop was equipped with all the modern aids including a mighty travelling gantry, capable of lifting the heaviest locomotives. The fairly modest shear-legs (shown) were thus consigned to the scrap heap.

*H.C.Casserley*

Longer wheelbase locomotives had by the 1900s been introduced on all major routes. Exmouth Junction turntable was inadequate at 55ft. and there was 'considerable difficulty in balancing and turning engines'. On 21st May 1914 there was furher news.....*Read letter from the Locomotive Engineers of the 14th inst. as to the necessity of providing a larger engine turntable at Exmouth Junction and stating that the present 55ft table could be enlarged to 65ft. diameter, at an estimate cost of £740, being £480 for the alterations to be carried out by his department and £260 for the work to be done by the Engineers Department. 'TO BE DONE'.....* Delay dogged all developments at Exmouth Junction and the new turntable drifted, lost, through various committees and records until after Grouping.

**Exeter's New Concrete Engine Shed**

The shed at Exmouth Junction was a vast creaking barn, the innumerable sheets of corrugated iron with its endless edging and countless fixings provided perfect conditions for corrosion, and decay advanced rapidly. Only a few years into the new century the building was in a dismal state. Large holes had appeared in the roof and walls; the iron framework in its contortions had broken most of the glass and warped doors were barely usable. Some repairs had been effected to the gables but the replacement wooden slats had in turn perished. For such an important location conditions were poor, draught and rain assailed those working in the shed and the combined effect of gale and locomotive blast tore flapping panels of rusty iron from its fixings. The whole frame became insecure and its slow movements only added to the damage.

To remedy all this, in 1920 an innovative scheme of mighty proportions appeared. Along with a sister establishment, Feltham, Exmouth Junction was to be erected entirely in concrete, a novel medium being widely explored for railway purposes. The Chief Civil Engineer's Exmouth Junction Concrete Works, occupying the western part of the yard, had experimented for some time in the use of this material and had established an impressive range of artefacts and building components. The LSWR works were set up as a production line for a (relatively) restricted range of buildings and components, produced on a vast scale (see for instance *Southern Nouveau 1, Wild Swan, 1987*); large capital projects such as the Exmouth Junction shed required private contractors, though design elements rested largely with the Company. As with its predecessor construction was a protracted affair, much of it left to the newly formed Southern Railway.

While the work went on it was necessary for the old shed to function more or less unhindered and construction was neatly arranged to proceed in stages, each complete part coming into service to minimise disruption. Thus the new building was placed at the rear of the old shed; the turntable necessarily then was the first part of the transitional scheme and it was resited to the south, closer to the main line .....*3rd October 1923. An order has been placed with Messrs. Stothert and Pitt Ltd. of Bath for the supply and erection at the Company's Exmouth Junction Locomotive depot, Exeter, of a 65ft. electrically operated turntable at the total price of £1,419 with delivery in four and half months from 22nd. August last. Approved.....* The old turntable was nevertheless deemed fit for further use elsewhere on the system .....*Recommended that 55ft turntable at Exmouth Junction be transferred to Dorchester (presently 50ft). Exmouth Junction turntable is redundant due to the rebuilding of the shed, estimated cost £1,200.....*this never in fact took place and what became of this ageing unit can only be wondered at.

It was not until December of 1923 that tenders for the main part of the building were requested, A. Jackman & Sons bid of £57,6812d accepted in preference to Holloway Bros' £59,700. Work started in the summer of 1924 and was to take some four years in all, a protracted affair necessary if the depot was to remain operational .....*20th May 1925, with reference to the new engine shed now under construction at Exmouth Junction, Recommend twelve engine pits outside shed, £200 each*
*£2,400 less savings on revised layout of yard, £860*
*Total £1,840.....*
*.....The engine shed will be 270ft long by 235ft wide with thirteen roads*

*traversing it, one of which is designed as a lifting road, and will be spanned by an overhead travelling crane. Accommodation is also being provided for running repairs staff*

## 'Observation shows that seldom, if ever, is an engine held up when moving to and from the Engine Shed'

'The Junction' was the locomotive centre of The West; a quasi-independent system more after the fashion of some inaccessible hill kingdom, its affairs were conducted semi independently, communication with Waterloo HQ limited to a single-needle telegraph. Both the Traffic and Locomotive Superintendents therefore enjoyed freedom from interference from above. Single lines led off through deep cloven farmland and over brooding moor to remote places where engines were sometimes absent for days or weeks at a time.

Exmouth Junction needed sophisticated repair arrangements to avoid engines engaging in a journey to Eastleigh. Capable therefore of all but the heaviest work a high lifting shop was built on the north side of the shed .....*8th October 1924. Tenders accepted for a 50 Ton travelling crane for Exmouth Junction shed, authorised by the South Western board on 21st December 1922. Messrs. Herbert Morris of Loughborough to erect at cost of £1,198.....* The ancient coal stage was demolished as a modern concrete coaling plant came into use, with a capacity of some 300 tons. The small three road carriage and wagon repair shed was demolished and rebuilt adjacent to the concrete works. By May 1926 the project was well in hand, the *Southern Railway Magazine* reporting that .....*The new locomotive shed at Exmouth Junction is gradually nearing completion and seven roads are in use for the stabling of locomotives. The Blacksmith and Coppersmith shops are in full use.....* It is difficult to say when the new shed was wholly complete; as late as October 1929 alterations were still being carried out to the repair shops, but it must have been substantially operational by late 1926 - early 1927. Guests from the *Railway Engineer* were invited along to inspect the new works and the visit was described in February 1928.

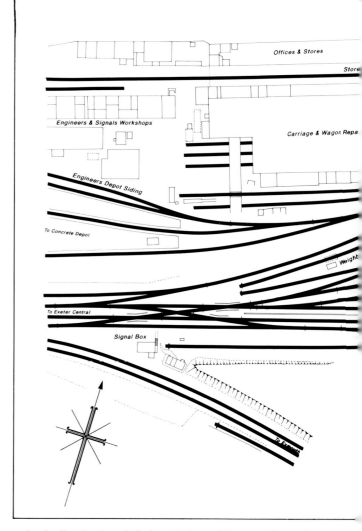

*....The new engine shed, which is situated at the extreme eastern end of the depot, has been constructed entirely of ferro-concrete. It consists of thirteen bays, each 270ft. long, and each bay is provided with a pit throughout its length. The roofing of the last bay on the north side has been especially raised in order to accommodate an overhead travelling gantry crane, capable of lifting loads up to about 63 tons, and all repairs involving lifting are carried out in this bay. The crane, which was supplied by Herbert Morris Ltd., of Loughborough, is electrically operated.*

*On the north side of road No. 13 are the offices and shops, the latter comprising a fully-equipped fitter's shop, machine shop, smith's shop and store. Slotting, shaping, planing and drilling machines are installed, also an axle-box lathe and four lathes for dealing with other classes of work. In addition, there are a tube cutter, a power hacksaw, grindstone and emery wheels, together with a hydraulic press for dealing with coupling rod bushes. In the store a wall crane having a radius of 12ft. has been provided. The various machines derive their power from two lines of shafting which, in their turn, are driven by a 30 H.P. electric motor. At the eastern end of the lifting road is the wheel lathe, which is independently driven by a 20 H.P. motor. The above plant, indeed, the whole section of the depot devoted to locomotive work, is incorporated in the Chief Mechanical Engineer's Department.*

*The roof of the engine shed is of the saw-tooth type, the ridges of the individual bays running north and south; the easterly slopes are glazed and the westerly slopes formed of concrete panels covered with asphalt. Excellent diffused light therefore, is obtained during the daytime. An interesting feature is the smoke hoppers, which run from end to end of the shed over each track excepting the lifting bay, and are constructed entirely of reinforced concrete. They are provided with special channels along the inside of the bottom edges to collect any moisture condensing on the inside,*

*and such collected moisture is discharged at intervals by means of gargoyles clear of the tracks.*

*The roof is supported on concrete columns measuring 12ins. by 12 ins. and approximately 18ft. high. The base of each column is carried on a specially designed concrete raft in order to distribute the load to the extent necessitated by the fact the whole shed stands on made up embankments formed some 50 or 60 years ago. The floor is paved with brindle bricks laid on concrete, and each of its longitudinal pits in the engine shed is carried on a concrete raft of similar design to that used for the column bases. The contractors for the construction of the shed were A. Jackman and Sons Ltd., of Slough. Electric lighting is provided throughout. All water collecting in the engine pits as a result of engine washing is passed through a special purifying plant before being discharged into an adjoining culvert. In this plant the water is freed from solid matter, whether floating or in suspension, and also from oil.*

### ENGINE TURNING AND COALING

*An electrically operated 65ft. turntable is located in the south eastern corner of the locomotive yard. A mechanical coaling plant constructed by the Mitchell Conveyor Company, in ferro-concrete, was nearly completed at the time of our visit. This plant is located near the south-west corner of the running shed. The wagon hoist and other machinery for operating the plant will be electrically driven.*

*The bunker will accommodate 300 tons of coal and two locomotives can be fuelled at one time. In addition to the coaling plant, provision has also been made for the standing on the ground of some thousands of tons of coal to serve in case of emergency.*

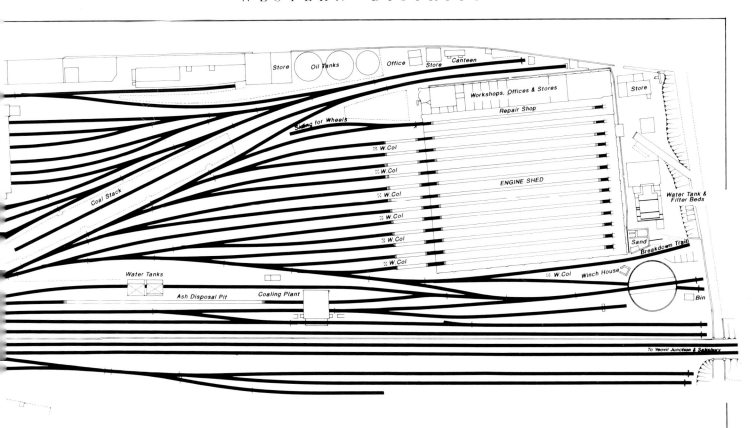

Store    Oil Tanks    Office   Store   Canteen

Workshops, Offices & Stores

Repair Shop

Store

Siding for Wheels

⊠ W.Col

⊠ W.Col

Coal Stack

⊠ W.Col

ENGINE SHED

Water Tank & Filter Beds

⊠ W.Col

⊠ W.Col

Sand

⊠ W.Col

Breakdown Train

Water Tanks

⊠ W.Col   Winch House

Ash Disposal Pit    Coaling Plant

Bin

To Yeovil Junction & Salisbury

*The new shed in 1950. Its entire arrangement is seen to have a more modern quality, with the whole of the yard and its operation fixed for the principal movements to the west. 'The Junction' lay at the centre of a web of lines in the West and every week its far flung engines (crews as well, particularly in summer) would trail in from their various outstations, 'comin' 'ome to roost'.*

**Construction of the new shed was, as we have seen, a prolonged affair, due principally to the need for engines to continue in traffic. To this end the new turntable came first, whilst the new concrete building was put up in the 'back end' of the yard. A fraught period, no doubt. 4-4-0 No. 0162 and Urie 4-6-0 No. 744. 18th July 1925.**
*H.C. Casserley*

## LOCOMOTIVE YARD LAYOUT

*A special feature of the layout is direct access to and from the locomotive shed from the main line. Practically all the engines entering the shed come from Exeter, similarly nearly all engines leaving the yard proceed to Exeter to pick up their trains and a reference to the plan of the new layout will show that the connections have been so arranged that their engine movements are absolutely direct whereas with the old layout several shunts were required. Observation shows that seldom, if ever, is an engine held up when moving to and from the engine shed when going on or off duty.*

*The Railway Observer* of September 1929, belatedly, recounts *.....the new sheds at Exmouth Junction are nearly complete. The old depot has been entirely reconstructed and includes a new engine shed, workshops, marshalling yard, mechanical coaling plant for 20 ton wagons and a new large signal box. Construction is in concrete.....* 'The Junction' was ultimately responsible for all locomotive work in the west and all the sheds in some sense were outstations, only Wadebridge and Barnstaple having a measure of independence and the associated repair work. Other outstations corresponded more closely to the foreign term 'sub sheds' and were generally run by a 'driver in charge' with engines changed at regular intervals. Crews were usually local men though cleaners, drivers and firemen out of Exmouth Junction were constantly relieving, and promotion usually involved a transfer to the main depot. Lyme Regis, Bude, Exmouth, Seaton, Okehampton, Sidmouth until closure and even Exeter Queen Street (the turntable, coalstage and water tank were at last done away with in 1930) operated much after this fashion to the end of steam.

The City of Exeter was heavily bombed during World War Two. With relatively little strategic importance the bombing was no doubt intended to cow the civilians into submission. In 1940 the workshop staff at 'the Junction' was augmented by fitters from Dover and Ashford where locomotive stock had been reduced owing to their close proximity to occupied France. Devon was considered less likely to be invaded and held

very few military objectives apart from Plymouth Dockyard. Exmouth Junction therefore became a 'reserve workshop', a safeguard against other workshops being knocked out by bombing in Hampshire and London. Major operations, however, were carried out on the Bulleid Pacifics, of which the first ten were confined to the West of England main line during their most unreliable phase, 1942-44. (Later in the 1950s, Exmouth Junction was to be Concentration Depot for over a third of the entire fleet of Pacifics). Several bombs fell either in or around the shed, on Prince of Wales Road (now a swathe of housing) and at the side of the shed, with a few direct hits. The shock from one of these bombs removed whatever good glass remained and the great repair shop doors, in heavy planking and normally firmly shut, burst open in response to the sudden pressure gradient.

The immediate post war years saw little change, the bomb damage not being made good until the formation of British Railways. However, a new turntable was installed in 1947, described by *The Railway Magazine* thus *.....A new 70ft articulated turntable was recently installed at Exmouth Junction to replace the balanced 65ft. table, enlargement of the pit being carried out while the old table was still in operation. A 40 ton steam crane removed the old table on 17th March and the new turntable was placed in position and ready for use by 30th March.....* It was about this time that the experiment with oil fired locomotives took place. Fratton shed at Portsmouth was chosen, along with Exmouth Junction, and oil storage tanks and pumps were installed. This ill-conceived idea had received Government backing with further installations planned for Plymouth and Wadebridge, but the scheme collapsed when its basis in economics proved false.

The depot was transferred to the Western Region in 1963 which later saw the downgrading of the Salisbury - Exeter route to a single line. By 1966 the shed was in a bad state of decay, the turntable was demolished and the remaining staff transferred to

**Tank No.68 and crew, oblivious to the surrounding chaos.**

**The finished shed. These LSW/Southern buildings were pioneering efforts after their fashion but the design with its vents and numbers, and even** *gargoyles* **was far from the crude slab structures associated with concrete in more modern times.**

Exeter St.Davids or any other location they were lucky enough to obtain. Some diesels lingered on until the spring of 1967 when the shed finally closed, ending some eighty years of association with the site.

### 'The Junction'

The shed and various works at Exmouth Junction lay in a fold of land out by Polsloe; the Great Western is habitually regarded as the dominant power in the west, a picture belied by this South Western enclave. In comparison indeed the GWR engine shed and traffic arrangements were regarded as relatively primitive. The GW attitude to freight working in particular was regarded as reprehensible.

The rivalry GW - LSW came down the years, wandering threads deriving from a contest which waxed and waned in intensity. There was great resentment when 'The Junction' closed and the men were asked to work from the old Great Western shed at Exeter St.Davids, a miserable neglected place by any measure. The LSWR fought hard to win and then retain its Devon and Cornwall traffic and there was always the imperative to bear favourable comparison with the larger rival. This continued certainly through Southern days and into the 1960s. It is in the hearts of men even now! Every goods ('The Perishables' in its infinite manifestations) and passenger train off the Plymouth road, without fuss and 'to time', was a daily victory over 'The Western' a slumbering giant whose freights habitually ran hours late over schedule - 'days, some of 'em...' The ubiquitous 'Double Homes' were regarded both as a symptom and a cause, dulling the imperative to run 'to time' on humble goods. Exmouth Junction men had lodged in London in former years but the practice seems to have faded out, certainly by the 1920s and possibly much earlier, when the new shed at Salisbury opened.

The path of memory and reminiscence can be a treacherous one, and in recounting the experience of so long ago, ancient rivalries continue to insinuate themselves. Great Western men, from Exeter across to Plymouth need almost to be reminded of the very existence of the 'Southern', whilst those who worked at 'The Junction', Salisbury or any other shed in the West retain even now an almost indignant memory of the great rivalry. Much of this centres upon the (perceived) Great Western attitude to goods working, the almost universal view that a GW train ran according to the necessity for tea, rather than traffic. The Great Western remained safely aloof from this, confident in its own vast superiority.

The Great Western of course had the advantage of direct access to the populous South Devon and Cornwall peninsula, whereas the South Western's later arrival dictated that its line, and therefore traffic, would draw upon the sparsely populated and comparatively unprofitable areas of North Devon and Cornwall. The connection between the two companies at Exeter, moreover, did little to favour through-working and under Nationalisation the Southern route was less and less regarded.

It is hardly thinkable that flesh could now be put on these old gnawed bones of contest. That it seemed so to South Western men cannot be doubted, yet the GWR was a vastly different railway. Devon and Cornwall were but small part of a great empire yet the main line to the west suffered more so than the LSWR from disadvantages of terrain. The LSWR was able to 'focus' its goods services more effectively; essentially it ran fast daily trains for the London market and was less troubled by the demands of a wider 'catchment' area - London, the Midlands, the North and beyond. The best LSWR goods were the various perishable traffics, requiring exact timings but the GW worked similar trains and though endless coal empties clumped from siding to siding, slotted in between were painstakingly planned

4-4-0 No.710 outside the great repair 'hall' on 4th August 1928. This host of 4-4-0s and tanks, in all their guises, characterised Exmouth Junction for years, really until Pacifics and Standards appeared in numbers from the 1950s.

*H.C. Casserley*

'Z' No.30950 clumping about with wagons, part probably, of one of the innumerable 'Tavies'. This road down by the side of the coaling plant (it dispensed 'a tray of sugar' when breakage and crushing was bad) seems to have played little part in the servicing procedures, unless it stored coal wagons but appears to have provided a useful goods siding.

*R.C. Riley.*

van trains, running at accelerated schedules with engines specially provided for the 'season'. The brocolli trains were justly famous. All these trains, GW and LSWR had to reach their markets by an appointed time. The merchant cart or lorry would be waiting at Nine Elms or wherever and lateness could mean an absolute loss. Both companies faced classic difficulties which were to prove near insurmountable, problems which came to bedevil the roads in even worse fashion. Routes for the GWR, in especial, 'funnelled' in from north and east, traffic heaping upon itself to meet successive problems of gradient, or line occupation. The LSWR main line in a sense thrust through much of this and free of Exeter, could race to the west on its sweeping hillside curves. 'The Junction' lay at the very heart of this operation, drawing trains off the attenuated lines to the west and transforming them into expresses for Waterloo, goods for Nine Elms. 'The Junction' was thus unlike almost any other engine shed in Britain (Stratford would be one exception) in the complexity and range of its duties, much of it conducted in far flung places across a network of outstations. It was not unknown for over 140 locomotives to end up at Exmouth Junction on a Sunday and the awesome volume of work was mastered, week by week, over years. Such adversity demanded peaks of efficiency and nurtured a highly developed *camaraderie*, wholly beyond that experienced at most large sheds.

### Cleaning, the Black Gang and the Taveys

From LSWR times, throughout Southern days until the changes of the BR period, Exmouth Junction operated some ten links, or 'gangs' as they were frequently known. They were rigidly delineated, the work varying throughout in complexity and arduousness and all men did not follow the same path by any means. Men were constantly moving up and down; some men through availability (or choice) were destined to remain in certain links, other jobs were 'non-progressive'. Drivers were not able to transfer from depot to depot (unless by special dispensation). The fireman who chose not to apply for promotion elsewhere had to remain, despite age, until seniority enabled him to step into a vacancy at his own depot.

All men began as cleaners, awkward youths who were initially 'sorted' under the baleful gaze of the Running Foreman, a fearsome figure wielding unimaginable power. It was a good job for any boy, preferable to the farms and the primitive, mainly farm-based trades available around Exeter and there were plenty af applicants. Exmouth Junction's web of outstations demanded constant 'relief' and cleaners were frequently sent forth for weeks or more, sleeping under a tank perhaps, with an old overcoat and employed principally in the role af 'shedman', labouring, coaling, lighting up and whatever other tasks might be found. The Exmouth Junction 'cleaning gang' thus underpinned work in the district, forming an adaptable pool of general labour. The gang was accordingly of considerable size with 72 cleaners in its ranks in 1929. The Superintendent at this time - the awesome 'Peggy', took a personal interest in the cleaning duties and how they could be arranged to benefit the depot accounts. 'Nightwork' at this period comprised the hours 10pm to 4am and no less than 60 of the gang were due on at 4am precisely - no later. This reduced to a minimum the numbers able to claim the night work pittance, whilst usefully weeding out those unsuited to the labour. There were scarce half a dozen cleaners rostered for each of the other two shifts, so the great bulk of cleaning took place throughout the mornings. The sixty would shuffle, blinking, in for breakfast (strictly, twenty minutes only) in two batches, such were the numbers involved and moved off into the gloom in groups of four or five, shuffling past the fearsome 'Peggy'. Leaving his lair he would stand and watch this abject

procession, his lingering daily memory designed to instil an awareness of omniscient authority throughout a day spent in the shed. The guv'nor or a foreman was likely to descend upon errant cleaners with appalling prescience, efforts which reinforced, as much as they deterred, the harum scarum antics of cleaner boys. Nevertheless no recollection of oppression or unfair treatment appears to come down from those years; all was ordered much as everyone expected and 'The Junction' enjoyed a sort of 'family' atmosphere, the like of which is probably impossible today, among so many hundreds of men, working hard on shifts. Some of this was unique to the institution of the 'loco', across the country, though the atmosphere at some places could almost be poisonous and it was relatively less highly developed at many sheds the scale of Exmouth Junction. Everyone wanted 'off early' on a Saturday and while some remained on an unofficial roster basis it was usual to work exceptionally hard in the afternoon. This got the job done in four and a half hours, for an early 'away' and a Saturday night at home, or elsewhere.

'The Royal Gang' was the pinnacle of cleaning achievement at Exmouth Junction, satisfying enough but potentially unnerving through the personal interest the job attracted from 'Peggy'.* This group of five spent their time on the shed's two Lord Nelson 4-6-0s. No effort was spared given the guv'nors practice of watching the engines off shed, a figure of Sea Lord dimensions and association. Other gangs laboured on King Arthurs, S15s. T9s and so on; the King Arthurs received treatment almost to 'Royal Gang' standards, the smaller and older locomotives attended by lesser, more junior gangs.

The traditional 'Top Link' at Exeter was the 'Main Line', occupied with express work to Salisbury. The LSWR main line was worked in sections to an unusual degree, a practice marked for its survival (in modified form) even until dieselisation. Thus the work of the principal link was peculiarly restricted - to and from Salisbury, invariably with the same engine. Through working of engines to London but not crews, became common place in the 1950s. To work the Salisbury jobs was to reach the lordly heights; the combination of banks and curves with stretches of great speed demanded the keenest touch and the various branch junctions added a unique dimension, a variety of complex procedures timed in minutes. There seems little doubt that the Bullied Pacifics and in particular the Merchant Navys mastered this sort of work. Enginemen recall the various technical faults (from the everyday to the near catastrophic) but the Pacifics are rarely remembered in less then glowing terms. There can have been few heavy express jobs on a winding and hilly road, punctuated by a number of standing starts and periods of high speed to compare with the 'main line' of the Exmouth Junction (and Salisbury) men. At Exmouth Junction (indeed across much of the Southern) there seems to have existed a readiness to grasp, to take hold of whatever machines were provided, to an extent not obvious elsewhere. At the Junction it was apparent that the Pacifics had drawbacks (more serious indeed than many types) but they were overcome without the damaging rejection that could mar the introduction of engines elsewhere. The SR men in turn took to the BR standards immediately, in contrast to their colleagues 'down at the Western'. At Exmouth Junction the Bulleid engines were viewed with some pride, despite their outlandish antecedents and unfamiliar features. The Pacifics were pushed to extra-

*From 1929 - 1939 the Running Shed Superintendent was W. O'Neal who was an ex-SER man and mariner. He was nicknamed 'Peggy' after the famous actress on the London stage, Peggy O'Neil. Despite the terror he inspired in cleaner lads his memory remains one of affection. He did the job.

**A familiar Junction type, T9 No.733, on 19th February 1928. These were the engines of the 'Plymouth' and 'North Devon' Links, of the 'North Cornwall' Link and others.**

ordinary levels out of Exeter; their idiosyncrasies were simply catered for as part of the lot of men and rapid repairs were commonplace. Pacifics, it was insisted , could come 'onto a pit' at about 1.45p.m. having worked down the 11 O'clock Waterloo. It might have suffered a warm coupling rod bush or big end, which would require immediate dismantling of the motion; the shop would stop whatever routine work was going on to push out the bush, remetal and turn it, place it back in the rod and return it to the engine in time for it to go up on its booked duty at 7 o'clock. Apocryphal or not, it indicates the mood at the Junction.

Junior to the top 'main line' men was the 'Plymouth Link,' 12 sets again, working the passenger turns to Plymouth with a few Padstow jobs. Eight sets of men comprised the 'North Devon Link', concerned with the Barnstaple and Ilfracombe lines, intermingled like all the secondary lines 'westward' with men from the smaller local sheds and outstations. The 'North Cornwall Link' operated in similar fashion, to Okehampton, Halwill and beyond. Holidays, sickness, special work and vacancies usually ensured that the Junction men spent time 'at some country place or other' and an Exeter career would take a man to most sheds in the District. Placed somewhere in the middle yet relatively senior was the 'Heavy Goods Link' with around sixteen sets of men; it varied over the years and could even be adjusted seasonally. Its work included the 'Tavys', fully fitted goods trains running overnight, non-stop to Salisbury, except for a 15 minute check at Templecombe by wagon examiners. Railway working terms were most effective when combining the merest factual fragment with some sort of anarchic joke. ... 'Tavys' derived from the fact that Plymouth stood on the River Tavy and that most of the villages down that way began with ....Tav.    This sort of work was most important

for Exmouth Junction; much of the agriculture of the West depended in large part ultimately on London (or the North) for its markets and a mass of traffic, of astonishing variety often peaking with the seasons, was carried by the South Western. There was an enormous volume of livestock traffic - sheep and cattle and any variety of poultry, rabbits, game, winter crops, summer crops, spring crops, fruit and vegetables from France and beyond, cut flowers; all 'timed' traffic to catch specific markets. Trains like the 7.38 and 8.37 a.m. worked out of Exmouth Junction with S15 4-6-0s, a continuity of such work spanning thirty - forty years or more. 'The Black Gang' was the link responsible for much of this traffic, the latest turn coming at 5 a.m. All their work was booked 5 p.m. - 5 a.m., 'all at night, with black engines', hence the faintly lurid title for the link. Mixed goods and other Sunday tasks were given over to the 'Yeoford Link' men often on their first driving turns proper (other than banking or yard work) and passed firemen. Underpinning all this was the enormous 'Spare Link' at Exmouth Junction, rivalled for size only by the cleaning army. There were *forty-eight sets* for much of the time, reflecting the great variety and enormous fluctuations in the Exeter work. The 'Spare' men covered all the duties at the depot, including main line passenger, doing 'anything and everything'. At one time it was even subdivided into senior and junior gangs. An 'Exmouth Link' existed, an agreed backwater, a 'stopped' or 'non-progressive' link where drivers who did not want more onerous work could be accommodated. Its occupancy was discussed and agreed with the Exmouth Junction LDC, the firemen passing through in the normal way of things. There were something like fourteen sets involved, on local turns, seven on Sidmouth trains, seven on the Exmouth branch.

At the bottom was a fairly amorphous band, principally of 'Not-to-go-men', invalids or miscreants who would perform more or less any of the 'home jobs' in and about the depot and yard but also (for those destined to leave the gang), the St. Davids bank work. A disposal gang was also generally available from men in the 'Spare Link', a striking illustration of how varied was the work it encompassed.

The basic essential of locomotive servicing had been worked out on the LSWR very early on; engines were coaled and disposed (firebox/smokebox attention), moved forward a suitable distance away from these operations to turn and then reversed back on a separate track to gain the shed yard as quickly as maybe, leaving behind the choking clouds and guttering flares of the disposal roads. The Salisbury shed had early on embodied these principles, making the best of a layout and avoiding for instance a turntable marooned on a separate siding. Even in the first Exmouth Junction shed the coaling and turning procedures had been laid out in logical fashion though it suffered unduly, like Nine Elms, from a dependence upon the turntable. Wear and tear, and accidents as well, were directly related to the intensity of use and it was essentially wasteful to operate a turntable merely to direct engines rather than turn them for the next job. The old Exmouth Junction turntable was located as part of the servicing procedure and use was accordingly intense. Turntables did not suffer from the rotational process, this can happily take place for decades given elementary attention to lubrication, but are deranged through the constant clattering assault of heavy engines, every indiscreet approach above the stipulated snail's pace leading to wear and damage. In the building and rearrangement of the depot, initiated by the LSWR and concluded by the Southern, the whole of the servicing was shifted to the strip of ground at the south side of the shed. Engines could then approach the coaling plant over the ash pits for disposal work or directly if the bunker

simply required topping up, as was customary with some of the local branch engines or bankers.    On the LSWR and Southern, as noted eleswhere, crews traditionally disposed their own engine but it was always necessary to roster some men specially for the work. The 'Disposal Gang' might comprise eight or ten sets of men, (more in summer) booking on perhaps every two or three hours and *rostered* for certain engines off particular turns. They thus knew more or less precisely what to expect and what the shift would entail. The system was flexible and if a crew moved on shed with half an hour 'to do', the fireman would clean the firebox whilst the driver might look the engine over. Fires were in any case run down towards the end of a turn to minimise work; few of the ill chances of the world could bear comparison with a disposal man's wrath, anxious to 'do the off' and confronted with a firebox 'piled up to the 'ole'. If a crew were late they might be inclined to walk off immediately on bringing the engine to a halt but life at Exmouth Junction was such that if the blokes in front were particularly hard pressed those arriving on the ash pits behind would probably lend a hand.

Engines, as at any depot, even of modest dimensions, were put away 'in time order' the first out at the front of the shed or the head of the yard. The shed turners had a daunting task, impossibly complicated to any outside observer yet straightforward, logical routine to those charged with this nighmarishly complex operation. There were an extraordinary number of rosters at Exmouth Junction and every road might be full on a summer weekend. The turners, armed only with a list of engines, and what the next duties were, set about their labour with absolute confidence usurping one suitable engine after another for the various heavy pulls required to get everything in order. There was a 'shed pilot' of sorts, often an Adams tank like 204 or 207 or a 'Brighton Billy' (E1R). This served as the 'shed shunter', that is the engine for shunting the shed, rather than an

**No.740** *Merlin.* **This engine would have received punctilious cleaning, only slightly less devoted than that administered by the 'Royal Gang'.**

*H.N. James*

**Pacifics at the Junction, on 7th April 1949. The shed received a batch of the first West Countries in 1947 and despite the perplexities of the encased oil bath gear they proved popular.**

**V2 at Exmouth Junction, No. 60896, along with** *Sir Kay* **on 24th May 1953. This would be the period of the Merchant Navy axle problems.**

*C.H.S. Owen*

engine specifically used for shunting other locomotives about the yard. This 'pilot', such as it was and despite its apparent unsuitability to the task, was brought on about 5.30 in the morning, its first duty to place wagons along the ash pits ready for the reeking stuff to be hand shovelled for disposal. For some years a grab crane had been made available for this work but it was frequently out of action. Whether it was required at the ash pit or no, the 'shunter' put in the various oil supplies, spares or whatever was needed by the fitting department, shunting the 'Store Road'. It then arranged for the coal wagons to be lined up for the coaling plant, bringing in rakes of wagons from Exmouth Junction Yard. The concrete works also required a daily shunter; beginning at about 8.15 a.m. and finishing around 2 p.m., it also attended to the carriage and wagon works.

## The Bank

The banking of trains, now almost entirely vanished in Britain was once commonplace, an everyday part of railway operation. There were innumerable instances, usually little known though the 1 in 37 St. Davids bank from the Great Western station up to the LSWR at Queen Street (later Central) was amongst the most remarkable. It was very short and had little of the elemental contest of Beattock or Shap (it leapt across streets and houses rather than moor and stream, and an ascent was measured in minutes) yet the sudden plunge from the heights above the River Exe, a lurching motion by the (frequently) troubled waters, was intensely dramatic. The road from Waterloo was more or less conventional for the railway

*Elder Dempster Lines* **on 20th May 1964. The Junction also maintained a complement of these bigger Pacifics. Their first runs with the** *Devon Belle* **are recalled as odd; 'cream and chocolate amidst all that green, even with them down the road an 'all' (the Great Western were usually 'them' though the Southern turntable was readily made available in the event of trouble at St. Davids).**

*K.C.H. Fairey*

73

traveller; breakfast perhaps and then (after barely noticing the toing and froing at Queen Street) an abrupt careering descent from tunnels and cuttings, the train at once at rooftop level, dropping at an unnerving rate to water meadows and St. Davids Station, with great suddenness. Here the railway was conventionally arranged once more, with a comforting familiarity, the alarming cliff railway episode safely behind. Progress to the west through Exeter was made over the Great Western lines to Cowley Bridge Junction (once mixed gauged); this had proved awkward enough at times but the principal obstacle remained the awesome curving bank. The arrangements necessary for up trains to successfully negotiate it was the responsibility of Exmouth Junction. A loosely defined 'Bank Gang' worked the incline, men junior in driving terms but learning rapidly in the daily pell-mell that weather and breakdown could bring to 'the bank'.

For years there were invariably two bankers out, all the time, with a third engine often manned by drivers 'who didn't want to go anywhere else' and firemen more or less on their first job on the road. The Meldon stone trains worked by Exmouth Junction, an N mogul with ten hoppers would require the full banking panoply - two engines at the rear and one at the front. The two rear bankers lurked in a spur by Exeter Middle Box at the Cowley end of St. Davids station and were out all day from about 7 in the morning until one o'clock the following morning. The 11.30 train if it ran, was the last 'big un' of the night. The front banker was not required continuously and its wait in the loop by the West Box was punctuated by spells on the Exmouth branch. It was exceptional for trains not to be banked - even two coach locals could be so indulged - but the fiery drama achieved its thunderous crashing heights at night, with 'Meldon stone'. An N mogul or S15 4-6-0 would draw slowly into St. Davids,

invariably on the up through road and an almost mystical process of shouts and whistles began. Classically small tanks 'Drummonds or Brighton Billys' were used, an odd choice for such heavy work it might be thought but by no means uncommon in British practice. Small tanks were in regular use on the Lickey say, and 0-4-4Ts were regarded as specially suited to the Beattock bank. The big Z 0-8-0s later enabled one rear banker to be dispensed with and only two were required, one at the front and one behind. When a stone train shuddered to a stand the rear bankers gave two short crows and on reply from the train engine set off, guided by the yell of the 'bobby' in the signal box and the waving lamp of the guard. The front banker at this time would have observed the stones' arrival and would 'get the off' from the West Box man, leaning from his window with the traditional cry 'he's about'. Amidst a few reluctant barks of exhaust and a brief trail of steam the front banker trundled a short distance up the bank, to then set back onto the front of the train. The great cavalcade set off with an abrupt explosion of noise, the disparate exhaust beats brought together in a single volcanic outpouring of smoke, fire and noise. The tumult shook the very fabric of St. Davids, incandescent cinders and sparks fading in their fall and mingling with the ghastly firebox glare. The bank made its daunting, intimidating, presence felt almost immediately, the noise growing to a thunderous clamour, an echoing roll across the flats to the hills above the Exe. The shower of sparks continued up the curving bank, a hazard to cyclists, their faces bathed in glare and registering acute alarm in the road below. Conditions in the mercifully short tunnel were made hideous, temperatures rising with alarming suddenness; a smoke blast and noise of an appalling intensity.

**Late days of blasting up the bank. The full panoply would charge off 'rather like the March from *Aida*' to an assortment of pyrotechnics. Mogul No.31858 and 2-6-4T No.80042, on 2nd July 1963.**

*R.C. Riley*

**Z tank on 26th August 1959. They could toy with the various heavy shunts round about and could take the place of two smaller 'tankies' on the rear banking job. Concrete blocks in a neo-classical office, behind the engine, are interesting touches.**

*K.C.H. Fairey*

**'The Junction' in the evening of its years.**

*R.C. Riley*

# Budleigh Salterton

A small shed for the branch engine was erected at the west end of the yard when the station opened for traffic in May 1897. Very little documentary evidence exists about this tiny establishment, and surveys of the early layout are similarly scarce.

The Budleigh Salterton Railway had been promoted by a 'private' concern, authorised in 1894 and was to run from Tipton St. Johns on the LSWR Sidmouth branch to a terminus inland from the sea. Worked from the outset by the South Western, Board of Trade notes state that 'only tank engines are to be used'. Set amidst land 'of the eminent Lord Clinton' the shed was of very simple construction, executed in wood and measuring 50 ft. x 18 ft. A pit was located inside the building, a coalstage and wooden water tank directly outside.

The station was of a fairly basic nature - goods shed, weighbridge, cattle pens and a single platform, which was later, on rebuilding of the site, to become the down platform.

Plans were proposed in February 1902 which were to completely change the station from a terminus to a through station on a new line linked to Exmouth. Powers to construct this railway had been granted some years earlier in 1898 which allowed for a service to run from Exmouth to Sidmouth Junction direct. Amended plans were subsequently put forward on 25th March 1902, ratified and recommended 'to be carried out'. Considerable work was necessary at Budleigh, a new up platform was constructed and an additional '16 perches of land' were obtained for a roadway. The line had formerly been worked under the 'one engine in steam' principle, although signals are shown on contemporary plans of 1899. The link to Exmouth was eventually complete when the line opened for traffic in June 1903.

The line now extended past the shed over 'Dark Lane' and on to Littleham and Exmouth. Doubling was allowed for, although this was never deemed necessary. The shed had, prior to this, been responsible for all branch workings to and from Sidmouth Junction, the loco outstationed from Exmouth Junction returning to the main shed weekly for washout and repairs. Through working from Exmouth inevitably led to the demise of the shed although it was retained for some time to service early and late services starting and ending at Budleigh. With changes in timetabling the shed was effectively put out of use and although still standing in 1911 the work would now have been largely in the hands of Exmouth tanks. It had been demolished by 1925 but the sidings remained until closure of the whole line in March 1967.

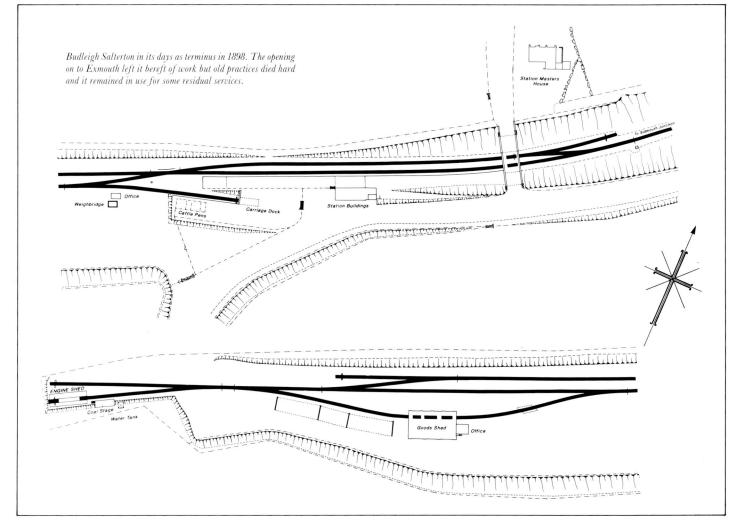

*Budleigh Salterton in its days as terminus in 1898. The opening on to Exmouth left it bereft of work but old practices died hard and it remained in use for some residual services.*

# Sidmouth

*January 1874. Mr. Beattie was instructed to get as speedily as possible a locomotive similar to the one on the Ilfracombe line for the Sidmouth Branch.* This instruction emanated from the Locomotive Committee, busying itself with preparations for the branch opening later in the year, in July 1874. The Barnstaple and Ilfracombe Railway was indeed to open in the same month and presumably the 0-6-0 was duly delivered to the branch. In all probability Beattie 2-4-0WTs began the services, as used on the Swanage and other branches at the time, the class being the staple form of power in these early days. The branch left the main West of England line at Feniton, renamed Sidmouth Junction on the opening of the railway which had been constructed under a Light Railway Order. Obtained in 1871, this had been the second attempt by the Company, earlier efforts coming to nothing, the earthworks being abandoned through some misfortune.*

A copy of the first layout, dated 29th January 1878, is reproduced opposite, 'forwarded to Mr Fisher of Exeter.' All the original features are shown including, tank, coal stage and engine shed. The signal box was later moved to a new site at the head of the goods yard on the down side. The engine shed was of wooden construction and similar to the buildings at Exmouth and Holsworthy, measuring approximately 45ft x 18ft. A small turntable was supplied immediately in front, characteristic of the South Western at this time, and scales at 42ft. Coaling took place from a small stage set in front of the shed along with a small yard lamp and water column. Water was fed by gravity;

the local relief was used to some advantage, the tank being sited on the raised ground at the west side of the Tipton road. An adjustment to the supply was made late in 1897 when an offer was received from the Sidmouth Water Co. to improve it 'at rates which will reduce the cost from £60 as paid at present to about £30 per annum.'

It was not unknown for these small wooden sheds to suffer damage through fire etc; such disasters were partly responsible for the LSWR fascination with 'Muribloc'. Such a misfortune consumed the shed on the night of 7th January 1900 :

*In the small hours of Sunday night* a devastating fire reduced the building to a charred mess. It was reported thus in a letter from the Locomotive Superintendent ....*at 1 o'clock on the morning of 7th instant the engine shed at Sidmouth was destroyed by fire, the origin of which is unknown, and engine No.195 which was stabled there was slightly damaged. The cost of repairs is estimated at £200.* O2 0-4-4T No.195 had in fact been unattended and but for the swift action of the local fire brigade would have suffered more grievously. Nevertheless the building was the major casualty, *a number of supporting columns being the only remains* to greet the shed staff the following morning. Although the paint had been burnt off the loco the enginemen managed to prepare 195 for duty the next day and returned it to Exmouth Junction Monday evening. Shed staff repainted her in due course.

*\*R.A.Williams, History of the LSWR, David & Charles.*

**Postcard view of an ideal country terminus, an institution the LSWR enjoyed in more than usual measure. The fire disturbed this tranquility on a Sunday night and 'raged for a couple of hours...the locomotive within becoming red hot'. This was fortunately something of an exaggeration.**

Sidmouth in the 1930s. The reasons for the closure of the shed are far from clear; carefully rebuilt it was the only one of the Junction's outstations to be closed in Southern days. Engines it remains clear, used the single road long after closure.

*W.A. Camwell*

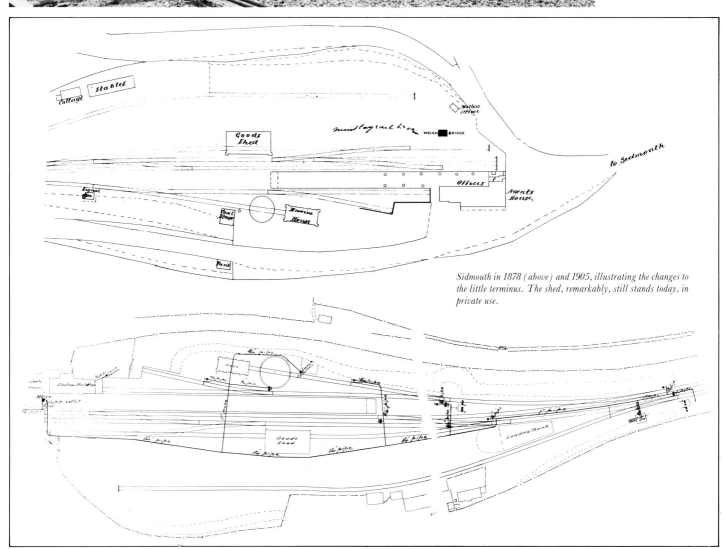

*Sidmouth in 1878 (above) and 1905, illustrating the changes to the little terminus. The shed, remarkably, still stands today, in private use.*

Little was recovered from the building, but the foundations and pit remained, put to further use as a replacement building was erected on the site. Chastened by the experience and similar instances the Board determined upon brick construction. Opportunity was not taken to enlarge the building for it housed only a single passenger tank sent out from Exmouth Junction; the turntable thus saw little use and was eventually removed in the late '20s. 'Old and somewhat worn' the unit was taken out by a local contractor and sent for scrap. The shed itself was by this time out of use, engines making the journey from Exmouth Junction to work the branch. Locos still took water and there was an emergency supply of coal but tracks leading to the shed were cut short and stop blocks added.

The station underwent some renovation in 1935 the General Manager* commenting on his visit in August of that year:

*The Booking and Parcels office at this station is quite inadequate for dealing with the summer traffic, and is also very dark.*

*A sketch was submitted showing how the office could be enlarged by taking in the passageway running from the Booking Hall to the Ladies Room, access to the latter being given direct from the platform.*

*The Chief Engineer was asked to prepare a plan for this and also to include the replacement of a portion of the platform roof outside the station offices in glass, and extend the covered way a further 150ft.*

*At the present time there is no footpath leading from the station entrance to the junction of the two main roads, both of which are fairly busy. It is considered very desirable that such a footpath should be constructed, and the Divisional Engineer was instructed to negotiate with the Local Borough Surveyor with a view to seeing what would be best arrangement to suit the requirements of both the Local Authorities and the Railway passengers and report thereon.*

*The space available for the parking of cars and buses in the forecourt is somewhat restricted. It could be enlarged by an alteration to the fence enclosing the Cattle Dock, thus giving a larger area for the parking of vehicles to carry out the work in consultation with the Divisional Superintendent.*

*ENGINE SHED*

*This has been out of use for some years and work is currently in progress in converting it for further use.*

*GOODS SHED*

*Although the Goods Shed is generally satisfactory for dealing with the Goods Traffic, the work etc, etc....*

Traffic as on most of the South Western branches waned as the 1950s came to a close. The through coach to Waterloo was withdrawn after transfer of the line to the Western Region in 1963. The branch nevertheless survived for some considerable time not closing until March 6th 1967, Sidmouth Junction closing at the same time.

**LOCOMOTIVES**

The plethora of small branch lines in the Western District of the LSWR made this particular part of the railway system a haven for railway enthusiasts in later years. A variety of locomotives could be sought out, unseen anywhere else on the system - Adams Radial Tanks on the Lyme Branch, Beattie Well Tanks at Wadebridge, E1Rs working the Torrington Halwill line and so on. Although the Sidmouth branch could not boast locomotives with the longevity of any of the above the variety was nevertheless over the years most interesting. As mentioned previously an 'Ilfracombe Goods' 0-6-0 was ordered by the Locomotive Committee to work the initial services. It is, however, speculation that this locomotive ever worked over the line but in these early days the ubiquitous Beattie 2-4-0WTs would have been much in evidence. The Drummond locomotives were later to dominate the branch services, M7 and T1 0-4-4Ts covering the passengers with the occasional Adams O2 helping out. Mixed traffic locos of the L11 and K10 classes were also common on the line, supplied from Exmouth Junction.

M7s were push-pull fitted in later years but this did not stop the arrival of the BR fleet of Standard locomotives, 2-6-2Ts and 2-6-4Ts taking over the services. The line was 'dieselised' in 1963, multiple units handling most of the passenger work although summer traffic was augmented by Hymek and North British Type 2 diesels.

*There was a first class hotel in Sidmouth much favoured by S.R. chief officers.*

**No.133 at the Sidmouth 'shed', in the 1930s. The branch engine usually changed at Sidmouth Junction once a fortnight; two sets of men were required and at one time a cleaner saw to the engines overnight needs.**

*R.S. Carpenter*

The wooden shed, hoarding-adorned, through the tracery work of the station.

No.188 by the elderly Exmouth tank(s). Washout as with all outstations, took place at Exmouth Junction though the changeover period was usually seven days

# Exmouth

Originally planned to run from the broad gauge South Devon Railway at Exeter the nominally independent Exeter and Exmouth Railway eventually fell to the standard gauge of the London and South Western. The branch proper began at Polsloe Priory opposite the site of the later Exmouth Junction shed on the main line into Queen Street. Passing Whipton the line swung southwards past the hamlet of Clyst St. Mary and onto Topsham where a ferry linked the village of Exminster on the west bank of the River Exe. The last five miles of the branch ran alongside the river through Lympstone and onto Exmouth, opening to traffic on 1st May 1861. A small wooden engine shed opened in that year close by New Street at the east side of the small terminus. There was no turntable at first but Beattie soon arranged for one to be put in ..... *8th July 1861 : I recommend the erection of a water column at the end of the platform at Exeter station for the use of the Exmouth line engines, and that a Turntable should be placed at that station.....*

The original water tank was of a limited capacity and in 1871 a new tank at Exmouth shed was recommended, at a cost of £40. Two tanks, therefore, stood side by side in the shed yard for many years until the complete remodelling of the station in the 1930s.

Exmouth led an untroubled existence during these early years though traffic at times approached commuter proportions, increasing markedly after opening of the Budleigh Salterton line in 1903, enabling a circular service via Queen Street, Sidmouth, Tipton and Budleigh. Several proposals for complete rebuilding of the station subsequently appeared from the Drawing Office at Waterloo including 'Scheme No.2' which although rejected interestingly enough was resurrected many years later as the basis of a new Southern SR terminus. Sanctioned by the General Manager in October 1916 'Scheme

No.2' envisaged a new station in the goods yard, by the banks of the River Exe. Four platforms each some 600ft. in length were planned and the Dock Line previously skirting the edge of the site was to be directed through the station itself. Strangely enough the engine shed did not figure in this (or other) proposals during these years. The traffic people confined themselves to the station and a plethora of plans, projects and revisions conveniently left the shed and its working to whatever peculiar demands might be deemed appropriate by the Running Department. None of the schemes were approved and were only dusted down after the formation of the Southern Railway, the Company setting forth on something of a campaign to renew many parts of the system. 'Scheme No.2' eventually resurfaced in 1925 but no intentions were disclosed with respect to the engine shed until 1927. In that year correspondence was first exchanged *as to the provision of engine shed accommodation at Exmouth Station....26th January 1927. The General Manager submitted plan for a new engine shed at Exmouth. The building will be in Ferro-concrete supplied from our own works at Exmouth Junction and, as will be seen from the accompanying drawings, will be surmounted by a new water tank. This will allow us to dispense with the current supply which is unreliable and fed from two very old water tanks. Their removal will allow us to make considerable improvements for the stabling of locomotives at this station. The turntable which has not been required for some time and is out of use was recently inspected and found to be beyond repair. This should be removed by a local contractor for scrap. The total cost of the scheme will be £2,200. APPROVED.....*

The building which eventually emerged from these proposals was a single road shed constructed, as determined, 'entirely in concrete'. The tank occupied part of the roof at the rear, the rest being felted and tarred. A small office and messroom adjoined the eastern wall, a W.C. and store also being supplied. A pit and

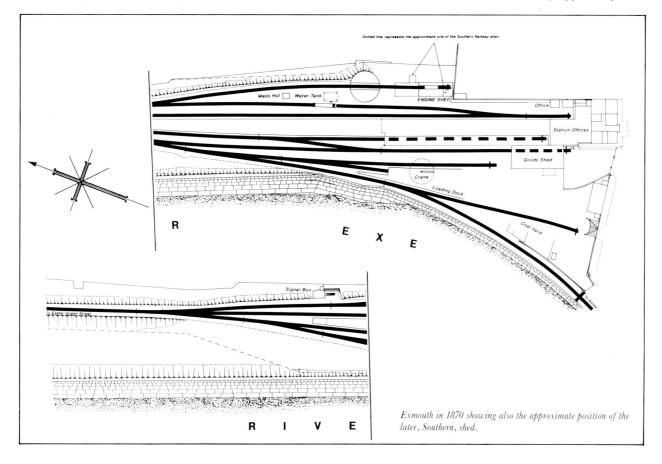

*Exmouth in 1870 showing also the approximate position of the later, Southern, shed.*

No.328 at Exmouth. It was a busy little shed; the Exeter services were quite intense and there was dock traffic both here and at Topsham. The latter was frequently a job for The Junction but Exmouth engines and men worked a tile company siding and the Exmouth Dock line, in daylight only, at 4 m.p.h.and with a flagman!

The new Exmouth shed carried on the tradition of advertising, for the thousands of holidaymakers flowing past. A spare gang contingent from the Junction was necessary to help out in summer and there were also SR 'bosses specials' to keep an eye on.

*W.A. Camwell*

**Crowd at Exmouth. There were no less than eight sets of men based here but although two cleaners did whatever might be necessary to attend the engines there was no shedman. Fires were cleaned at Exmouth but coaling generally required a quick call-in at the Junction. A loaded wagon was available in cases of need.**

*W. Potter*

hydrant was provided inside the building whilst two further pits were located in the yard. The shed occupied a site almost identical to the previous building, alongside New Street Road. It measured approximately 70ft. by 20ft. with coaling (where necessary) effected from open wagons stabled on an adjacent road. Such activity was understandably kept to a minimum and there was usually opportunity during a days work to make use of the Exmouth Junction coaling plant.

Exmouth handled considerable amounts of traffic both passenger and goods (notably pilchards); trains from the Docks, Budleigh Salterton and commuter traffic to Exeter. It could be said that Exmouth had the nearest thing to a commuter service in the west of England, something the General Manager was keen to improve after his visit to the branch on 20th August 1935 ..... *In passing over the Exmouth Branch it was noticed that the service is a somewhat irregular one, and a scheme should be prepared showing how a regular hourly service in each direction could be given throughout the day in the winter months, and a half hourly service throughout the day in the summer months. It is understood that additional provision would have to be made during the one hourly service period for the morning and evening business service. The Traffic Manager was instructed to have a scheme prepared on these lines....*

The Western Region assumed control of the branch in January 1963 diesel units taking over the declining steam duties soon after. Little work now remained for the shed, the stabling of the odd permanent way wagon its only use. The shed closed on November 8th 1963 and although the branch still operates a regular service to the town the building has been demolished and the site covered by a new road.

## LOCOMOTIVES

The Exmouth line today can still afford panoramic views across the estuary of the Exe; unspoilt and mostly unchanged for more than a century. The popularity of the branch of course has waned over the years from the days of packed through specials from all over the south of England, Midlands and the North.

The locomotives in the early years were a variety of 2-2-2Ts whose cabs gave little comfort from the biting winds, which even in summer swept across the sands and mud flats. After 1876 0298 2-4-0Ts were introduced along with the more powerful Ilfracombe Goods 0-6-0s already finding favour on branches in the north of the county. 0395 class 0-6-0s made the odd appearance from Queen Street shed at this time but from c1893 0415 4-4-2Ts were used extensively on branch services.

Almost exclusively O2 and M7 0-4-4Ts covered the branch work after the Great War even double heading specials to and from Queen Street station. Steam railcars performed fleetingly on the branch, but as elsewhere found the work too strenuous and were soon transferred away.

The Dock branch, renowned for its pilchard industry, had many shunting and marshalling jobs worked by a variety of small tanks over the years. B4 0-4-0Ts were evident on most occasions but it was also possible to find an A1 or even a G6 0-6-0T performing on the tightly curved wharf.

Class 2 2-6-2Ts arrived in the 1950s along with the more powerful LM class 4 2-6-4Ts. BR Standard classes were also being used by Exmouth Junction at this time represented by class 3 2-6-2 and class 4 2-6-4 tanks. GW 0-6-0PTs were also noted on the branch with DMUS introduced in 1963.

**The old shed at Seaton, creakingly and alarmingly close to the water.**

*Lens of Sutton*

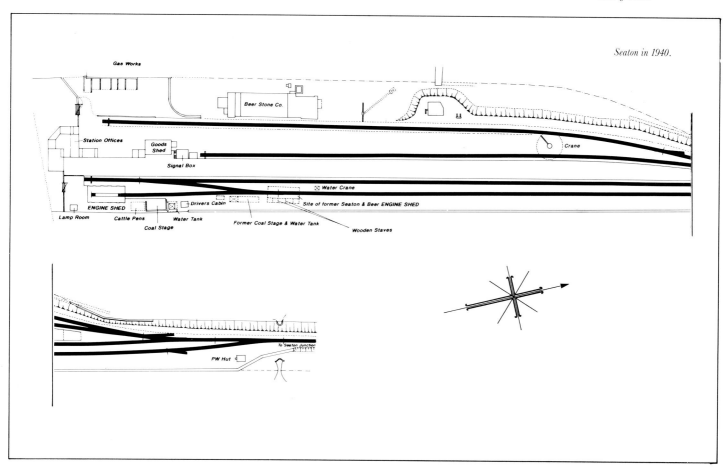

*Seaton in 1940.*

# Seaton

'Colyton for Seaton' had opened on 18th July 1860 as a small wayside station on the main line to Exeter. It was from here that the Seaton and Beer Railway, an independently constituted concern, decided to run a railway to the little seaside resort. For nearly half its course the line ran alongside the River Axe making full use of the level nature of the flood plain. Two small stations were erected en route to Seaton, a fairly substantial structure at Colyton and a second at Colyford, although here the facilities were a little sparse. On the opening of the line on 16th March 1868 the main line station was renamed Colyton Junction but this was to prove too confusing and was finally changed to Seaton Junction on 18th July 1869.* The London and South Western Railway of course had extensive interests in the small line; it worked the services from inception and officially absorbed the Company in 1865.

The station at Seaton lay hard against the west bank of the River Axe and was unremarkable in nature. The small platform had two faces, one used exclusively for branch services, the other for stabling coaching stock. A goods shed, crane and cattle pen completed the facilities in the small yard and a accommodation for the station master formed a considerable part of the station. A drab wooden building sufficed as engine shed, perched precariously above the lapping waters of the river. Its uncomfortable proximity to the water's edge was to lead in later years to problems of slipping foundations, made good by the expeditious use of wooden staves. The shed had originally been part of the plans of the contractor, Sampson, but failure to complete on time led the Company to seek the help of 'Birmingham & Co.' of Broad Clyst. Plans were again submitted

for *an engine shed in wood - foundations to be twice tarred and inspected. Total cost including ironwork ; £2103d.* Maggs and Paye, *The Sidmouth Seaton and Lyme Regis Branches, Oakwood, 1979* give the price at £200 but this may well have excluded ironwork, indeed there could have been very little apart from say the odd brace or stay. Maggs and Paye also note that Captain Charles E. Mangles, Chairman of the LSWR was unhappy at some of the proposed constructions on the line, including the engine shed. He wrote on 27th February 1868 suggesting *that the wooden engine shed and platform at Seaton, platform walls at Colyford and two timber bridges be replaced and also transverse wrought iron girders inserted in two other bridges.* Dismayed at the extra cost the Seaton and Beer Company sought arbitration, Maggs and Paye recording it thus : *To satisfy the LSW, the following month the S&B gave an undertaking that they would reinstate the structures in durable materials. A year later Charles Hutton Gregory giving judgement on 15th March 1869 said that the S&B was properly constructed but remarked that the Company should rebuild with brick, stone or iron the all timber bridges north of Colyford, etc. etc.*

The engine shed, remarkably, survived until the 1930s and was thus something over 60 years old when demolished on rebuilding of the station. It resembled the sheds at Exmouth and Holsworthy in the extreme simplicity of its construction; measuring only 45ft x 18ft it was unsuited even to the earliest locomotives such as the Beattie 2-2-2WTs. The later D1 0-4-2Ts were almost impossible to use, the crews having only inches to spare when boarding locos. A pit was supplied inside and a

*R.F.Clarke, A Southern Region Chronology

**The Seaton shed long resisted a slow slide into the mud below. It was declared 'worn out' and was in any case too small and closely confined for comfort. A pair of push/pull Drummond tanks were long its denizens (one at a time) manned by two sets and coaled by a single cleaner.**

*Lens of Sutton*

sleeper coalstage immediately outside. A water tank and crane were located contiguously but may not have been original features : *Seaton station. 27th January. Subject to approval by the Engineering Committee, by this minute of today have given orders for the water tank at Seaton to be enlarged as to provide storage capacity for 40,000 gallons of water instead of 2000 gallons as at present. The work estimated to cost £250, and if carried out will enable the water supply for engines at Colyton to be dispensed with. APPROVED.* Whether the tank was ever installed has not been ascertained - at 40,000 gallons it was unlikely to have been used solely for engine purposes.

Seaton was always under-provided for; witness LSWR concern at the length of platforms in 1868. Traffic became heavier every year with the 'holiday habit' together with a more modest goods traffic, including stone from quarries at Beer, fish and coal. The Southern determined upon the general rebuilding of the station in 1935; a large holiday camp adjoining it opened around this time and convinced the authorities *...as to the need to meet the traffic at Seaton in the summer months.... The difficulties experienced in handling the summer traffic at Seaton are considerable owing to the extremely limited accommodation. These difficulties have been accentuated by the opening of a large summer camp. The weekend excursion traffic has also increased and owing to the shortness of the platform and the absence of runround facilities etc. the traffic cannot be handled as efficiently and expeditiously as it should be.*

*It has been recognised for some time past that general improvements are necessary at this station, and it has already been decided to include it in the list of New Works to be considered for approval during 1936.*

The Chief Engineer was therefore requested to prepare a plan embodying as its main features the following:-

*(i) The platform to be lengthened to accommodate a train of 12 coaches.*

*(ii) A run-round road through the engine shed to be provided for trains of this length.*

*(iii) In tipping for the necessary run-round road, space also to be allowed for putting in a long carriage siding outside the run-round road if conditions will allow. The present station building to constitute Parcel, Booking and Enquiry Offices, and a new building including Booking Hall, Waiting Rooms, Lavatory Accommodation etc. to be designed in place of the present structures. The platform to be raised to standard height and to be covered to a length of 300ft.*

This was an aspect of so-called Southern *Nouveau,* an era when many 'standard' components emerged from the Company's works at Exmouth Junction. It was apparent, however, that the dismal original shed was to be retained. It was a place of great bleakness, the decaying shack afforded little comfort and was to be transformed into a through building, presumably restricting movements on and off shed to a minimum, stabling taking place only in the early mornings or after services ceased at the end of the day. Any structural alteration was likely to bring about the collapse of the building let alone such fundamental rearrangement and this was obvious once site realities became clear. Further plans were made, to include some form of proper shed accommodation, notice of this given in the simple caveat... *Locomotive Shed construction not included in this contract.*

The authorities cogitated upon this and found room for a shed off the lengthy runround, at the east side of the station.

*\*A useful catch-all term (despite certain drawbacks) to describe architectural developments, particularly with regard to the widespread and novel use of concrete, from the 1920s until the Second World War.*

**No. 224 at Seaton on 24th June 1928. The branch engine also shunted the little yard, the traffic including fish, livestock and of course coal and general goods. Excursion work in the summer brought 4-4-0s and Moguls and even a West Country it is said.**

*H.C. Casserley*

**30045 in July 1959. 64XX pannier tanks took over the push/pull with 'the London coach' (the connection for London) at the front and the auto at the rear. Sometimes two engines were at Seaton and one would return light, or as pilot to a local. The Western Region it was widely felt 'didn't want to know'.**

*J. Davenport*

Proposals submitted on 8th March 1937 for a shed *of brick and concrete construction with water tank incorporated in the roof* bear various pencil marks including a line through the water tank saying 'No'. The building was neat if plain, assembled from existing artifacts and making use of 'Muribloc', similar to that at Ilfracombe and Okehampton, for the walls and (separate) water tank. This was particularly ingenious, sitting upon a construction adapted from pre-cast concrete footbridges, then being erected across the Southern. The office was simply a pre-cast 'sectional' hut of suitable dimensions. The coal stage was put together from leftover platform supports and concrete steps and slabs. It could even double as a cattle dock.

Work was still in progress on 18th and 19th August 1937 when the General Manager made an inspection; the Isle of Wight and the West Country were particular favourites for these summer visits.
*The work in progress on the station remodelling was inspected. It was decided to provide a small elongated island within the Company's boundary on the station forecourt, with suitable 'in' and 'out' and parking direction notices. The Chief Engineer will arrange for a plan to be prepared. This arrangement will allow of better circulation of road traffic, and provide a definite standing space for the Associated Company's omnibuses.*

*Plan No.II/2623D/5 shows triangular space as pavement outside the gates leading to the engine shed (iron work delayed); it would be better if this were arranged as a bed planted with suitable shrubs. The General Manager instructed the Chief Engineer to arrange accordingly.*

Seaton shed was administered from Exmouth Junction, the locomotives outstaioned overnight to run the up morning service. As with all these West Country branches, change of boundary brought Seaton under Western Region control in 1963, and subsequent dieselisation. The shed closed on November 4th that year along with Exmouth and Lyme Regis and was subsequently demolished, a large factory now covering both station and shed site.

**LOCOMOTIVES**

Branch traffic running between the junction and Seaton would in the beginning have been in the hands of Beattie engines, 2-2-2WTs No.12 & 33; the pair are known to have been used on the line at this time although an 'Ilfracombe Goods' 0-6-0 was recorded working passenger services during the 1880s. Various other tank engines came to the line including O2 and occasionally T1 0-4-4s but by the 1930s displaced LBSCR D1s were covering the passenger traffic.

Seaton, a notable holiday resort at this time, catered for an astonishing variety of trains on excursion work and consequently witnessed many classes of locomotives. M7 0-4-4Ts, T9 4-4-0s, Q and Q1 0-6-0s, U and N 2-6-0s, Bulleid Pacifics and even some 'foreign' locomotives working through. GWR pannier tanks of the 64XX class were allocated to Seaton on the Western Region takeover in 1963 and dieselisation in the form of multiple units covered the passenger traffic from withdrawal of the 0-6-0PTs until closure.

Branch engine at Axminster. The 'Big Wheelers' were used on light work when absent from the branch 'and the spare pair was generally treated gently' during 'off' weeks at the Junction, either stored or shunting the carriage sidings/concrete works. 8th July 1949.

*H.C. Casserley*

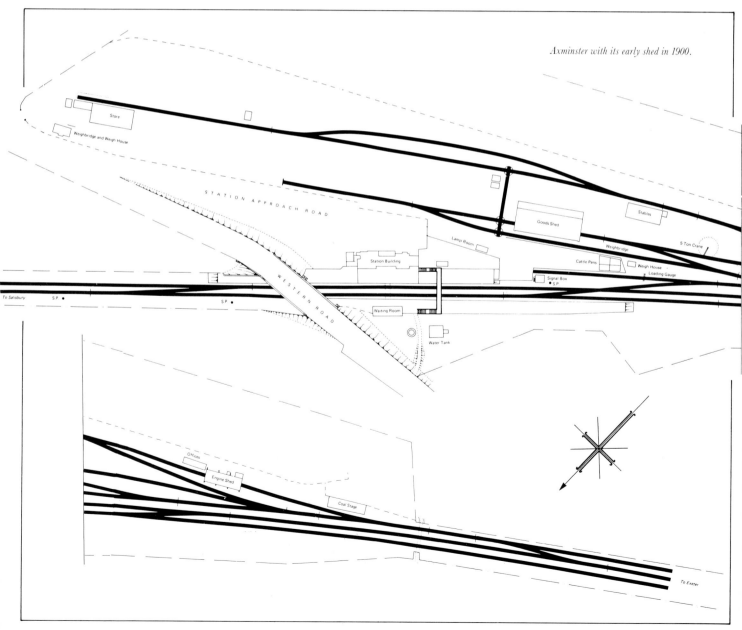

*Axminster with its early shed in 1900.*

# Lyme Regis and Axminster

The Lyme Regis branch passed through some of the most beautiful and spectacular parts of Dorset and was considered the 'best introduction one could wish for'. The charming woodlands carpeted by bluebells and primroses in spring attracted ramblers in their hundreds, the undulating chalkland coming to an abrupt halt on the magnificent cliffs overlooking the Channel. The station lay perched on this hillside above Lyme and afforded breathless views over land and sea. Passing through a small cutting on the approach to the station one was suddenly confronted with a sweeping view of Lyme Bay, which Lewis Cozens (*The Lyme Regis Light Railway*) alludes to in his publication of 1952 .....*From the station superb views are obtained to the east, stretching from the great fossil bearing cliffs of Black Ven (between Lyme Regis and Charmouth) past Golden Cap (619ft the highest cliff on the south coast of England) onwards by the curving Chesil Beach to distant Portland Bill, with the English Channel to complete the picture.....*

The Axminster coal stage and water tower, almost an 'outstation of an outstation'.

## AXMINSTER

The branch proper began here, a small wayside station between Chard and Seaton Junctions. One of the many intermediate stations on the west of England main line it acted as a railhead to the surrounding parts including Lyme itself. Axminster station had opened in July 1860 and included a small goods yard to handle local commodities (Axminster Carpets later a notable product of the town). A minute engine shed was established in the yard, along with coal stage and offices. Mess facilities were also provided, the building it is thought, constructed in corrugated iron. Very little is known of this early building and apart from one official plan there is almost no other documentary evidence - save an allocation of 1882 unearthed by the late D.L.Bradley who wrote .....*A 2-4-0, previously a locomotive in the Engineer's Department and numbered 4, was stationed here to assist trains over Honiton bank, which although not that servere by some standards, was nevertheless a test for the smaller locomotives in those days.....* The locomotive was *Locke*. Believed to have been out of use by 1896 the shed is nevertheless recorded on plans of 1901; shortly afterwards it was swept away as the embankments for the Lyme Regis branch were thrown up. A small servicing area was established on the down side by the road overbridge comprising coal stage, water column and water tank fed by a pump. Here the locomotives working off the Lyme branch would replenish their tanks and bunkers before returning to Exeter or work on the branch. Axminster was an outstation of Exmouth Junction, locos returning light weekly for washout or repair.

## LYME REGIS

Steeply graded and with exceedingly tight curves the branch wound its way up to the summit at Compyne 500 ft. above sea level to drop to Lyme at 250 ft., still a mile from the town .....*It was impossible to connect Lyme with the railway system of the country without engineering works of considerable magnitude; but the facilities offered by the Light Railway Act, and the skill of Mr. Arthur C. Pain, M.Inst.C.E. who has made a special study of this class of undertaking, have at last brought the expense of a line to Lyme Regis within practicable limits.....* An engine shed was established more or less from the first; it was of considerable proportions, to house two ex-LBSCR A1X 'Brighton' tanks supplied for the 'Special Work' needed on the line.

The building measured a generous 100 ft. x 20 ft. with a sleeper coalstage outside. An LSWR pattern water column stood by the entrance, fed from a small tank perched on land overlooking the station approach. Almost no details have survived of this early building, only that construction was executed in wood, along with the buildings at the terminus. The little 0-6-0Ts were soon in trouble, the stresses deriving from the sharp curves exacting a toll in the form of excessive flange wear, strained frames and gland leakage. 02s took over in 1907 but proved unsatisfactory, suffering various problems; nevertheless they were to remain for some time, until the arrival of the Adams 'Radial' tanks, a class which was to become synonymous with the line until their withdrawal in the early 'sixties.

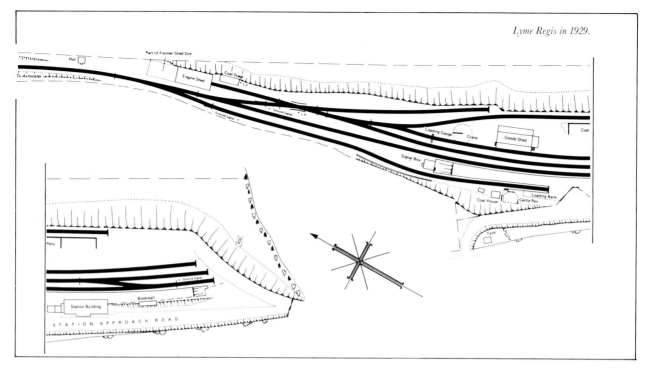

*Lyme Regis in 1929.*

**No. 3520 at Lyme shed on 11th June 1935; 3125 was the branch engine, the pair presumably double heading the heavier trains.**

*W.A. Camwell*

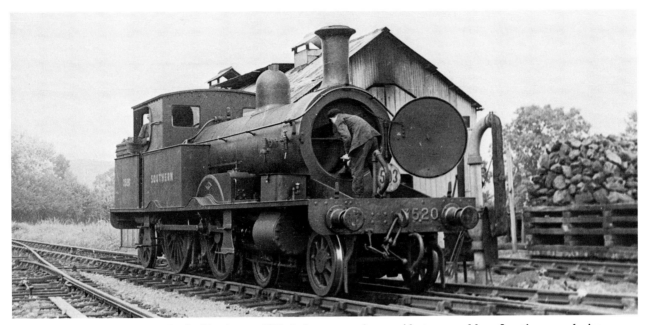

**Disposal work at Lyme Regis, 31st August 1935. A cleaner was long resident; covered by a Junction man during sickness, he performed the coaling duties together with the crew if necessary. Lodging throughout the Exmouth Junction summer empire demanded a certain resourcefulness - you could cycle home to Barnstaple from Ilfracombe for instance and still claim the allowance whilst at Lyme one genius had digs in the** *Victoria Hotel,* **his keep paid by working in the bar.**

*H.C. Casserley*

Opportunity was taken at this time to try new motive power on this difficult line. Whether the branch 02s had in fact been damaged in the fire is hard to say but whatever, the South Western were not happy with the wear and tear suffered by the locomotives. D.L. Bradley relates in his book *Locomotives of the LSWR*, RCTS, 1967, that .....*In 1913, the provision of different locomotives for the Lyme Regis branch had again to be considered, for the Adams 02s which had been in charge since May 1907 were not proving really satisfactory. As an experiment therefore, Urie took No. 0125 into shops in mid-September, 1913, to give its bogie greater side play and thereby make the negotiation of the severe curves abounding on the branch easier. Leaving Eastleigh works on 11th October this engine was tested five days later between Axminster and Lyme Regis with both goods and passenger trains, when it gave a much better performance than that achieved by the small Adams 0-4-4 tanks. Apart from recommending that the quantities of fuel and water carried should be restricted, the Civil Engineer was also quite satisfied with the tests. Therefore in the new year two more of the class were similarly modified, their details being: No. 521, 24th January 1914; No. 0419, 7th March 1914. Like No. 0125 the latter was provided with double slide bars and crossheads, but No. 521 retained the single pattern. One of these engines was normally sub-shedded at Lyme Regis, while the other two were kept at Exmouth Junction and employed mainly on the Exmouth service. At busy periods the Lyme Regis branch required the use of two engines, but with three available it was usually possible to cover routine repairs without resorting to 02s....*

Exquisite situation and long decrepitude made Lyme amongst the most endearing of the gaggle of Exmouth Junction out-stations. Two engines had traditionally been outbased with two sets of men supplemented as required from the 'Junction', often passed cleaners, especially in summer. The job was no sinecure and the branch was a hard one to work. One lodged for a spell of firing and Lyme was considered one of the least attractive for this purpose; of all the Junction jobs 'it was an awful place to get anything' and in the 1940s Exmouth Junction took to booking two cleaners so difficult was it to get a lad to go there. A Lyme posting could with uncanny certitude induce all manner of minor illness and incapacity.

Ashes were dumped outside at Lyme shed but much of the engine work as already mentioned took place at Axminster. Shifting foundations imparted a lop-sided look to the little shed and the fragmentary doors proved almost impossible to use. The 'Radials' reign ended in the early 'sixties when extensive track realignment took place, enabling class 2 2-6-2 tanks to take over the remaining services, something which they did with considerable ease. The line passed to the Western Region in 1963 the transfer bringing 'one engine in steam', and all signals were removed with haste. The inevitable happened later that year, the shed closing along with Seaton and Exmouth in November.

The Running Department, particularly in the West, suffered regular fires at its remote outstations and a typical incident occurred late in 1912 ...... *The Engine Shed at Lyme Regis was discovered to be on fire on the morning of 28th December and before the flames could be extinguished the structure was burnt to the ground.....* Whether or not the locomotives were involved was not reported, but the board were swift to move, approving plans for a new structure in April 1913 .....*Referring to minute of 23rd January, a detailed drawing of the new engine shed which it is proposed to erect at Lyme Regis in place of the one destroyed by fire in December last was submitted. The cost of the building is estimated by the engineer at £400 as mentioned in the Engineering Committee minute of this date.....*

This shed emerged as a shack like building, destined rapidly to fall into disrepair. It was set upon the original foundations to reduce costs but was only about half the length of the former building, the first having proved to be over generous with respect to space. A steel frame was used, clad in corrugated iron, doors were of wood and windows were steel framed. A pit ran the length of the building and a washout hydrant was located alongside. Two small raised vents in asbestos ushered the smoke away, the roof being of similar material. Whether this was an improvement on what existed before is doubtful, steel framed buildings of this period could derange rapidly and the flapping corrugated material eventually transformed the shed into a mocking reflection, in miniature, of the parent shed at Exmouth Junction.

Okehampton, gloriously sited on the fringes of the Moor. It was an odd place in many respects, for years (if ever at all) there was no proper allocation and it stood as a retreat for engines off all manner of sheds, Salisbury, Plymouth, Exmouth Junction and Wadebridge. It is best associated with 'the stone' engines, principally Moguls but other types following the installation of its fine new turntable.

W.A. Camwell

# Okehampton

Okehampton nestles close to the very edge of northern Dartmoor and the little shed seemed almost to echo the exposed, almost tenuous hold of the town. The building clung perilously to the slopes of East Hill, on one of the alarming, heroic curves of the LSW main line. The route to Plymouth was driven on through Okehampton in the 1870s; it acted as a terminus of the line from 1871 until the section to Lydford came into use in 1874 but it is not known what, if any, arrangements were made for locomotives. A 42ft. turntable is shown on a plan of 1885 and in all likelihood this had been put in some years before; even from the earliest days, Okehampton was an important exchange for trains from Plymouth and the North Cornwall line from Holsworthy.

*November 8th 1893 Okehampton : Additional sidings on the east end of the station and erection of an Engine Shed. Estimated cost £5,530. TO BE DONE.* With this terse instruction a shed was at last established; The sidings were hewn out of the hillside providing spoil for the embankment supporting the shed; accounting for the not inconsiderable cost of construction.

The shed was probably completed towards the end of the following year or possibly in the early part of 1895. In June and July of 1894 there are various brief references to the 'Locomotive Department' and its needs and a further note regarding the replacement of the turntable....

*27th June 1894 Read Report ...as to the requirements of the Locomotive Department in connection with the general improvements ordered at Okehampton.*

*25th July 1894 Additional Accommodation for Locomotive Department ...£965...Recommended.*

*May 1895 ...Read letter from the Engineers of 16th April reporting* that the 40ft. engine turntable at Ilfracombe station requires renewing and recommending that the recently recovered turntable from Okehampton, be erected at Ilfracombe at an estimate including strengthening of £200. TO BE DONE.

The new turntable at Okehampton was 50ft, for 'the biggest locomotives now in service' and lay outside a modest engine shed of 'lap board' construction, sufficient to house a single tender locomotive. Water came from a large tank at the Exeter end of the up platform and this caused some problems; on 17th March it was necessary to order *that steps be taken to ensure a sufficient supply of water for engines ... all the year round at Okehampton.* On 14th April a supply was approved from the River Okement, at an estimated cost of £1200 but there were (unspecified) 'legal problems' and on 21st July 1897 the 'improvements' were estimated at only £200.

The shed had not been built with a generous regard to space and some difficulty had been experienced, locomotives 'fouling the doors'. There follow one or two more or less oblique references to the cramped nature of the accommodation but no serious consideration appears to have been given until 1913; in October the Traffic Officers Conference were advised of a variety of 'new works' including a proposal for:

*increased accommodation at Okehampton Engine Shed ... Reported that a saving of £500 per annum could be effected in running expenses if the engine shed at Okehampton was enlarged so as to admit of the ballast engine that works the stone trains from Meldon Quarry being housed there instead of it being brought daily from Exeter, and Plan No.9, 420 was submitted showing how the necessary work could be carried out at an estimated cost of £610.*

The plans were duly authorised and subsequently forwarded for

**Okehampton on 9th June 1935, with two Moguls presumably for 'the stone' secreted in its fireproof interior, 1835 and 1845.**

decision by the Engineers Committee :

*Ordered: subject to approval of this committee the Engine Shed accommodation at Okehampton to be increased as shown on the plan submitted at an estimated cost of £160 as recommended by the Traffic Officers at their meeting of the 25th October last. APPROVED.*

## MELDON QUARRY

It is a convenient moment to discuss, albeit briefly, the locomotive accommodation at the quarry itself. The Company had begun these workings in 1897 for stone used chiefly as ballast. As mentioned above the 'stone engine' eventually found itself housed in the shed alongside the station. Duties of course would have included shunting and marshalling trains ready for departure to Exeter and eastward to London. The quarry and the work steadily grew in size to warrant in later years a permanent shunting engine. Records show this to be ex-SER No.313, a Manning Wardle 0-4-0ST originally destined for the Folkestone Harbour branch and allocated to the quarry in the mid 20s. Although designated a 'Departmental' locomotive, operations were necessarily closely linked with the Running Department.

A small shed of wooden construction, covered with the usual corrugated iron sheeting, was erected to house the variety of locomotive which came to use the quarry. Needless to say the building suffered appalling decay over the years and was replaced by the concrete building still evident today.

The Meldon Manning Wardle 0-4-0ST trundling through the ordered chaos that was (and is) the quarry workings.
*H.C. Casserley*

## A DISASTER

To return to Okehampton shed; the building was more or less doubled in length, the new work again in wood but it was not to be enjoyed for long. A 'disastrous fire' occurred in June 1920, notified thus to the Locomotive Committee a month later :

*It was reported that the Engine Shed at Okehampton was destroyed by fire on 7th June last and that the Engineering Committee had ordered a shed to be constructed with concrete blocks and corrugated asbestos roofing, shown on the plan (No.16658) subject to the approval of this committee. The estimated cost of the work is £1500. APPROVED.*

The Engineering Committee had indeed been swift in supplying drawings of new accommodation, a reflection probably of the shed's importance. Similar speed was shown by the committee of inquiry; the exact reasons behind the incident and its findings are detailed thus.

**The ruinous Meldon wooden shed with tank engine faithfully stabled inside. In proper Southern tradition its successor was put up in concrete.**
*Lens of Sutton*

### FIRE ON COMPANY'S PREMISES OKEHAMPTON 6th JUNE 1920

*At 12.45 a.m. on June 6th a Shunter and Porter, who were performing night duty at Okehampton, discovered that the engine shed, which is situated at the London end of the station, was on fire. They informed the signalman, who communicated the information to Yeoford Junction, and a few minutes afterwards about 50 yards of the telegraph wires, which were run on poles close to the engine shed, were burnt out and all communication east of Okehampton destroyed.*

*The shunter took immediate steps to obtain fire hose, and with the assistance of the Porter and the Driver and Fireman of the Shunting Engine, appears to have done everything possible, but was unable to prevent the engine shed, which was a wooden building with a slate roof, being entirely destroyed. They were unable to remove from the shed the two tender engines which were considerably damaged.*

A joint enquiry was held on the 14th June. The officers report as follows:

*The last two men in the shed before its demolition were Herbert George Newman, the Fireman of the shunting engine (who had been sent over by his driver (Bennett) about 11.30 p.m. to ascertain why the gas lamps in the shed were alight) and Loco Cleaner Tanton of Exeter. The Driver and Fireman belong to Okehampton and had signed off and left the shed about 10.0 p.m.*

*We regret there is a direct conflict of evidence. Tanton states that having finished his work about 11.00 p.m. he was cleaning himself preparatory to travelling back to Exeter when Fireman Newman came to the shed and made some enquiries for an empty sack, subsequently opening a cupboard belonging to driver Wayburn and taking out some sponge cloths, afterwards having a further search at the western end of the shed for the sack before he left the building. During this search Newman is said to have used two or three matches at the cupboard and another match at the western end of the shed. Tanton also states that before Newman left the building he (Tanton) had put out all the gas lamps and was outside closing the doors of the engine shed before he noticed that Newman had gone away.*

*Newman, on the contrary, denies having used any matches in the shed. He further states that when he left the shed all the gas lamps were burning. With regard to Tanton, who states that he was washing his face and hands when Newman entered the building, Newman declares that Tanton was brushing his hair and smoking a cigarette, whilst Tanton emphatically denies he was smoking in the building at all.*

*No definite origin of the fire can be assigned; but it would appear to have resulted either from carelessness on the part of Tanton in connection with his work, or the result of Fireman Newman exploring the shed and using*

Okehampton and the country which this line pierced so magnificently, on 15th April 1938. On shed that day were two Moguls once more, 1844 and 1848 and No. 3083.

*W.A. Camwell*

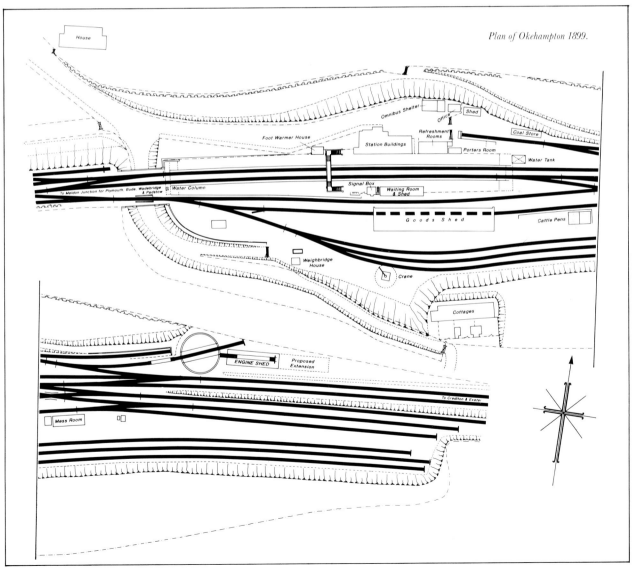

*Plan of Okehampton 1899.*

*the matches, which, when dropped, caused some inflammable matter to smoulder and ignite.*

*Cleaner Tanton gave his evidence in a very straight forward and lucid manner, the only weakness being that when he was interviewed by Messrs. Hale and Moore on the Sunday (6th June) he did not say anything about the matches which Newman is supposed to have used and this feature was not forthcoming until the next day.*

*Newman, on the other hand, was a very disappointing witness, and we feel we must call attention to the irregularity which he committed by opening the cupboard belonging to another man and extracting articles to which he must have known he had no right. Further, the object of his looking for an empty sack was to place in it some lumps of lime which he had picked up on the permanent way. Had Newman acted in accordance with his Driver's instructions by going to the shed and, after finding the Cleaner there, returning directly to the footplate, he would have escaped the suspicion of being implicated in the fire, which now must necessarily rest upon him.*

The wretched Newman's fate is unknown, presumably a fine at the very least and a poor bargain for a few lumps of lime. A new shed was authorised within a matter of weeks, on 22nd June 1920, with some considerable regard to the likelihood of further fire; 'Engine Shed, Okehampton ... destroyed by fire 7th June ... shed to be reconstructed with concrete blocks and corrugated asbestos roofing. Estimate £1500 ... APPROVED.'

The shed like its ill-fated forebear was furnished with one road, a pit running the entire length of the building and a small office/mess room where men could light matches safely, was attached to the side. The builders made use of the existing foundations and also installed a small coal stage. This was to prove awkward to use and enginemen latterly preferred the convenience of a coal wagon and small 'portable' stage.

The turntable by the latter part of the 1930s was nearing the end of its useful working life. Ballast trains, the staple work of the shed for many years were now considerably heavier and necessarily larger locomotives were increasingly used on these demanding turns, S15 4-6-0s permitted to work to Meldon in 1943. Baldwin 2-8-0s from Exmouth Junction also worked to the Quarry, but for many years the faithful 'Woolworth' 2-6-0s handled the bulk of the traffic. A 70ft turntable had been installed at Basingstoke in 1943 and one of similar dimensions and design was subsequently ordered for Okehampton. The 'table was laid down at the Exeter end of the station by the water tank and new pits, water columns and coaling shelter were all supplied in a rearranged yard. The building had some small modifications carried out, the wooden facade above the entrance was replaced with corrugated sheeting, the roof received further attention in the form of new smoke vents and the doors, by now inoperable, removed. These two sites, Basingstoke and Okehampton, were in some senses peculiar choices to make and can be explained, it is believed, by wartime traffic demands. Basingstoke in this period was a strategic and highly sensitive junction, Okehampton an important source of raw material. Meldon provided ballast for the entire Southern Railway and in wartime, beyond, and was also a useful refuge on a lengthy and crowded main line, which a heavy freight could take days to travel. Such strategic improvements were common from 1942/3 under Government control, for traffic increasingly funnelled to the south coast, on an awesome scale.

Okehampton was transferred to the Western Region in 1962 and closed some four years later, along with Wadebridge and Bude.

## WORKING OVER THE MOOR

The winter of 1947 broke upon a Britain debilitated by war and persistent shortage; the country suffered to a degree beyond the memories of most and it lingers today in the mind, a yardstick almost, for privation and harshness. It smote the West with a white fury, stifling everyday life and rendering the simplest movements more or less impossible. The railway, especially the Dartmoor limb of the LSWR, had for years served as lifeline in these circumstances, abandoning established procedures and practices in the salvation of people and livestock. This role had traditionally been performed in concert with farmers, workers and townspeople and in particular elements of the armed forces, of which there were (and are) many stationed close to Dartmoor and Plymouth. Okehampton shed awoke to a hushed world, flurries of snow lacing the hillside; this was unremarkable enough and held but scant hint of the trials to come. The gloom deepened through the day until the snow had become relentless; it was soon clear that it would be a difficult time, and slowly, things came to a halt. Snow drifting off the Moor reached depths of nine feet in places bringing down telegraph poles for miles around. Communications were thus scant and signal boxes for several weeks after the first falls of snow were forced to use the time interval system for train working.

The crew of the late turn T9 that evening could only gaze down upon the (faltering) lights of Okehampton far below. They were there to take a train to Exeter but were instead directed back towards Lydford, *tender first*, in an attempt to clear the road as the snow came in. With great foreboding they set off, 'slow and careful', crossing Meldon amidst a gale; the great viaduct successfully negotiated, the engine proceeded, with slow purpose, to then bury itself in a colossal drift a mile and a half beyond, at Sourton Down. Nothing of this was known until some hours later when the fireman at last staggered back to Meldon signalbox .... 'in a terrible state', as might be understood. Meldon telephoned through to Okehampton, where a glum crew crouched in the shed, hopeful that their own T9 4-4-0 might not be called upon. Forewarned of the drifts it set off chimney first (carrying the slowly recovering fireman), crossing Meldon Viaduct, on past the lonely junction signal box, only to hit the same snowdrift, forced to a halt yards from the first stricken T9. The driver of the first engine was found to be in some difficulties; the canvas cab sheet had long been carried off and he had to be gingerly levered from his refuge close in the corner of the cab.

The numb driver could only nod his head in some simple form of gratitude, tongue cleaving to his mouth. All four now retreated to the doubtful protection of the second T9, where at least an impoverished brazier, a bucket with holes knocked in it, gave some rudimentary comfort. It was 9 o'clock in the evening by now and past midnight when the Exeter plough eventually pulled alongside the four huddled shapes and their brazier. The ordeal nonetheless had some hours yet to run; the plough set off amid solemn oaths to return in half an hour and instructions to cast out the fire. This only evinced a few muttered curses and knowing nods - this sort of thing had been heard before and indeed as dawn broke hours later, glittering white, still no sound or hint of the Exeter plough came across the shrouded hills to the weary footplate band. The dawn brought the kind of exquisite morning that can only follow a tempest, and a walk to the nearest farm, for a fry-up of heroic proportions. This was to prove later an even greater fortune for at Okehampton the water had frozen in the night and remained so for many days. An engine eventually appeared to take the refreshed crews back to a thoroughly miserable 'Okey' and further waiting about. The marooned T9s were eventually dug out by the Royal Marines, dragged back to Okehampton and re-lit for working back to Launceston.

'Okey' consistently proved both refuge and operational centre in these times. Snow ploughs were made ready every winter, from Salisbury to Exeter with loosely defined spheres of work. Exmouth Junction and Salisbury for instance divided the main line between themselves, the boundary traditionally fixed at Yeovil. In the 1963-64 winter, which recalled to many the dark days of 1947, there were no less than seven engines and trains marooned around Dartmoor at one point. Ploughs on setting out were routinely powered by '140lbs 0-6-0s,' unsuited for the toughest work. In 1963 much of the rescue work was carried out by Q 0-6-0s, the trains dragged back to Okehampton for the passengers to be decamped and the engine seen to. Confronted by the worst of the drifts Okehampton could only double up on power, coupling an N mogul to the usual Q and the plough; in despite of this, mountainous drifts came close to halting the cavalcade and the first of the rescued trains only crawled forth after many anxious hours. The forty or so passengers, though grateful enough, were still marooned at Okehampton and were housed for the duration in coaches, steam heated by an engine. With strict railway sense of propriety they were fed in a handy refreshment car. In times such as this the plough would serve a multiplicity of purposes, ferrying people about, including the Army and delivering foodstuffs, especially bread, to Meldon and other places. Bales of hay were thrown on the tender for cattle and sheep, often only reached from the lineside. Given this interlacing of interest and common adversity any farmer would be glad to provide a breakfast for crews caught on the line.

## LOCOMOTIVES

Okehampton's strategic role on the main line to Plymouth made it both an important and interesting location. Many classes of locomotives were allocated to the small shed over the years with a facinating mixed-bag of visiting types. In the very earliest days 302 and 273 class 0-6-0s handled much of the mixed traffic, whilst Adams 395 0-6-0s were familiar engines staying at least until the outbreak of hostilities in 1914. Adams 46 class were 'allocated' new to Okehampton to work the Holsworthy line in 1879 but they would have been serviced and housed at the small shed at the terminus. Beattie 4-4-0s, the 380 'Steamrollers', were used some time later on the mixed traffic turns to Plymouth and Exeter and whilst tank engines handled all traffic on the branches, 4-4-0s worked the Okehampton - Launceston North Cornwall line.

The familiar O2 and M7 0-4-4Ts were later outstationed from Okehampton to work the Halwill - Bude line (opened in 1898), with the more powerful T1 0-4-4Ts making the odd appearance. Adams Radial tanks also became a familiar and popular class of locomotive used on these services. Various Drummond types were used on the mixed traffic work notably the K10 and L11 4-4-0s which performed admirably on the difficult route to Plymouth and Wadebridge for many years. S11s came to work passenger trains to Wadebridge, Plymouth and Exeter and were later replaced by the ubiquitous N 2-6-0 mogul and T9 4-4-0. These two classes above all others came to dominate mixed traffic work throughout the west until Standard types started to arrive in the late fifties and early sixties. S15 4-6-0s, allowed to Meldon in 1943, were occasionally used on the 'stone' but the service was more or less the preserve of the Moguls - a job they were eminently suited to.

**The new turntable looking towards London. Great engines rumbled onto this 'table out of some mist-shrouded wilderness, stayed a while and crept away much as they had come.**

M7 No. 42 at Bude on 9th June 1935. A simple shed at the end of a long branch, workings were characteristically convoluted. 'Okey' men for instance would work the 'Bude Goods' with an N or U Mogul from Exmouth Junction, shunting stations on the way including Bude, turn and work back 'to Okey'. The Mogul would then be ready for another crew to take it to Wadebridge, say.

*W.A. Camwell*

# Bude and Holsworthy

The LSWR had opened its station at Okehampton in 1871 and extensions westwards proceeded amidst the usual trials. The line, destined to serve the faintly *bourgeois* settlement of Bude and Stratton opened to a terminus at Holsworthy in January 1879 whereupon the familiar squabbles broke out. Conducted principally in the local press they punctuated the period prior to extension onwards to Bude, in 1898.

## HOLSWORTHY

The progress of the LSWR lines across the more remote areas of Devon and Cornwall was marked by a succession of minor terminus stations, usually accompanied by a single road engine shed. It was invariably provided with a turntable, often immediately outside (a sensible disposition but also at the rear, rendering the shed, carefully laid out and constructed to a high standard, for much of the time useless. Holsworthy was typical of any number of small branch line sheds to be found in the west - a simple 'stable', access off a turntable immediately outside, with a crude open coal stage. Sufficient to get an engine off towards Okehampton or some similar point representing the outside world, early on a Monday morning.

The shed opened with the line and the detail of its years of operation (ending, to a considerable extent, at the turn of the century) must remain largely inexplicable. The shed served in simple fashion as did its successor at Bude and only a few Minutes and plans allow of some comment. It might have been expected to have gone immediately out of use on the opening to Bude in 1898 but apparently some duties kept it in intermittent use until 1917.

The constant concern with water supply brings the shed to notice as early as May 1878:
*WATER SUPPLY HOLSWORTHY: Read minute of Officers Committee of the 20th May recommending arrangements for the above by the construction of a reservoir with a drain to the engine shed and two hydrants and fittings at the estimate of £475, subject to an agreement with Lord Stanhope for obtaining the necessary supplies from his spring at a rent of £5 per year. Recommended to be carried out.*

This supply was piped along the line in a 3 inch main past the coal stage and turntable to a tank opposite cottages on the Launceston road. Later in 1881 a new supply was proposed from a well and pump house directly under the viaduct, tapped into the shed supply and dispensing with the 3 inch piping along the line from Okehampton.

The shed itself was of wooden construction and identical in almost every detail to the first shed at Exmouth. It had enough room for one tank locomotive working the local services to Okehampton. A 42 ft. turntable was sited immediately in front of the shed and Pryor and Bowring, *An Historical Survey of Selected Southern Stations*, OPC 1980, refer to the Board of Trade report *.....that a turntable was provided and that traffic was controlled by train staff and ticket.....* A pit was also provided inside the shed, a second alongside the small stage. Enginemen were originally accommodated on the station platform but by the 1890s a small lobby had been provided by the shed. A second building alongside the south wall afforded shelter for the local permanent way team.

The turntable was reported 'out of use' in 1911; this reveals essentially nothing of the status of the shed at this time but apparently (see Wroe, *The Bude Branch*, Kingfisher, 1988) Holsworthy continued in use as some kind of a stabling shed after Bude had opened. The turntable was actually removed in 1915 and the building is said to have been officially dispensed with two years later. It was subsequently used as a store and was not finally demolished until after Grouping.

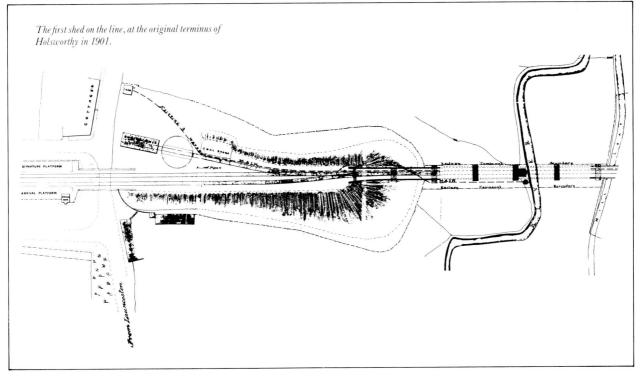

*The first shed on the line, at the original terminus of Holsworthy in 1901.*

## 'ONTO BUDE'

The elegantly laid out terminus at Bude opened in August of 1898. Engine accommodation was provided in the form of a small brick building, similar in detail to the shed at Swanage, but slightly larger than that at Holsworthy - 58 ft. x 20 ft., enough for a single tank loco. A pit was located inside and a second alongside the adjacent coal stage. Water was taken by pump from the Bude Canal to a large tank in the shed yard and a 50 ft. turntable was put in at the rear of the building.

The shed at Bude was not built immediately though presumably some rudimentary arrangements were made, a heap of coal at the least. Holsworthy indeed did not close for nearly twenty years and it is apparent that the line did not operate in straightforward fashion, with Bude as terminus. Plans for the new shed did not appear apparently until September 1898, a month after opening of the line; the tank had necessarily been constructed immediately and the plans directed that the 'building be constructed in similar style to that of the water tank', red brick with blue corner stones. 'Best Delabole slate' was used whilst smoke was ushered away using raised louvred vents. It is not clear what accommodation was afforded the enginemen in these early years, but in 1904 a small lobby was erected on the western side. In keeping with its remote situation very little happened save the installation of a 'W.C. for enginemen' in 1916.

The shed underwent a small renovation in 1929, the SR replacing the slating and blackened timbers with new wood-work and asbestos sheeting and in a simple remodelling of the track layout carried out in 1939 the shed lost its run-round. Boundary changes in the west in 1963 took Bude into Western Region control and doom. The branch like so many lost its through service to Waterloo, a shuttle service to Okehampton the only link with the main line and Exeter. An outstation of Exmouth Junction the shed closed in September of 1964 the whole line succumbing two years later leaving Bude with a railhead at Okehampton some thirty miles away.

## LOCOMOTIVES

Bude was on the very fringes of the South Western system, a finger of the 'Withered Arm' reaching to a coast as rugged as the inland terrain. For such a wayside line an interesting mixed bag of locomotives came to the branch, toiling over its winding course on passenger and goods duties.

The first locomotives to use the line were those of the contractor who supplied Manning Wardle 0-4-0s *Pioneer* and *Jessica*. These two sturdy locomotives were later purchased by the LSWR for use elsewhere but the first reported revenue earning locomotive was a Beattie class 302, No. 369. Loco-motive Engineer Adams later provided three of his new 46 class 4-4-0Ts to work services along with a variety of Beattie 4-4-0

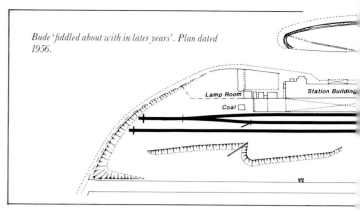

*Bude 'fiddled about with in later years'. Plan dated 1956.*

classes - 380 'Steamrollers' followed in due course by 348s. 46 class 4-4-0Ts proved too troublesome due to weight problems and the successful Radial 4-2-2Ts replaced them.

After the extension of the line from Halwill to Launceston, thence to Wadebridge and Padstow - the Halwill - Holsworthy - Bude line became 'the branch' and it was now that the small LSW tank engines came into their own. By 1905 Adams O2 0-4-4Ts were covering the local passenger duties with goods traffic in the hands of Beattie 0-6-0s. 'Jumbos' were later to monopolise the goods work to Okehampton and beyond. 'Jubilee' A12 0-4-2s came to the line in the late 1890s and more powerful T1 0-4-4Ts replaced the O2s on passenger work after 1910.

Some of the Drummond M7 0-4-4Ts, displaced by London suburban electrification schemes, were sent to Bude to replace the T1s now wanted elsewhere. By 1920 S11 and T9 4-4-0s were used on mixed traffic with post war troop trains double headed by T9s and N 2-6-0s. K10s and L11s made occasional visits to the branch at this time on mixed traffic work and even the odd E1R from Torrington would put in an appearance in the summer months. N class moguls were drafted into the west of England from Exeter and were powerful and well liked, ideally suited to the variety of work available on the branches in Devon and Cornwall. Shunting the wharf line, local passenger, goods and mixed trains to Okehampton and Exeter were all dealt with in heroic fashion by these machines, which were associated with the branch until closure.

Bulleid Pacifics, although making the occasional appearance were rare visitors owing to the fact that the turntable was unable to accommodate any engine larger then a 2-6-0. Standard 2-6-4 and 2-6-2 tanks saw traffic through until the cessation of steam hauled services west of Exeter in 1964. Twin and single unit DMUs were sent to the branch by the Western Region in that year and handled the traffic until closure.

*(For an exhaustive account of the locomotives and workings on the branch readers are advised to consult 'The Bude Branch' by David Wroe, Kingfisher, 1988)*

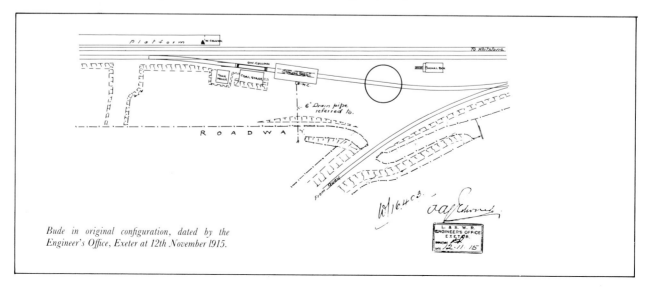

*Bude in original configuration, dated by the Engineer's Office, Exeter at 12th November 1915.*

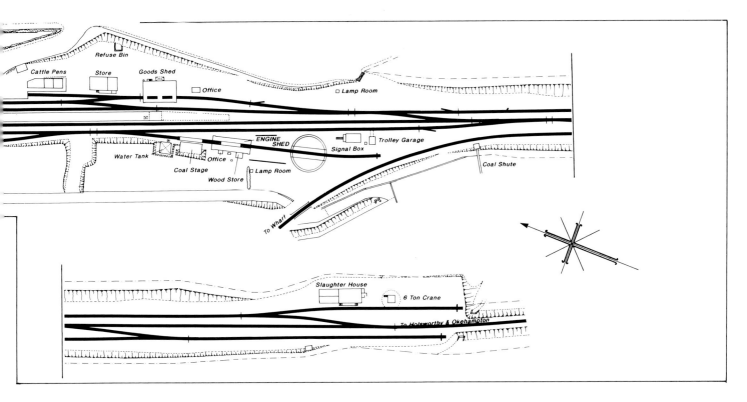

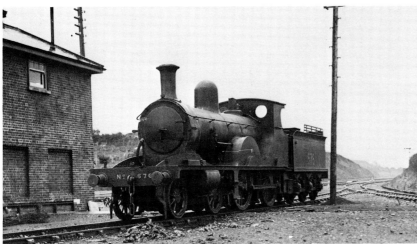

4-4-0 on the turntable approach, a useful link off the wharf line. The loss of this run round was odd for it meant the shed had to be cleared for any approach to the 'table.

*H.C. Casserley*

Bude on 20th April 1962. It had a pair of tanks (frequently only one in winter) with four sets of men and a pair of cleaners.

*P.J.Kelley*

The Barnstaple Junction turntable in 1925. The photograph is a glory of detail, from the entirely makeshift spur road (on the lower right) to the vegetable plots, casually discarded items and odd puddles. The goods yard, such a commercial necessity, was similar in character. It was full of little spurs and 'wonky' sidings, demanding exact positioning. A trader would frequently come forth to demand a wagon be moved an extra 18 inches, to mutterings from the engine crew. The various bits tended to have names, 'Mr. Reid's siding' was one, a road dealing mainly with sugar beet, manure and so on. An engine down this siding once ended up in the station master's garden. Barnstaple was that sort of place.

*National Railway Museum*

# Barnstaple

## A QUESTION OF GAUGE

Barnstaple lay at the mouth of the Taw and was to become an important railway junction. Branches set off for Torrington and Ilfracombe, the main line led to the south and Exeter and the Great Western had established itself over the river on the far side of the town, at Victoria Road

The history of the LSWR shed is a tangled one, with horse-drawn lines, lines laid but unused and a sequence of gauge changes. Two other long forgotten sheds also enter the story, short-lived establishments at Crediton and Bideford. The whole is perhaps best understood through a straightforward chronology; it begins simply enough.....

The first line to Barnstaple had been the horse-drawn Taw Vale of 1848. Goods only, it ran from Fremington Dock, a short distance to the west on the bank of the Taw. The unfortunate and ostensibly narrow gauge 'Taw Vale Extension Railway' was built southwards to Umberleigh but lay unused from the late 1840s. A broad gauge 'North Devon Railway' was to run from Barnstaple to Crediton, where a broad gauge line had opened from Exeter in 1851. Barnstaple thus opened to a broad gauge service throughout to Exeter over the Exeter-Crediton line in July 1854. A shed with workshop is believed to have opened at this time or very shortly after. Brassey, the contractor, held the lease of the line for the first seven years, having *...locomotives from the Bristol and Exeter Company..and ...subsequently ... his own...(Nicholas, Lines to Torrington, OPC).*

The LSWR had held a controlling interest in the line from Exeter through Crediton and Barnstaple on to Bideford, obtained at an early stage from under the noses of the broad gauge interests. With the LSWR a hundred or more miles off the company was necessarily content to see its lines worked on the broad gauge - it could not be otherwise. The narrow gauge

LSWR finally forced its path to Exeter in 1860 and the Barnstaple line was made over to mixed gauge, to Crediton early in 1862 and throughout to Bideford the following year.

The problems with Barnstaple shed now begin. It is a familiar building, a big wooden shed with low, stone-built workshops of an even more ancient aspect alongside. There was already a shed or some equivalent locomotive establishment at Barnstaple when the LSWR finally came into its own in 1863. This would have been broad gauge, put up by Brassey or by the direction of Ogilvie his manager *(Nicholas)*. One of Beattie's first tasks, whilst getting the LSWR narrow gauge service underway, was to attend to the engine accommodation - he alludes to existing arrangements in a letter to London:

'April 1863, read letter from Mr. Beattie as to the provision which will have to be made at Exeter for the repairs of the Company's narrow gauge engines running between Exeter and Bideford, *the present workshops at Barnstaple* - authors italics - it being no longer available for the purpose. Referred back to Mr. Beattie and Strapp for estimates.

This would imply that Brassey's building(s) had not (at least at first) been offered up to the LSWR. It is suggested that the company erected a new shed of its own, probably in 1863/4 - the timber building familiar until the end of steam. Confirmation of what took place remains tantalisingly out of grasp and evidence is by implication. The LSWR replaced the original (Brassey) building if a record of 1878 is considered correct. An inspection of several sheds by the Directors took place in July and August (Company jaunts have a long and noble tradition) of 1878 and part of their recommendation was thus drafted ..... *That the old engine shed at Barnstaple be examined and seen if worth repairs before any expense is incurred in removing it.....* The LSWR timber shed whether erected in 1862 or a few years after was in any event

The wooden shed had a novel if unique form of illumination with frames (probably redundant from elsewhere) placed in likely spots. E1R No. 2608 on 6th July 1949; christened 'bugs', they were perceived as awkward to fire and thereby unpopular.

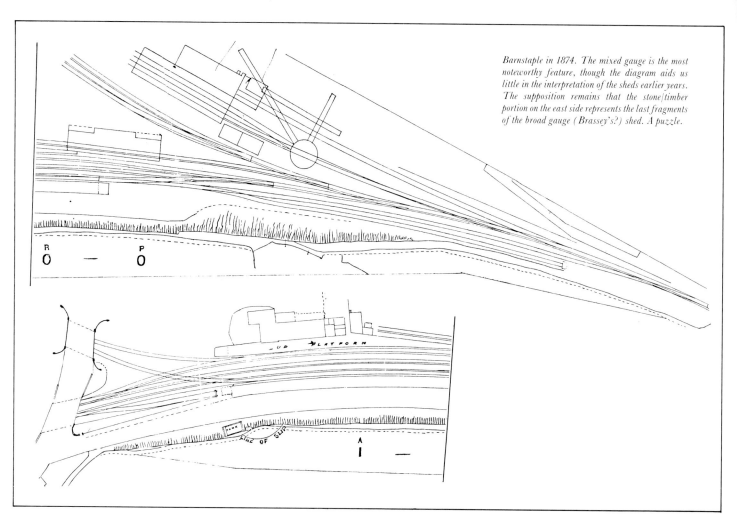

certainly in use by 1874 - a plan issued (and illustrated) in that year shows the two-road building in place, but laid to the broad gauge on one road, with the turntable mixed. This is slightly peculiar in that it would not be expected that such broad gauge provision would still be in place. The LSWR 'took over Brassey's motley collection of broad gauge rolling stock and continued to use it to run services for a time' but Nicholas doubts that any broad gauge passenger trains ran after 1872 and from 1870 until the abolition of broad gauge in 1877 only four suitable engines remained in service. From 1877 the Barnstaple shed would have been narrow gauge only. In 1872, however, a fire had nearly put paid to the whole lot:

*Because of a fire in the loco shops at Barnstaple, a brick wall is to be constructed separating the furnace from the rest of the wooden building. Approved £22.....* Coaling had been carried out from open wagons from the first but in April 1874 £50 was approved for the 'construction of a coal stage at Barnstaple shed.' Though small it was a most welcome asset; a larger turntable followed in the 1890s and much later a rudimentary shelter appeared over the coal stage. Apart from this Barnstaple over the ensueing decades is characterised by little more than lingering decline and decay.

# Crediton

*For the better there to promote their traffic*

As previously mentioned, Crediton away to the south had been served by a railway since 1851. The broad gauge Bristol and Exeter worked the 'Exeter and Crediton Railway' although the LSWR owned the majority of the shares and awaited only its line to Exeter before coming into its inheritance. *The

Crediton terminus from the first required some sort of shed and a Minute of 16th May 1851 authorised expenditure thus *.....It having been recommended to the Directors of this company by Mr. Bass and Mr. Gregory the respective engineers of the South Western and Bristol and Exeter Railway Companies to expend the further sum of £500 in station and engine accommodation at Crediton for working the coal line and other goods traffic there......* Quite what the work entailed is not clear but, by the following year the committee recommended the sale of the 'Turntable, now not in use.' Broad gauge trains ran through to Barnstaple and Fremington in 1854 and very soon, in August 1862, with the advent of narrow gauge and the LSWR, Beattie found himself concerned with 'loco' matters: 'further as to the fire which occurred at the Crediton station engine shed on the 20th, Assistant Fireman Thomas Butler to be given a gratuity for his conduct on the occasion'. The fire evidently destroyed the shed and desultory efforts were eventually addressed to some simple method of replacement; indeed it wasn't until January of 1864 that Beattie next referred to Crediton engine shed *.....Read letter from Mr. Beattie recommending the erection of an inexpensive wooden shed for the broad gauge engine when standing at Crediton station. To be referred to the Way and Works as to the cheapest mode of providing the necessary covering.....* Whether it was erected immediately has not been ascertained, but plans for 1872 show a small engine shed at the Barnstaple end of the layout. A small turntable was sited immediately outside with a number of radiating stub sidings. At the Exeter end of the station on the up side a small turntable is also shown in place although it is not clear whether this was the unit 'not now in use' in 1852. Changes in working arrangements would have put paid to the shed in the early 1870s, Exeter and Barnstaple supplying locomotives needed for any shunting work.

*Dendy-Marshall, History of the Southern Railway*

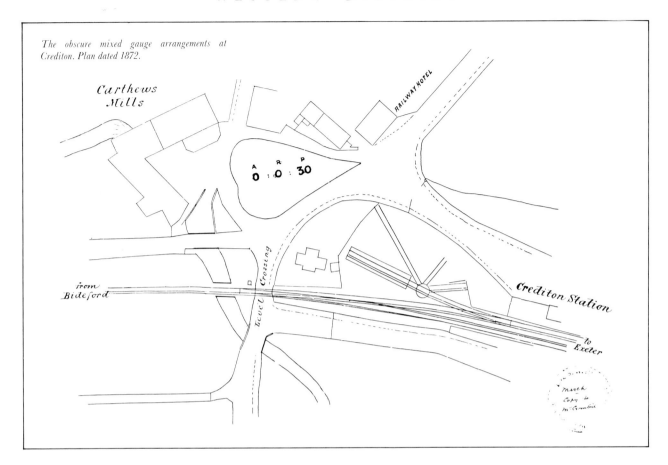

*The obscure mixed gauge arrangements at Crediton. Plan dated 1872.*

**Crediton station in mixed gauge days looking south. The van on the extreme left occupies the shed road.**

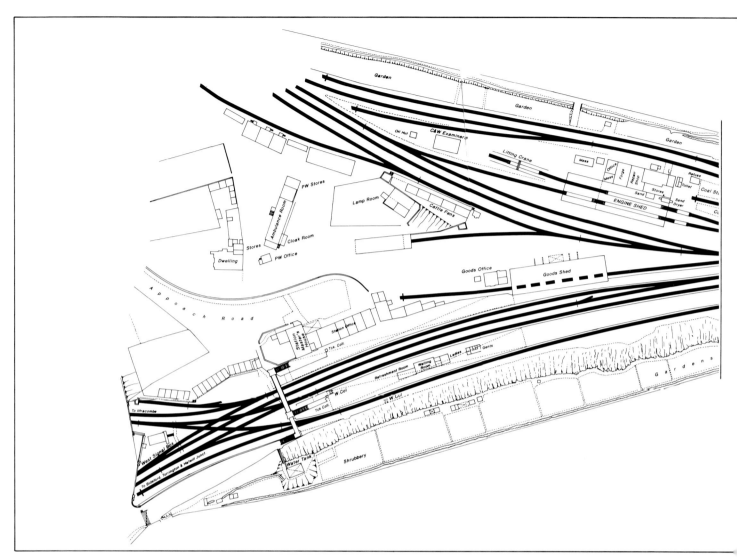

**Barnstaple in 1925. The usual mixed rafts of wagons could be found between the goods and the engine sheds. Mr. Reid's ill-starred siding lay in this part of the yard.**

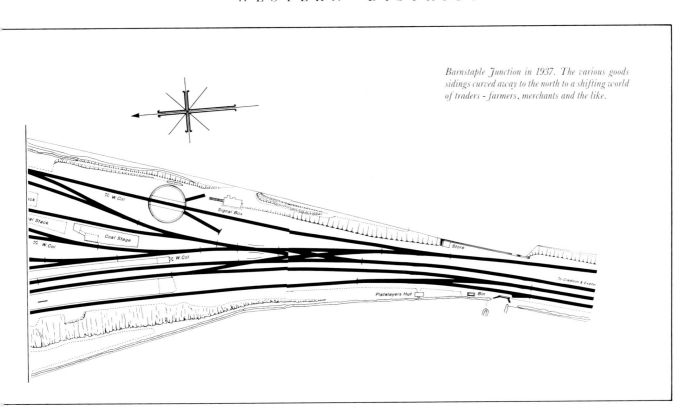

*Barnstaple Junction in 1937. The various goods sidings curved away to the north to a shifting world of traders - farmers, merchants and the like.*

## A Good Little Depot

The railway at Barnstaple enjoyed a place in the community, the only link with a world beyond North Devon that was for many only dimly perceived. It could provide a fine job for a lad, a security of employment almost unknown in any other endeavour available locally. The Southern foreman at Barnstaple took on school leavers most years and in 1945 five from the same class were started off as cleaners. They began on one of three shifts, early, late or night. This last was barred to the youngest and was the realm of the senior cleaner, who principally acted as steam raiser. Engines to be attended (frequently the Drummond tanks) stood on the 'Cleaning Road' leading off the turntable past the shed building but cleaning also took place inside the shed. 'Stopped' engines or those undergoing washout stood on the 'Repair Road' ending in shear legs at the rear whilst the 'Through Road', which engines approached or left from either end, could serve for locos simply awaiting a following turn. There were usually two coalmen available, working in ancient fashion even as Nationalisation dawned. They carried round wicker baskets, creaking with coal hacked into suitably sized lumps and slung over the shoulders. Both men loaded the baskets, the *mauns* of Devon usage, in calm moments and subsequently divided their labours, one to hump the mauns forward from the stack, the other to help the fireman sling the contents into the tender with a simple one-two-three-up! hoist. A conveyor belt turned up around 1946, outlandishly modern and regarded with some suspicion. It broke down regularly though plenty of time was usually available at Barnstaple for some sort of repair to be effected. The workshop gang was capable of almost anything, six or eight men with mates and a lad or two they coped with almost any bearing work, running out wheels from the various old tanks and tender engines working from the shed. The gang included a boiler-smith and mate. Engines stayed for years at Barnstaple and the mechanical staff grew to know them intimately; a man could develop an instinct for wear, so familiar did the engines become. The best two Drummond tanks in the 'forties, Nos. 250 and 670

were driven by two brothers, early and late men (one a hellraiser, the other a lay preacher) and the combination of fiercely possessive crews and the protective eye of equally concerned fitters made for pampered, beautifully cared for engines. Cleaners were adjured to take especial care; every pipe gleamed and small pieces of lino, carefully tacked in, adorned sundry flat surfaces - lids and so on. No. 23 and No. 247 were also at Barnstaple in the late 1940s; they were not confined so closely to particular crews but were still maintained 'in lovely nick'. The Drummond tanks were ancient machines even by steam locomotive standards and in this perhaps lay their greatest strengths. They could be kept going almost indefinitely at a shed like Barnstaple and the independence at such a place made various novel additions possible. Ash pan watering cocks and coal watering pipes were, according to legend, added (entirely surreptitiously) by the Barnstaple fitters. Such modifications proved useful for work around Barnstaple and going down to Ilfracombe say, last thing at night, when it was customary to sluice out the ash pan (along the track), the cocks operated with some force off the injector. Unofficial fittings were adopted at a number of sheds but care was taken to remove the offending appendage if a trip to Eastleigh Works was due. All drivers of the Drummond tanks carried a 'gadger', a nut and bolt three or four inches long and some three-quarters of an inch in diameter. This prosaic item was of inestimable value on the banks - attacking Mortehoe. 5 miles at 1 in 40 from the south the reversing lever required to be dropped forward beyond Fox-hunter. Steam would have to be momentarily shut off to alter the cut-off and sometimes on Drummond engines the reversing lever shot forward to full gear thereby losing momentum just as the bank began to make itself felt. A nut and bolt suitably placed in the 'ratchet' and 'couple of nicks' from the end rendered this unnecessary and the lever slammed forward to just the correct point, its progress arrested abruptly by the bolt. Pull on the drawbar was thereby maintained and progress up to Mortehoe would be described in thoroughly non-engineering fashion in terms of 'nicks up'. An ascent in 'one and 'alf nicks'

Inside Barnstaple shed with No 0475 on 21st July 1925. Despite the grim dereliction of its last years the wooden shed was cared for with some considerable zeal. Geoffrey Jewell, a private contractor (it was his men that were killed in the Plymouth bombing) did the whitewashing and creosoting and carried out a similar service at Torrington.

*H.C. Casserley*

The usual LSWR travelling hoist at Barnstaple lay 'out the back' and whilst repairs at these 'remote country sheds' were regarded as rather crude, this ignored the local ability to triumph over odds and adversity. The locomen held the fitting staff in some awe and they were in any case assessed to be vastly superior in technique and skill to 'the Junction blokes', or any other foreigner for that matter.

30253 at Barnstaple. A proper coaling shelter was put up largely in corrugated sheeting and similar material was applied to the roof. Within the shed notices promised dire consequences for allowing engines to blow-off. It was not long before portions of the new roof blasted skywards.

*K.C.H. Fairey*

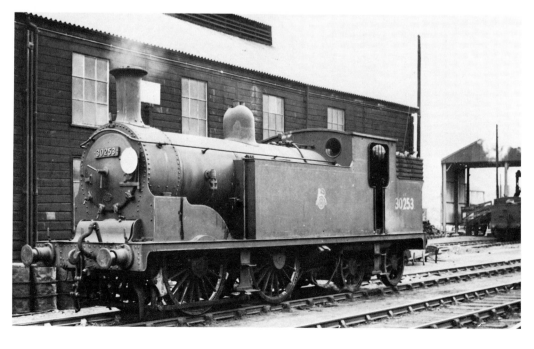

described a satisfactory effort.

The Drummond tanks and their regular drivers constituted the 'Old Boys Link', though Barnstaple was not big enough for a more formal system of conventional links. The 'Old Boys' would not dream of working any other turns and would be most put out if a 'personal' engine were even put aside for a day for washout. Some eight crews were in this 'Tank Gang', to Torrington and Ilfracombe with Drummond tanks and four coaches - nothing before 6 a.m. with the last train frequently the 10.20 p.m. to Braunton. Often loaded with service personnel after a night in the Barnstaple pubs, *The Boozer* might load to *ten* coaches, with revellers crowded even on the footplate, WAAFS in disarray and even worse. There were only some twenty crews in all, the younger men generally dispersed amongst the remaining passenger work and on goods trains.

There was much relieving work to be had at Barnstaple; in keeping with practice all over the West, it took young men to Torrington and Ilfracombe and often thereby provided early experience of firing. It was a case often of sleeping rough or close by the sheds but local girls added a vicarious element to the first time away from home, a young man's life until then crowded with brothers and sisters. Summer days at Ilfracombe, the seaside penny arcades and long evenings made for an abiding firing memory.

## LOCOMOTIVES

Barnstaple was the rail centre for North Devon with lines radiating out to Exeter, Torrington, Ilfracombe, Lynton and Taunton by way of the Great Western. The locomotive shed, therefore, was of primary importance supplying locomotives and staff to a bewildering variety of sheds and stations.

The early days of these North Devon lines are understandably difficult to chronicle in brief; however, Nicholas does reveal in his book *Lines to Torrington* that several Beattie 2-4-0s were outstationed from Barnstaple to work the Torrington line; Eagle class No.30, Vulture and Volcano class No.89 and No.61 *Snake* .

Barnstaple received Beattie's special 0-6-0s (Ilfracombe Goods) to work the difficult Ilfracombe route in 1874, No. 300,

393 and 394. The tiny 2-4-0 well tanks, a type so long associated with Wenford Bridge, worked much of the traffic in these early years and gave good service. With the advent of heavier loads they were soon replaced by the larger and more powerful Adams Radial class 4-4-2Ts. 'Steamroller' 4-4-0s were also working from the shed heading the heavier passenger and goods turns to Exeter.

The later LSWR period saw Drummond locomotives start to monopolise the work at Barnstaple, 'Large Hopper' and 'Small Hopper' 4-4-0s, K10 and L11s all on mixed traffic duties. Although the Drummond types came to dominate the allocation at this time, Adams locos were still evident, A12 class 0-4-2s and 'Jubilee's' engaged on mixed traffic work for many years.

The 0-4-4Ts came virtually to monopolise the branch line work in the early 1900s. O2, T1 and M7s taking on the responsibility of the Torrington and Ilfracombe branches replaced the ancient Radials. T3 class locos used primarily on the Torrington line and Adams 460 class 4-4-0s were also evident at this time.

After grouping the ND&CJLR had opened, with specially converted ex-LBSCR E1 0-6-0Ts (E1R 0-6-2Ts) running services over this line and outstationed from Barnstaple to Torrington. Much of the work centred around the passenger and mixed traffic duties to Halwill Junction but shunting at Fremington Quay played a major role in the daily routine of these engines. A variety of types came to the shed at this time notably the N class 2-6-0s, fine performers over the difficult Mortehoe Bank and on various goods and mixed traffic work.

A number of Bulleid light Pacifics worked out of Barnstaple to Exeter and Ilfracombe on the heavier passenger turns such as the *Devon Belle* and *Atlantic Coast Express*. These powerful machines revolutionised the work in the West and, although not without their critics, were well liked by the men. Ivatt 2-6-2Ts arrived in 1953 taking over much of the work of the ageing Adams and Drummond classes and in the late 1950s GWR engines (and men) transferred over from Victoria Road when the depot there closed. Standard 2-6-4 and 2-6-2Ts arrived prior to dieselisation, which came in turn in late 1963. North British Type 2 and multiple units handled most of the remaining work with Western Region 'Warships' running services from Ilfracombe to Exeter.

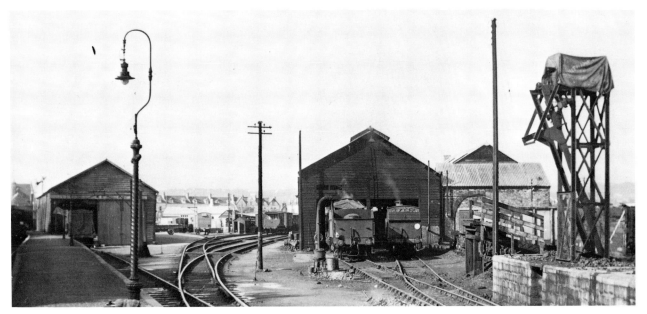

**Barnstaple Junction on 28th September 1956 with the latest generation of coal 'plant' - the newest 'opper' and its predecessor, a home made ramp suited to wheelbarrows. Barnstaple's great moment came with the naming of 21C105, *Barnstaple* (obviously) coming to the shed new and named locally.**

**Ilfracombe station on the heights above the town 'from Cairn Top'.**

# Ilfracombe

The railway had reached Barnstaple from Crediton in 1854 and subsequently proposals were made to extend the line northward to Ilfracombe. The terrain was not encouraging, with hills only a short distance from the town; the line opened in 1874, running northwestwards from Barnstaple along the banks of the Taw river and thence to Braunton and a site high above Ilfracombe itself. An engine shed was established from the first, an outstaion of Barnstaple, which was developing into something of an operating centre for North Devon.

The Ilfracombe shed was sited adjacent to the station on its eastern side and measured a modest 55ft x 25ft, construction executed in wood. The gabled slated roof had a single smoke vent and inside the building a bench and vice were available for simple fitting jobs. A small office was attached to the west wall and various bins, small store and a 40ft turntable lay outside - a straightforward arrangement characteristic of smaller establishments on the LSWR.

Ilfracombe shed, on the very fringes of the South Western empire, sat upon its hilltop over slumbering decades, housing an engine or two overnight, in all likelihood attended fitfully by a night cleaner or shedman. By 1895 the turntable, which had been causing 'considerable concern,' was the subject of debate at an Engineer's meeting, in May. Some time later the prospect of costs arose .....*Estimates (for new table) at £1,100...as against £200...required for making the 42ft turntable recovered from Okehampton available for use at Ilfracombe.....* This latter suggestion proved attractive and the old Okehampton machine was duly put in, suitably strengthened.

No alterations or improvements were necessary for the first decade of the new century at Ilfracombe though this was altered in startling fashion, in 1910, a wretched incident when a locomotive failed to come to a halt:

*Report submitted from the mechanical engineer of 11th July stating that an engine ran through the engine shed at Ilfracombe on 7th July. The resident engineer estimated the cost of repairs to be about £40.*

The building's wooden construction almost certainly saved it from total destruction the engine taking out a few planks rather then demolishing an entire wall; had the loco continued on its unofficial journey there would have been a very rapid descent into Ilfracombe and a less sanguine response from the Committee in London. This sort of incident and associated near misses were not uncommon at Ilfracombe; for two miles the terminus was approached down 1 in 36. A report states that even the egregious Drummond who went to Ilfracombe in his 'saloon' rammed the stop blocks; the old man was later to agree that the brake blocks on the single driving wheel were inadequate. As if suddenly reminded of the sheds existence the company now addressed itself to some further improvements :
*1st December 1910. Read letter from the Mechanical Engineer of 29th November recommending that an engine pit, 120ft long be provided in the new siding at Ilfracombe, the cost of the work being estimated by the resident engineer at £261.*

The pit was to be part of an extended stub siding adjacent to the shed. The Mechanical Engineer showed some reticence over this proposal recommending that it...'be provided but, the length to be reduced to 60ft..' Work was duly carried out. Further work at the shed before Grouping saw the Enginemen's cabin replaced by the increasingly popular 'Muribloc', a concrete product produced at the Company's plant at Exmouth Junction :

*It was recommended that the structure in use as a cabin and store for Enginemen at Ilfracombe which is in a dilapidated condition be replaced by a small 'Muribloc' building as shewn on plan No.17456 submitted (at the far end of the yard) at an estimated cost of £113.*

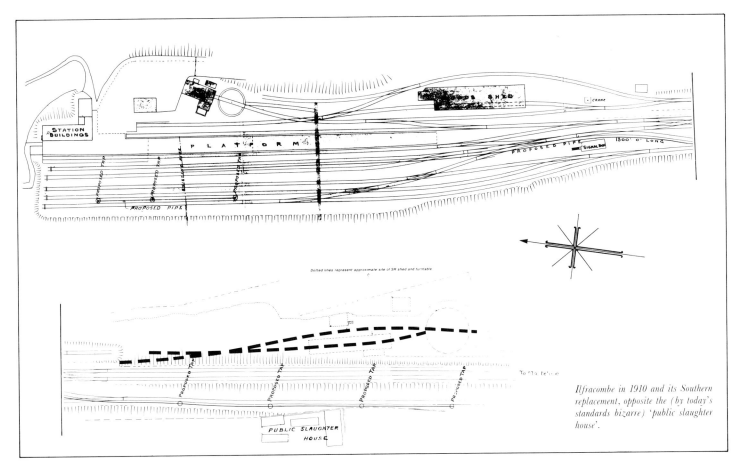

Ilfracombe in 1910 and its Southern replacement, opposite the (by today's standards bizarre) 'public slaughter house'.

## The Southern Railway - a 'Muribloc Age'

The Southern carried out a quite remarkable programme of improvement works at Ilfracombe; expansion had long been contemplated and in 1925 removal of the 'Locomotive Department' to a site further to the south began. The second hand turntable was now some fifty years old and inadequate, land in and around the station was very limited but cliffs and high embankments surrounded the Barnstaple end of the layout. Nevertheless a site on the up side was selected, demanding considerable excavation and appropriate expense - the Southern Railway Engineer reporting 'the cost of the new turntable at Ilfracombe being £9,000.' Progress was fairly swift and a short article in the *Southern Railway Magazine* describes the work thus:

*The new turntable at Ilfracombe is one of four to be installed, the others being for Redhill, Ramsgate and Dover. Sixty five feet in diameter, it is capable of taking the biggest and heaviest engines of the Company, and is hand operated and is fitted with ball-bearings to ensure smooth and easy working. It replaces the old 42ft diameter turntable near the engine shed at Ilfracombe, and is situated in a new position on the up side of the line. As will be seen .... the work entailed a considerable amount of excavation, the height of the cutting in the hillside being some 35 feet.*

The site so cleared was later to provide space for a new engine shed of rather more substantial proportions than the original building. Late in 1928 a proposal arose to erect *.....a new engine shed at Ilfracombe to replace the old building there which is now totally inadequate for the engines using the line.....* It was to be in concrete, a material the Southern was enamoured of and was to stand between the turntable and the station, on one of the approach roads. It was constructed of pre-cast concrete sections infilled with 'Muribloc' concrete slabs. It is not clear, however, if these were actually manufactured at the Southern's works at Exmouth Junction; certainly much of this sort of work in these years went to outside contractors. The roof was to be of corrugated asbestos and a pit ran the entire length of the building. Toilet, store and drivers' mess room were installed although the submitted plans were subsequently altered to allow for a less sharply inclined roof. A large water tank lay perched on the adjacent cliff whilst below, the Southern installed a coal stage and ash pit, equipped with a small crane.

With the installation of the new turntable longer wheel-base locomotives, mainly Maunsell 2-6-0s, could work the branch, a most welcome development on this steeply graded line. The shed stabled and serviced locos working in from Barnstaple and from this time did not have a regular allocation of its own. Three crews were latterly stationed there during the summer traffic when the shed staff were stretched to the very limit. After the war light Pacifics were introduced on services such as the *Atlantic Coast Express* and *Devon Belle*. The 'Belle', a particularly heavy train, was equipped with an observation car which required turning at the shed before returning to London. In the 1950s and 1960s engines off the last train (usually a light Pacific) stabled at the shed but ex-GWR and Standard types were frequent visitors after transfer to the Western Region in 1962.

The turntable was removed in 1964 and singling of the line came in 1967. The shed effectively closed on the cessation of steam but for some time diesel locomotives made use of the sidings, etc, The line closed completely in October 1970.

## LOCOMOTIVES

The difficult route from Barnstaple to Ilfracombe, reaching gradients of 1-40 and 1-36 in places, required Beattie to find a locomotive of sufficient power but within a strict weight limit. The line had been constructed to Light Railway specification and accordingly caused problems with axle loadings. *Maggs, The Barnstaple and Ilfracombe Railway, Oakwood Press* states that Beattie designed an 0-6-0 *Merlin* especially to handle the traffic. However this design proved unsatisfactory and consequently advice was sort from elsewhere. Beyer Peacock supplied their standard 0-6-0 *Ilfracombe Goods* which as we know became synonymous with the early life of the line.

By the early 1900s the 0-6-0s were life expired and were being superseded by more modern machines. Maggs goes on to note that at this time Adams A12 class *Jubilee* 0-4-2Ts were also recorded on the branch, but the main stay of the work was now in the capable hands of the ubiquitous T1 0-4-4Ts. M7 0-4-4Ts were later to join the T1s mainly used on pilot work and banking duties. N 2-6-0s came to the line in 1925 and were used principally on passenger and goods work to Exeter; however with the arrival of the larger and more powerful Bulleid Pacifics in 1945 they were relegated more and more to local work and banking duties.

Nationalisation brought Standard locomotives in the form of class 4MT 2-6-4Ts and the occasional Ivatt 2-6-2Ts. *The Devon Belle* and the *Atlantic Coast Express* of course stayed in the hands of the larger locomotives (and in the case of the ACE) until the end of steam in 1964. GWR locomotives had used the line over the years, mainly with through workings in the hands of their 2-6-0s of the 43XX class. Dieselisation brought Western Region Warships to the line and local work was dealt with by multiple units.

**No 57 on an 'Engineers job' aiding in the construction of the new shed.**

The new 'Muribloc' shed. Ilfracombe could be a dizzy place to work, it was non-stop in summer despite wind and rain and with many of the (younger) summer staff outstationed 'from afar', opportunities for *liaison* were a principle attraction of the job. Props from summer shows were stored on the nearby 'Theatre Road' (what else) and the headshunt of the goods shed (see plan) was used for ash and clinker. Taken from the shed it was wheelbarrowed to a makeshift 'chute' and dumped onto a waiting wagon, positioned out of the way of the shed yard.

*W.H. Whitworth*

Mogul in June 1935, a time when queues of holidaymakers complete with luggage could be marshalled at Ilfracombe, ordered about by Tannoy.

*W.A. Camwell*

*W.A. Camwell*

Torrington in the 1930s. It was a popular posting of Exmouth Junction - cleaners and young firemen sent in the summer especially looking forward to endless social diversion. Torrington men worked to Halwill and Barnstaple, men at the latter place at one time never went beyond Torrington but later this changed and even Exeter men went over the line. At Torrington as at Ilfracombe and other small places, the senior driver was in charge; engines did not normally take coal, this took place at Barnstaple - an 'ash loader' working by day at Torrington.

# Bideford

The broad gauge Bideford Extension Railway was completed throughout from Barnstaple, over the old horse-drawn Fremington portion, in 1855. The terminus was at Cross Parks, Bideford, with a generously-built engine shed at the head of the yard, 100 ft. long by 25 ft. in width with a gable slated roof. It was later to be converted to handle mixed gauge engines (presumably in 1877) and the turntable (latterly 42 ft. in diameter) was converted also. The shed's duties would have begun to wane in any case on opening of the extension to Torrington in 1872 and a new station was constructed some distance down the line, Cross Parks, latterly becoming Bideford (Goods). A small shed had been constructed at Torrington and this, along with Barnstaple, handled traffic on the branch. The Bideford turntable was still in place in 1879 but was subsequently taken out. Not long after this the shed was abandoned, though it found further use as a store and delivery agents van shed, standing until at least 1960.

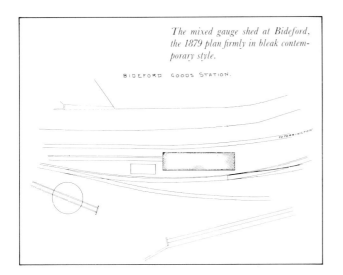

*The mixed gauge shed at Bideford, the 1879 plan firmly in bleak contemporary style.*

BIDEFORD GOODS STATION.

TO TORRINGTON

# Torrington

Torrington shed was a simple wooden building which remained little changed throughout some eighty years of use. Great Torrington, an 'ancient market town' stands high above the River Torridge and is some eight miles south of Bideford. The station lay to the west of the town in the valley bottom near Rothern Bridge and opened to traffic on 18th July 1872. Plans for an 'Extension' from Bideford had been laid as early as 1865 but construction proved troublesome; markedly more so than the previous section, Barnstaple - Bideford. LSWR interest paled and in attempts to abandon the project the company was twice defeated in Parliament by local Devon interests. Mr.J. Nicholas describes the railway development of the area in entertaining detail in *Lines to Torrington, OPC 1984*. The LSWR finally resigned itself to the task in 1870 and the line opened to a terminus at Torrington in 1872. The wooden shed, seated on a dwarf brick wall opened at the same time; it measured some 110 ft. by 20 ft. and had a small lean-to office at the rear. A store was supplied in one corner of the office along with some primitive benching and a sink. The gabled roof was slated and had a central raised vent although it appears to have been of little use. An inspection pit ran the entire length of the building and a 42 ft. turntable was located immediately outside. Three sidings radiated from it, one short, the others terminating in private lime kilns. A generously proportioned coal stage was located at the head of the yard and water was supplied from a tank on the hillside overlooking the station.

The shed could accommodate two small tender engines and its opening necessarily saw the demise of Bideford shed, which could now be turned over to different use. Colonel Yolland had inspected the line in July 1872 and Nicholas quotes part of his report thus:-  *the line was not ready for re-inspection prior to yesterday, and I delayed going there until there was a reasonable prospect of the works being sufficiently advanced to render another visit unnecessary.*

*Torrington station and yard is now all but complete, a crossover road at the end of the platform only being required to enable the engine to run round the train. It is covered by the proper signals, interlocked with each other, and provided with a catch siding and stop block on the 'up' and 'down' lines to prevent vehicles from escaping from the station which is partially on an incline.*

**Broad gauge days (though the years have not been kind to the photograph) at Bideford**

*I would suggest also that the lever which now works the points leading to the turntable and engine shed work on another pair of points - or even a single point in the nature of a safety switch, to prevent the engine from coming out except when required.*

The narrow gauge Marland Railway was put through to Torrington in 1881. It was intended to enable a cheaper and more convenient removal of the Marland Brick and Clay Works products and ran to interchange sidings in Torrington yard. This 3 ft. line was eventually converted to standard gauge and extended to Halwill, opening in 1925 as the North Devon and Cornwall Junction Light Railway.

Torrington was a distant outpost of the LSWR and not surprisingly very little documentary evidence has surfaced concerning the shed. Nonetheless some small changes are known to have occurred in the late 1890s, the most significant being the enlargement of the turntable to 50 ft. The Torrington supply was of some interest and for years was fed under gravity from the hillside tank. Various plans and minutes complicate the matter; in 1897...*a new supply direct from the River Torridge.....estimated at £740 for tank engines, pump, etc....* was approved but how, if at all, this was accomplished is unclear. On the hillside overlooking the shed stood a pair of cottages and two plans of May and August 1901 show, firstly, a tank some yards to the south of the cottages with a 'pump house' and well adjacent and, secondly, a spring-fed tank to the north of the dwellings opposite the signal box. In August 1901 a new tank is shown at this point 'fed by overflow from old collecting tank'. A further spring 'with chamber for collecting sediment' was tapped in 1908-9 but much of this appears to have been for purposes other than the engine shed.

By 1908 the rear of the shed had altered slightly, for what reason is not clear. An old carriage body had been installed on the platform side of the building and was used as a messroom for drivers. Smoke vents had been added to the roof and a door put in, allowing easier access to the shed from the platform.

Tender engines, 0-4-2s and 4-4-0s had customarily been used on the passenger services to Torrington but the turntable was evidently giving some cause for dissatisfaction; in 1921 it was ordered taken out .....*Turntable and a siding.....at Torrington original cost £160 - estimated cost of removal £41 - estimated saving £5 per annum.....to be removed.....*

The company however was to forego these momentous savings and the turntable lasted until 1925 (coinciding with the opening of the North Devon & Cornwall Junction line - see earlier); in the summer of that year with various improvements at Ilfracombe, Torrington services were reduced, relatively. Through trains afterwards ran from Ilfracombe with Torrington workings in branch line fashion attached at Barnstaple. With tender engines no longer required the turntable could be quietly done away with and Torrington shed settled into a long dotage, caring for a handful of tanks engaged on the leisurely services to Halwill and Barnstaple. With the 'table removed the lime kiln sidings were rearranged onto a new shed road and a pit built outside the shed itself. The various bins and lean-tos were necessarily removed and the doors, by now inoperable, were taken down.

## LOCOMOTIVES

Nicholas covers the evolution of engine types at Torrington more or less exhaustively charting the progress from various tanks and tender locos, 4-4-2Ts, 2-4-0s and 0-6-0s, 0-4-4Ts and 4-4-0s of LSWR days, to the converted EIR 0-6-2Ts of the Southern and the 2-6-2Ts of British Railways. Two or three tanks, EIRs or perhaps a pair plus a Drummond tank were outbased from Barnstaple through the bulk of the Southern period and crews from the main shed frequently worked from Torrington on relief, customarily in the summer and also to cover illness. They were generally younger men, sent out for a week and sleeping rough in the cabin at the rear. Torrington was considered to be unduly remote from the town but, as at Ilfracombe, local *liaisons* proved a compensation.

The shed survived the years well enough, the smoke vents more or less disintegrated at the last and new roof cladding appeared but by the time of closure in 1959 the building had an exhausted, sagging look to it.

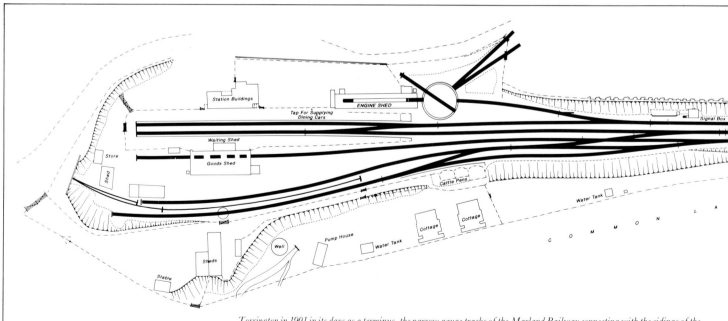

*Torrington in 1901 in its days as a terminus, the narrow gauge tracks of the Marland Railway connecting with the sidings of the LSWR. The conversion of the 3ft line to standard gauge on to Halwill opened the horizons of the Torrington crews, their EIR tanks (variously liked and disliked) clattering about the district.*

Torrington as terminus, the sagging roof of the wooden engine shed a contrast to the solid station itself. The building quickly disappeared at the end of steam, ushered away to leave a small patch of rubbish-strewn ground.

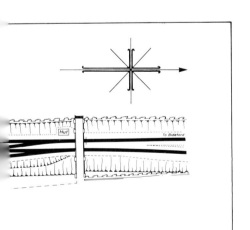

Familiar view of *Snake* on the Torrington turntable, an odd variation of the over girder type.

'The new Plymouth shed', with youthful onlookers. This is the south side of the building and the hoist has yet to be put in; the roads were numbered 1 - 3 (from right to left in this view) with No.3 given over to washouts and valve/piston work - all the repair jobs not requiring lifting.

# Plymouth
## Devonport and Friary

### DEVONPORT

Plymouth had drawn the London and South Western Railway from the very earliest times, its halting progress to the West the harbinger of years of antagonism with the incumbent GWR. The Company was eventually to establish three locomotive sheds, one at Devonport, then outside the conurbation of Plymouth, a second at their Friary station and a final building, familiar latterly, outside Friary itself, by Lucas Terrace Halt. They were of course not all in use simultaneously, Devonport opening in 1876 with the Plymouth Friary sheds following much later in 1891 and 1908 respectively.

By 1874 the South Western had reached Lidford (sic) a small station on the broad gauge line from Plymouth to Launceston. To allow LSW trains forward from here into Plymouth it was necessary for the line to be mixed and this was carried out under previous Agreements between the rivals. Taking the route via Yelverton and Laira Junction, LSWR trains entered the city from the east in 1876 and ran to their own station at Devonport, a small terminus at the end of a short branch west of the GWR 'Millbay Junction'.

LSWR trains to Plymouth at this time were at the very extremity of an attenuated, winding route, a physical remoteness made palpable by a baleful, all-encompassing Great Western. Opened with the station in 1876, the solid stone and 'Portland dressings' of the Devonport engine shed matched the high standards of the station .....*elegant commodious and superior to any other LSW station. Designed by Galbraith its light and graceful ironwork roofing from Belgium surmounted buildings of local stone. (Williams, David & Charles, 1973)*.....

Ornate in its styling the shed was nevertheless small, room for little more than a pair of tender engines. It had two roads, pits running the full length of the shed with two others outside. Both

tracks converged to meet just short of a 40 ft. turntable, a large 'coke stage' occupying most of the embankment between it and the shed. The building measured approximately 100 x 36 ft. and a large water tank was situated on the end of the down platform, built hard against the embankment which formed the station approach from Lower Stoke Road. There was very little stabling available at all; a small head shunt extended under 'Paradise Road' bridge allowing at least some siding space and locomotives apparently used the goods yard at busy times.

Devonport served the South Western's beleaguered Plymouth outpost in unremarkable fashion and it was intended that it be put largely out of use as the new direct line into Friary was made ready. New arrangements were in mind by November of 1888 .....*Locomotive Committee.....Letter from the Locomotive Superintendent as to the arrangements of the Drivers and Firemens duties at Devonport, by which there will be a saving of about 29/6d per week in overtime and the allowance of £10 p.a. hitherto paid to the Station Master at Devonport for keeping the Locomotive Department returns will cease.....* The new route at last brought the LSWR into a position of strength at Plymouth, such to rival effectively the Great Western. 'Originally surveyed by Locke in 1846', the line enabled a London schedule better than that of the GWR but the South Western entered Plymouth almost it might seem under conditions of stealth, creeping along the banks of the Tamar in the very shadows of the Brunel Bridge.

Friary station came into use for passengers in 1891 having opened for goods (much to the chagrin of the Great Western) in 1878. An engine shed was put up more or less from the first. Devonport then entered something of a decline but still had two engines in 1899 to shunt Stonehouse Pool (the South Western's Harbour Branch) and Devonport Goods. A minute of May 1917 noted .....*The turntable at Devonport is now surplus to requirements. Original cost £520 - estimated cost of removal £80 -*

**Devonport in the 1930s, with its engine shed in private use.**

*W. A. Camwell*

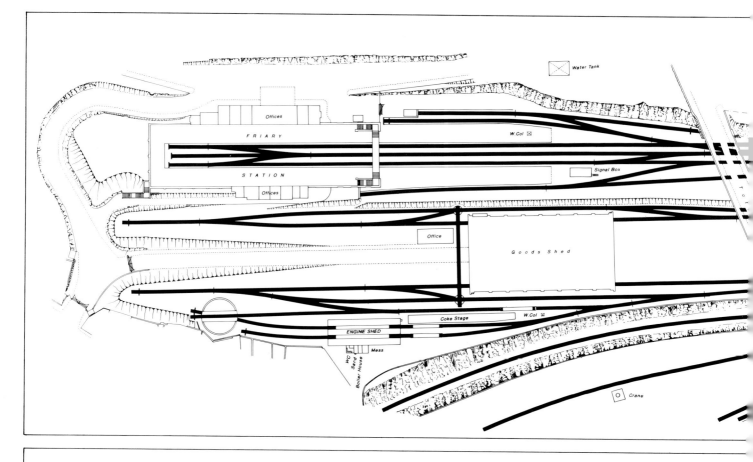

Water Tank

Offices

F R I A R Y

W. Col

S T A T I O N

Signal Box

Offices

Office

Goods Shed

Coke Stage

W. Col

ENGINE SHED

Mess

WC

Sand House

Boiler House

Crane

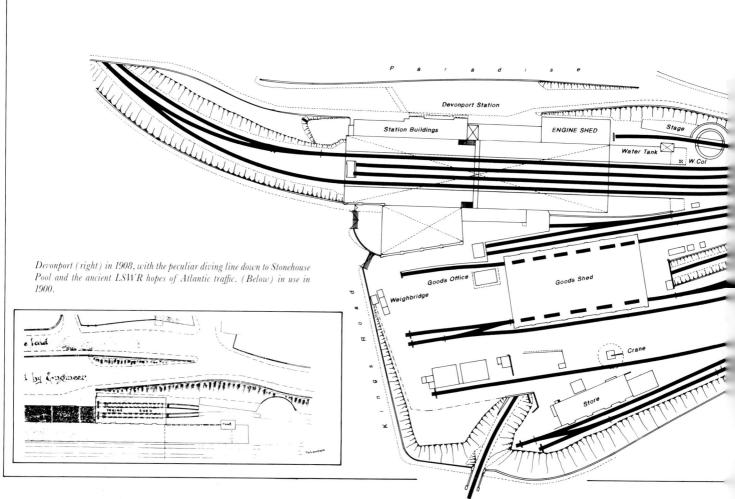

*Devonport (right) in 1908, with the peculiar diving line down to Stonehouse Pool and the ancient LSWR hopes of Atlantic traffic. (Below) in use in 1900.*

P a r a d i s e

Devonport Station

Station Buildings

ENGINE SHED

Stage

Water Tank

W. Col

Goods Office

Goods Shed

Crane

Weighbridge

Store

Kings Road

e land

t by Engineer

Tank

To London

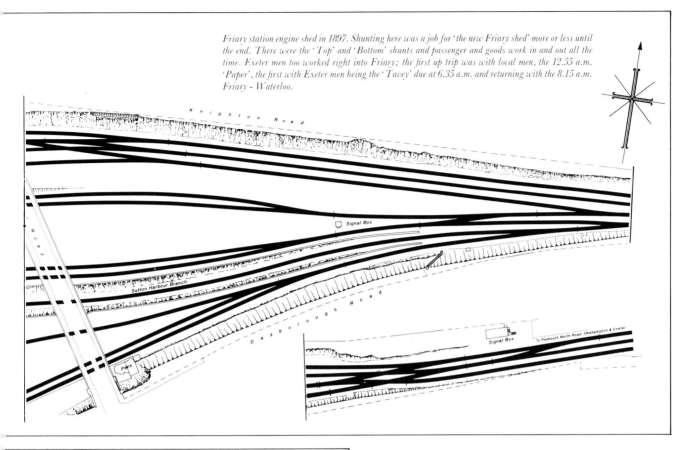

*Friary station engine shed in 1897. Shunting here was a job for 'the new Friary shed' more or less until the end. There were the 'Top' and 'Bottom' shunts and passenger and goods work in and out all the time. Exeter men too worked right into Friary; the first up trip was with local men, the 12.55 a.m. 'Paper', the first with Exeter men being the 'Tavey' due at 6.35 a.m. and returning with the 8.15 a.m. Friary - Waterloo.*

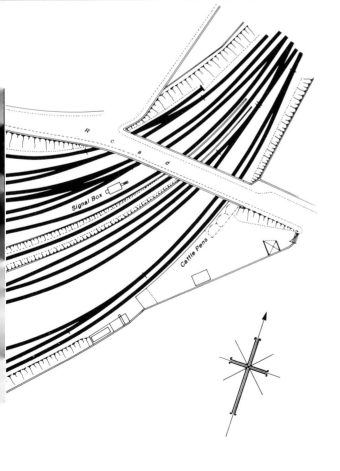

*estimated value £54 - estimated savings for maintenance £6.10.0d......* Few locomotives used the remaining sidings for stabling now save the odd one on shunting duties and they were eventually removed in 1919, the shed surviving until closure of the station under private use.

## FRIARY STATION

February 1890 *.....Friary station. With the arrival of the Company's line from Lidford* (sic) *it is necessary to provide accommodation for our locomotives at this station. The Locomotive Superintendent, Mr. Adams, to obtain tenders by the next meeting.....* The tenders were unrecorded but in May a 'sand drying furnace' was approved at £52 and the new shed appears to have opened later in the year, or early 1891. It offered few improvements over that at Devonport, a two road building 100 ft. x 35 ft., a 50 ft. turntable, a large coke stage and a water column at the head of the yard. Pits were supplied inside and out whilst a fifth was located alongside the coke stage. 'Mess Room, Boiler House and WCs' accompanied the Sand Furnace but conditions remained cramped and unsuitable. Despite mighty efforts the LSWR failed to overcome Great Western hegemony at Plymouth and though the Company's presence was certainly made felt, Friary retained all the air of 'the outpost'. Most repairs were supposed to be conducted at Exeter but 'the Junction' was many leagues distant and all sorts of minor adjustments - brakes, glands and so on were done at Friary. There were nine engines by 1899 with Devonport an odd sort of outbase, remote even from Friary and principally a place for various shunts. The two establishments clearly operated in some close form of association but the precise arrangements, how staffing and work varied, through both the seasons and the slow change across the years, is long lost.

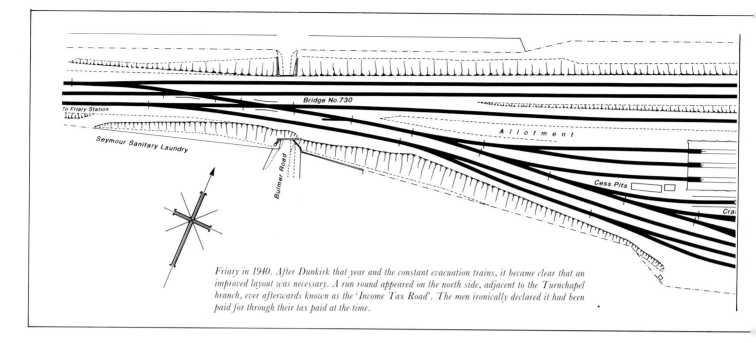

*Friary in 1940. After Dunkirk that year and the constant evacuation trains, it became clear that an improved layout was necessary. A run round appeared on the north side, adjacent to the Turnchapel branch, ever afterwards known as the 'Income Tax Road'. The men ironically declared it had been paid for through their tax paid at the time.*

**E172 and A865 at the east end of Friary shed, on 15th June 1926. There were well over a hundred men at the shed at this time engaged upon all manner of work - 'wandering about'- as the text relates. Friary even had a 'banking turn'- demonstrating the complex, interlocked nature of much of the work in the west - the 10.00 a.m. Sunday job to Exeter would help out for an hour or two on the St Davids bank, before returning to Plymouth.**

*H.C. Casserley*

**West end of the shed on 18th August 1923, with 4-4-0 No.280. The wide range of duties and 'ability to do anything' included familiarization of the GWR routes out of Plymouth. 'That lot down the road' were therefore familiar to the Southern men and there was a considerable co-operation between the two.**

*H.C. Casserley*

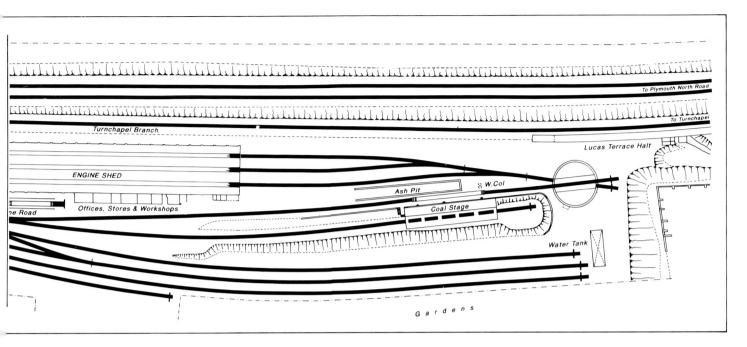

## THE NEW FRIARY

'Friary engine shed' proper, the LSWR Plymouth shed inherited by the Southern Railway, dated from the early 1900s - an entirely new development which brought together the two older establishments by now wholly inappropriate for the work. Both had been built according to ancient precepts and on the LSWR, approaching a peak of prosperity, sweeping changes were in motion. Friary station was a restricted site, constrained by the cutting of the Sutton Harbour branch and higher ground to the north. Only spare ground outside the city could provide the necessary space (the Great Western were forced to a similar course with the new roundhouse at Laira) and Drummond, unhappy with conditions at Plymouth sought out the necessary land. In November 1904 he reported, with customary under-statement .....*the present Running Shed at Plymouth, which holds 2 Tender Engines and 2 Tank Engines is inadequate for present requirements and recommend a new shed be erected to stable 15 Engines on ground belonging to the Company outside the Station.....*

The site lay on the south side of the line between Bulmer Road and Lucas Terrace Halt, the first stop out of Friary on the Turnchapel Branch. Plans were made ready only slowly, a broad outline of the scheme by 'JMB' of the Engineer's Office, Exeter, not sanctioned until 20th April 1906. Some months before in November 1905 requirements had been put thus .....*Read letter from the Engineer of the 27th October with plan shewing the position proposed for a new running shed at Friary capable of stabling 15 Tender Engines or 24 Tank Engines the cost of which, including connected works is estimated at £19,500. Approved.....*

The big steam sheds of the LSWR originated in the period around the turn of the century. The great corrugated iron barn at Exmouth Junction remained (with great good sense) the only venture of this type and a much more solid style emerged. Generous glazing and high roofs made the buildings light and roomy and the style could be adapted for layouts of different dispositions and sizes. Plymouth Friary was amongst the smallest - three roads running the length of the building. Drummond argued that the through type of shed was the most suitable though site restrictions made such provision difficult in many cases. Lighting at Plymouth was by 'incandescent gas lamp'; hydrants were provided between Nos. 1 and 2 roads, a

small crane was available for lifting adjacent to the fitters and stores, and an elevated coal stage of contemporary style and proportions was erected with 50 ft. turntable at the extremity of the yard. The depot was modern and well laid out and opened fully to traffic in 1908 when 'coal tips and trolleys' arrived from the suppliers. The old Friary shed is presumed to have closed immediately, Devonport apparently remaining much as before - 'closed' but in use for some sort of stabling or layover purposes.

Little change occurred in the years up to Grouping; 'much inconvenience' had been experienced in the Great War period though, with the arrangements for ash removal and to remedy this a new pit was put in in 1920 .....*It is desirable to provide an ash pit at the Friary Locomotive Depot and plan No. 15.924 was submitted shewing how this could be carried out at an estimated cost of £116. The Engineering Committee by this minute of today have ordered the work to be put in hand, subject to approval of this Committee.....*

Grouping brought the Plymouth Devonport and South Western Junction Railway locomotives from the Callington line. A small shed had been established there (and at Calstock) and locos from the branch frequently visited the main depot for washout and repair. A new lifting crane was installed in the late

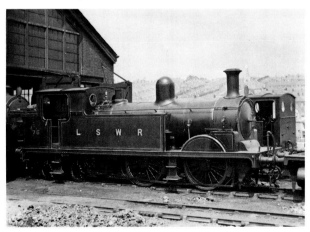

**0-4-4T No.75 on 13th June 1926. Motor fitted examples were used on Turnchapel jobs and later Brighton 'tankies' on e.c.s.**

*H.C. Casserley*

*Dartmoor* **one of the aptly-chosen Friary quartet of Pacifics, on October 3rd 1949. As well as seeing to the last of the roof, with their unfamiliar strong blast, the West Countries required a new hoist (the old one, pinched from Callington after 1923, was too small).**

**Tankies, Nos.222 and 223, in contrasting states, on 15th June 1926. It illustrates the sort of work embarked upon at this shed.**

*H.C. Casserley*

**No.712 on the Friary turntable, 16th July 1924. It was awkward to use and 4-4-0s were turned before taking water, to assist the balance. Most men preferred the Cattewater Junction triangle - a bit of a gradient it was known as 'going over the hump'.**

*H.C. Casserley*

**Bug No.E100** *taking* **coal on Christmas Eve, 1927. This stage was blown apart in a World War Two air-raid, two bombs on 21st March 1941 which killed fireman Geake, coalman Whiteside and two contractors employees, H. Lucas and F. Vivian.**

*H.C. Casserley*

'20s, of much greater capacity allowing the larger locomotives now at the shed to be dealt with. For similar reasons alterations were necessary to the coal stage in 1938 .....*Recommend that in order to minimise difficulties and delay at present experienced in coaling the high tenders fitted to modern engines, the floor of the coal stage at Plymouth Friary engine shed be raised by 18 inches. Estimated cost £300.....*

The shed was an early casualty of the Western Region take-over, *The Railway Observer* reporting the intended closure as early as May 1963. A West Country Pacific was 'seen' taking water and coal on 9th of the same month but by mid summer transfer of all locomotives, equipment and men to the nearby GWR shed at Laira had taken place. The site was sold off and is now covered by factory development

### Wandering About - Work at Friary

Smaller sheds could not of course boast the complexity of working to be found at a District centre such as Exmouth Junction, though as size diminished the quirky quality of the link arrangements seemed to intensify. At Friary it was long the practice to operate four links, without (in the main) the customary complement of 12 sets each. The usual throng of cleaners occupied in traditional fashion the lowest reaches of the promotion system, their first firing opportunities coming with entry to the No4 'shunting link'. Much of its work as the name suggests, was occupied round about in 0-4-4 and 0-4-0 tanks. It also had goods work to Cattewater, Turnchapel and elsewhere, 'but all local stuff'. Promotion upwards brought a man to the No.3 link, on local passenger trains to Tavistock, Callington and so on; obscurely the twelve sets of men making up No.3 were known as 'the milky dozen'. Eight sets of men occupied the next link, the No.2 or 'goods link' working mostly to Okehampton and Tavistock whilst the top or passenger was (logically)

No.1 - 'the Exeter link'. Their best job, remembered with wistfulness, had briefly been *The Devon Belle*, though no one at Friary worked further east than Exeter. There was thus a sense of 'apart-ness', nurtured by the brooding bulk of Dartmoor and relished by the Friary blokes. To the Salisbury men, coming upon them in the Exmouth Junction cabin, they could seem an odd lot but then so did 'the Londoners' and just about everybody else..... The top link as in most sheds throughout the country was carefully fashioned to reward long years of endeavour and no top link worthy of the name did not boast the best work, in terms of money and daylight hours. Additional to this would usually be the inbuilt 'soft job', a phenomenon common to most of these sheds. Taking place towards the end of the week it would be a relatively relaxed affair, not too taxing so the rigours of the more arduous work could be 'digested' as it were, at leisure. It would entirely derange today's computer-led flexible rostering but it was an efficient and very human system. Top link drivers after all could be expected to be in their fifties, working at a hard physical job, including lots of nights, for over 30 years. This sort of easing back was only right.

Goods work from Friary was concerned with a variety of traffics, originating from or destined for the docks. Perishables came into Cattewater where shunting went on, most of the time; there was even a late turn there, '1.15 am off for the 2.15 am Cattewater shunt'. The various commercial/industrial concerns were all of a time served by rail and Baileys at Orelston was a typical 1950s job. 'Baileys' was a timber yard which supplied 'The Western' with sleepers. SW men would shunt the yard and take the train so formed to Plymstock, moving on afterwards to shunt the wharf at Turnchapel. There would then be a trip back to Plymstock to offload whatever had been gathered together, the job ending with the return to Friary shed for coal. There could be three B4 0-4-0Ts, or 'bugs' on

Cattewater work in the height of summer. The bugs were not coaled under the stage at Friary in conventional manner; so small were they that this was better effected, by hand, *within* the coal shelter itself. Coaling in the usual fashion, on the road below the stage with 'the big engines' meant that most of it missed the tiny bunkers - in any case to extend the hours of the bugs it was necessary to construct a very edifice of coal lumps, to the level of the cab roof and beyond and as far as possible on the footplate itself; the narrow confines of the little cabs were restrictive enough but were made even more awkward by this sophisticated 'wall' of coal. The bugs, fitted with spark arrestors for the timber yard at Orelston were capable of prodigious feats despite their fussy air; at Cattewater they would lurch from one shunt to the next, dozens of wagons at a time, amidst a fine uproar.

The two 'Friary shunts' were usually entrusted to something bigger, M7s or O2 0-4-4Ts; one on the carriage sidings, the other on goods - the 'top' and 'bottom' shunts, respectively. They could at times operate almost round the clock. To avoid clashes at the head of the sidings, where the two could come together, the top (or 'carriage') siding job worked to a 'white' light in the hours of darkness and the bottom to a 'green' light. Between times the pilots could be called out on all manner of work - Gunnislake trips (passenger and goods) the Devonport shunt and trips to Keyham Dockyard or Callington.

Amongst the earliest working of the day into Friary was the down 'Tavy Goods' which after a bit of shuffling about formed the 8.15 a.m. back up to London. Probably the first train out of Friary was the 12.55 a.m. 'Paper' carrying the *Western Morning News* to Exeter Central; it worked back to Plymouth as the 5.12 a.m. 'Paper', getting to Friary about 7 o'clock. The 1.55 a.m. goods included the 'North Cornwall Paper' (picking up newspapers from Devonport) and restricted as to its weight to ensure quick running. The 4.15 a.m. took the Bere Alston and Callington papers and was a typical Friary job, the engine wandering about various Southern corners on all sorts of jobs. It

would shunt before making up the train, leaving it at Bere Alston to come off and work light to Lydford. There it picked up two coaches for the 7.05 a.m. Lydford - Friary train, doing some shunting before taking on the 10.45 a.m. Cattewater - Friary goods. All this was accomplished with an M7 0-4-4T, the crew relieved at Friary shed for other men to dispose the engine.

There was a 1.08 p.m. passenger to Tavistock which came back with the 4.23 p.m. Friary, timed to follow the *ACE* down. It then worked back to Tavistock with the 6.18 p.m. and returned with the 8.25 p.m. to Friary following the 3.00 p.m. to Waterloo. (Western men worked this one down from Central as part of their route familiarisation). The 5.58 'stopper' to Salisbury was nicknamed the '1st turn'.

Coal trains for the shed came from Newport or Bassaleg, in latter years worked by Western men but LSW/SR coal originally came by boat to Fremington Dock. Friary shed got through about three wagons a day. Before Nationalisation no tender engines were allowed to be coaled on a Sunday, the Southern stipulating (to save costs) that engines had to be coaled 'nearest the colliery' that is, Exmouth Junction. Friary had the West Country Pacifics for the major passenger turns spending most of their time between Plymouth and Exeter. They would work a variety of jobs, a stopper perhaps to Salisbury, coming back on the 'Brighton'. The next day's work might comprise the 7.58 to Exeter Central and back with a portion of the 1.12 Waterloo, or the 5.25 perishables (up Tavy) for Nine Elms, working back on the 10.24 to Friary (7.00 ex-Waterloo). Pacific work 'essentially meant variations on a theme - the up 12.55 to Exeter Central back with the 5.12 portion of 1.00 Waterloo, the up 3.50 Friary - Waterloo, back with the 8.07 stopper'.

Pacifics could not turn at the shed, so they used the Cattewater or Lipson (GWR) triangle. Nearly all Friary locos apart from the West Countries, thereby illustrating maybe, the generous provision of these locos on the Southern, were 'old 'uns' from somewhere else. The M7s for instance were passed

**The shed with the 'Callington 0-6-2Ts' in August 1955. Engines came on shed past here, on the south side by the hoist, coaled and turned and either left on the 'income tax road' or moved straight into the shed.**

*N.E. Preedy*

**Plymouth on 17th June 1958. It was reduced to a backwater even before takeover by the Western Region, which was interpreted as the final spite of the old rival. Southern engines afterwards used Laira, to the Western's embarrassment as it raced to eliminate steam. Friary had always had work there, round the Lipson No.1 curve,** *the Speedway* **past the Great Western shed, where almost any effort was worthwhile to put on a good show. The ignominy of a stuck West Country is still recalled, hauled into North Road by (horror) an Old Oak King with a** *London* **crew.**

*N.E. Preedy*

down from the Exmouth branch before they went to shops at Eastleigh. *Sort of got the last bit out of them.*

### LOCOMOTIVES

Plymouth, at the end of the South Western's winding route from Exeter, was responsible for all manner of goods and branch line work. On the opening of the 'direct' route via Lydford, Tavistock and Devonport in 1890, 380 class 4-4-0s were transferred to Friary shed for slow passenger and pick up goods duties. 460 class 4-4-0s were also used but proved not so popular with crews.

The work at Plymouth included many small branch lines and local passenger duties. For this, the shed was allocated numerous tank engines; the lines were often without turntables and threaded throughout with heavy gradients and tight curves. The small but powerful T1 0-4-4Ts had a varied programme: Tavistock and St.Budeaux locals, Turnchapel goods, Friary - Laira transfer goods and piloting at Friary station. So capable were these tanks that one was booked to work to Okehampton and back on a Saturday with a passenger train.

O2 0-4-4Ts were also much in evidence; motor fitted, they dominated the branch line work and were particularly used on the Friary - Turnchapel services. Their versatility allowed them to fulfil a mixed-bag of work - St.Budeaux, Gunnislake and Tavistock locals, Devonport and Friary pilots, goods at Stonehouse Pool and Keyham - later they were stationed at Callington to run branch line services from there.

The O2s were joined by a gaggle of the odd looking B4 0-4-0Ts, the 'bugs'. These powerful machines worked over the branches to Stonehouse Pool, Sutton Harbour, Cattewater and Turnchapel, both wharves and private sidings. The gradients and sharp curves on the lines allowed the B4s to perform well where other classes had been relative failures, ensuring their retention at Plymouth for decades. Transfer trips to Laira and Friary were also B4 duties along with piloting at Plymstock and shunting the timber yards at Oreston. The heavier and more powerful M7 0-4-4Ts arrived later for many of the services originally worked by the T1 and O2 tanks, especially the Tavistock - Okehampton and Brent locals.

Bulleid light Pacifics arrived after the war and took over the majority of the passenger work to Okehampton and Exeter which included some of the local duties too. 'The Brighton', a passenger service operating between Plymouth, Salisbury and Brighton, was also in the hands of the Pacifics, a Plymouth engine occasionally working right through to Salisbury.

Wadebridge shed and station; this really was isolation, where practice and custom owed little to outside authority. Cleaners lavished days on tank engines working a mineral branch, young men gained unheard-of driving experience, there was the usual close familiarity with the Great Western and breaking the Sabbath would deliteriously affect one's standing in the town.

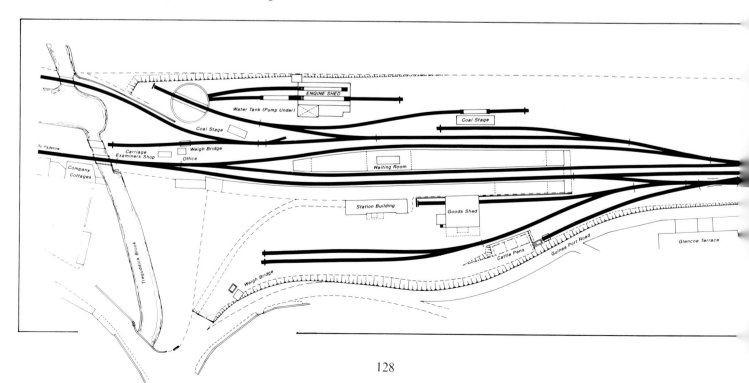

# Wadebridge

## Launceston, Delabole & Padstow

Shed accommodation had been provided at Wadebridge, in some form or another from the very earliest times. The Bodmin and Wadebridge Railway had opened a small station on the banks of the River Camel in 1834, the line running twelve miles or so inland to the terminus at Wenford Bridge. Two short branches were laid to Bodmin Road and Ruthern Bridge but most traffic is considered to have been concentrated on the 'main line'. In keeping with most railways at this time a small engine shed was erected at the main station and was sited amongst the works buildings of the Bodmin Co. near Molesworth Street to the west. Construction was not surprisingly of local stone with a small wrought iron water tank fronting the building. An unassuming structure, it was abandoned as an engine shed in 1895 but (remarkably) was to survive for another sixty years or more, only pulled down at last in 1962.

The LSWR by the late 1840s was still far away, some 200 miles from this part of Cornwall; long term aims, however, were to extend westward, to seize large tracts of Devon and Cornwall from under the very noses of its rivals. The frail financial position of the Bodmin and Wadebridge Company from the first made it an obvious target and arrangements were complete by 1847. Connection with the rest of the LSWR was not destined to take place for nearly half a century after the North Cornwall Line, pushing through from the north east via Launceston and Delabole, arrived in 1895.

The line wound its way down from the edges of Dartmoor through Halwill, the junction for Bude, and into the valleys of the Rivers Carey and Kensey. The ancient village of Launceston was chosen as temporary terminus, then further on Delabole, another temporary resting place, before making a final approach upon Wadebridge. At all these locations the LSWR determined that shed accommodation be set up.

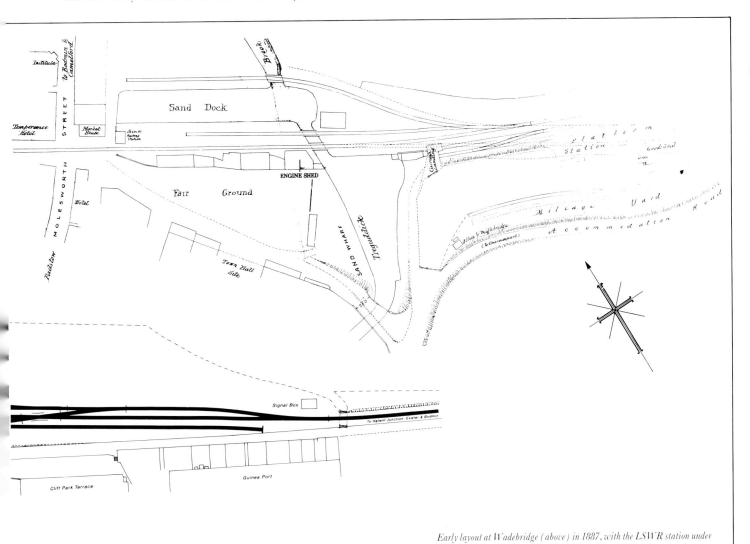

*Early layout at Wadebridge (above) in 1887, with the LSWR station under construction and (left) the shed in 1901, before its extension.*

**The old Bodmin and Wadebridge shed, demolished only in relatively recent times.**

## LAUNCESTON

'Lanstan' despite its obscurity boasted two stations. The Great Western example had opened in 1865 together with a small one road shed and turntable, coal stage and water tank. The line terminated just short of the Bude Road by the bridge over the River Kensey. The LSWR-inspired North Cornwall Line reached the town in 1886 and set up shop, as it were, alongside the GWR adversaries. The station, as intimated, was to serve as terminus until Delabole was reached in 1893, and the company therefore required some modest engine accommodation of its own. No plan of these earliest days has been unearthed but it would seem that the latter day building, albeit periodically renovated represents more or less the original provision.

The earliest reference occurs, oddly enough, on a plan of Delabole, of 1893, with the note ..... *The engine shed and turntable to be removed from Launceston and refixed here.....* What happened is not clear. Both sheds, Launceston and Delabole were regarded as temporary but some form of building is believed to have remained in place at Launceston; either it was removed to

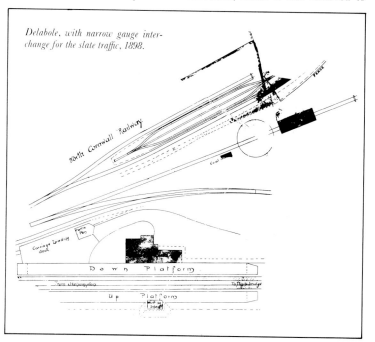

*Delabole, with narrow gauge interchange for the slate traffic, 1898.*

Delabole, reassembled there and a new Launceston building put up or, more likely (to judge from its periodic ruinous declines), it remained in place and an even less substantial building was hastily put up at Delabole. An LSWR plan of 1905 shows a small one road shed at Launceston, without turntable (adding more speculation to the Delabole plan) but sporting a generously-proportioned coal stage, at the Exeter end. All this is of little help in determining the precise sequence of events Launceston - Delabole and a reminder of the perils of fragmentary, contradictory evidence.

The tiny Launceston engine shed stood in the station goods yard; no runround line was established but a lengthy siding was provided at the rear of the building. Construction was executed in corrugated iron on a metal framework, doors and smoke vent also being provided. It measured only 50 ft. in length and some 20 ft. in width, mess room and stores - corrugated iron sheds - alongside. By 1913 a turntable was definitely in place, on the siding at the rear of the shed. 48 ft. diameter in a pit of local stone.

### LAUNCESTON AND THE GREAT WESTERN

In a minor instance of wartime operating expedience, the Southern shed at Launceston was abandoned and operations centred upon the Great Western shed in the autumn of 1943, shortly after two new cleaners arrived from Exmouth Junction. They were to act principally as steamraisers and a pair was deemed necessary for safety reasons, much of the work taking place at night. In September of 1943 men still signed on at the Southern 'cabin', a squalid lean-to attached to the shed; it had a table and fireplace and following 'amalgamation' with the Great Western formed a moderately cosy dormitory. Old overcoats served as blankets and the nearest toilet was at the station. The two Southern cleaners attended to both resident engines, the Southern T9 4-4-0 and the GWR Laira engine, a 45XX 2-6-2T. Both of them stabled in the Great Western shed. The 4-4-0 backed its coaches out of the Southern station at the end of the day having worked in from the Halwill line and moved forward, light, positioned for a morning turn onwards to Padstow. In the 1940s the Southern turntable was used only on a Sunday though in latter years it seemed to serve on a more regular basis. T9s on troop and p.o.w. trains always used the GW 'table which required extensions ('ramps') for tender engines. In 1943 there were ten men at Launceston, two crews for each company and the two Southern cleaners. Relations were highly amicable and one of the Southern lads did an odd turn on the GWR when a resident fireman was indisposed. He would fire to Tavistock where a replacement, Laira having been alerted by 'phone, would be waiting. Great Western men disposed their own engines at little places like Launceston but in 1944 a local labourer was taken on as shedman and the cleaners instructed him in the art of steam raising, before being recalled to Exmouth Junction.

### DELABOLE

Somewhat circuitously the North Cornwall line had arrived at Delabole in 1893 via Egloskerry, Tresmeer, Otterham and Camelford. As previously mentioned a plan of this terminus dated 1893 directed that the shed at Launceston be 'refixed here'. The Delabole shed was a small building with stage and turntable at the rear; it was considerably smaller than its 'contemporary' at Launceston, which serves only to add to the variety of possible outcomes. An LSW plan of existing features in 1898 shows a small engine shed 50 ft. long and 18 ft. wide. A turntable 50 ft. in diameter was supplied at the front of the building along with a small coal stack. It stood in a goods yard alongside some narrow gauge exchange sidings serving the nearby slate quarry. The line had been extended through to

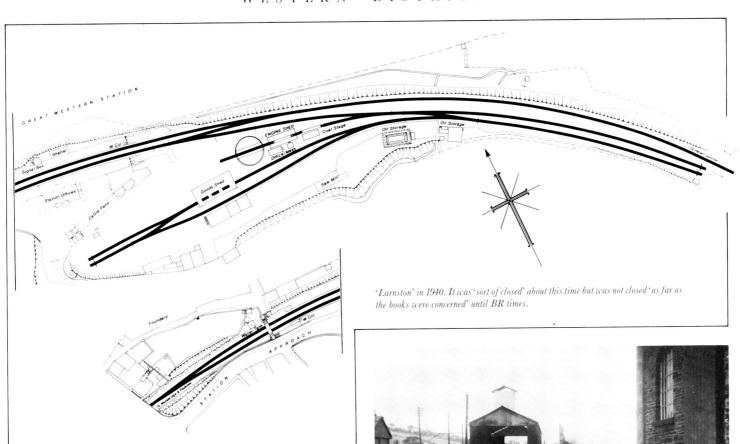

*'Larnston' in 1940. It was 'sort of closed' about this time but was not closed 'as far as the books were concerned' until BR times.*

**The shed on 12th October 1950. It remained 'open' simply, it would seem, for the sake of the turntable and the ex-GWR tanks would use it, though whether this depended upon a particular working, or problems with the WR 'table, is unclear.**

*D. Clayton*

'The new pier', a photograph taken by the Resident Engineer, G.H.Read. The train standing by the fish dock is an express, waiting to draw forward and set back into the platform. The work is a neat accompaniment to the drawing (below).

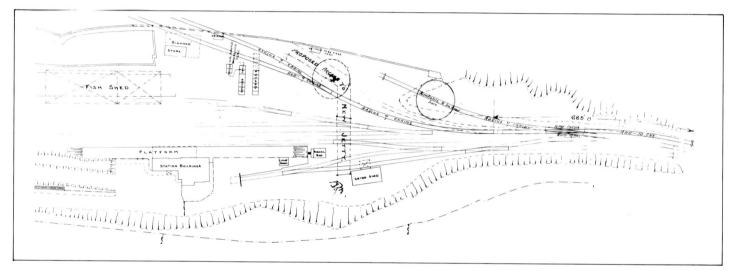

Wadebridge in 1895 and there is a tradition that quarry traffic kept the shed open for a year or two. If this was so it was a brief interlude, and a Minute of July 1900 'approved' the sale of 'the engine shed.....at Delabole to the Co-op - £20'. The Co-op simply removed it; the shed was doubtless built in the ubiquitous corrugated iron, on an easily dismantled frame. Such construction condemned these sheds to an early and ruinous demise but lent an unusual flexibility. Hence the unfortunate (from the chronicler's point of view) LSW habit of moving (or at least proposing to move) buildings around its lines. Parts of these sheds might still languish in some West Country barn or stable; certainly the Co-op found removal straightforward and plans of 1905/6 show shed and turntable site covered by sidings.

## PADSTOW

There was no engine shed at Padstow but it played a part of some note in the operation of the various lines out of Wadebridge. The terminus had opened in 1899, a route of great beauty and serenity along the south banks of the River Camel.

Suitably dramatic final approach to the terminus was made on the magnificent 'Iron Bridge' and through a rock cutting. A turntable was deemed necessary at Padstow, recommended by the Board of Trade, but it does not seem to have been put in until 1900.

For years Padstow like other villages along this coast had a tradition of fishing and the sea. The wider market afforded by the railway in those days enabled a great increase in the trade, recorded in *The Railway Gazette* of 1933 ..... *The Padstow Extension of the North Cornwall Railway was opened for traffic in March 1899. A small harbour had been constructed at Padstow many years previously for fishing vessels, and as it became insufficient to deal with the increasing number of east coast boats visiting these Western waters for herring fishing, the Padstow Harbour Commission, which had been created by statute in 1844, in conjunction with the North Cornwall Railway, obtained powers in 1910 to provide additional accommodation, including a wet dock.....* In conjunction with this work it was necessary to move the turntable some distance to the south of the layout and the original 50 ft. 'table was simply lifted out and placed in a newly prepared pit close by. *The Railway Gazette* elaborated .....*Only the outer wall, however, of this dock was constructed, in the form of a jetty 780 ft. long and after its construction complaints were made from time to time that vessels lying at the quayside were not adequately protected from the weather.*

*In order to meet this difficulty it was decided to construct on the north-western side of the old harbour a new jetty, about 450 ft. long, in line with that built in 1910, and to extend the latter by 50 ft. leaving the entrance 300 ft. wide thus enclosing the harbour. It is anticipated that the works, now in the course of construction, will be completed at the end of the summer. The jetty consists of concrete walls founded on the rocks with hearting of grouted rubble filling, the two walls being strengthened and held together by old rails embedded therein.*

*It is expected that the works, by improving the amenities of the harbour, will attract fishing vessels to the port to an increased extent, and that this will result in an increased revenue to the railway company from the traffic thereby brought. The contractors are Sir Arthur Carkeck & Co. Ltd., and Mr. George Ellson, Chief Engineer of the Southern Railway, is responsible for the design and supervision of the work.*

After the war Bullied Pacifics were introduced on the routes west of Exeter and to cope with these larger locomotives it was *.....necessary to enlarge the turntable.....by now some forty years old.....* A 65 ft. example was installed, the jetty wall being rebuilt somewhat to accommodate it.

## THE LSWR AT WADEBRIDGE

Wadebridge for long years lay in a remoteness almost absolute, despite its early railway developments. The LSWR, miles away nevertheless made its suzerainty felt. References are few but an Officers Committee of 1865 'Recommended' the sale of 'the two old and worn out locomotives now lying at Wadebridge shed. Offers invited for them but tenders to remain as proposed'. Later in May 1886 Adams reported the arrival of *.....the engine 'Bodmin' at Wadebridge and the consequent removal of the engine 'Scott.'* Distant and isolated Wadebridge is largely absent from the general flow of business recorded in the minutes, the clutter of orders, missives, instructions, admonitions, and reports that form much of the record of these times. A flurry of

activity occurs naturally enough (the minuting practice of pre-Grouping companies eschewed wordiness) in 1895, when a handful of references indicate the construction of a shed for the newly arrived railway. The old Bodmin and Wadebridge buildings were darksome hovels, crudely rural for a company of the prestige and power now gathering to the LSWR. The new shed though modest was at least of modern appearance and had none of the byre-like antecedents of its predecessor. Orders were issued to seek 'Tenders for a new Engine Shed at Wadebridge' from April of 1895, when the Committee 'authorised works at Wadebridge'. Estimates were put at £1700, 'viz:- 50 ft. engine turntable and connecting siding, with coal stage, engine pit, tank, water column, well and pump with gas or oil engine for the necessary water supply'. Further thought and modification led to the more specific 'Approval', on 29th May 1895 *.....for the Engine Shed WADEBRIDGE with pits Tank House and other connected works including an Engine Hoist.....Estimated Cost..... £2440.....*

The two road building was erected on spare ground on the north side between the station and the River Camel. The one inch weather boarding used throughout to clad the walls was supported on a framework of 'best Norfolk Larch', the whole resting on a brick plinth. Pits were supplied on both roads, an architects note stating that 'they should be in concrete, rendered inside in Portland Cement and similar in detail to the pits at Bodmin'. The finest 'Countess' slating was used on the roof whilst the water tower was dressed in 'Blue Staffordshire Brick'. underneath this commodious tank lay the 'Gas Turbine Pump', fitters shop and stores, whilst lean-to accommodation served for foreman's office, messroom, sand furnace and latrines. The shed was built to accommodate 'two tender engines or four tank engines' and measured a modest 70 ft. x 38 ft., whilst the tank held 12000 gallons, supplied from a well. The northernmost of the two roads terminated inside the building whilst the other ran through the shed onto a pit with hoist, drawings noting that 'The lifting road will be provided and fixed by the company'. Windows were provided along both

**Wadebridge with Beattie tanks and wicker coaling 'bauns' (though the term may have been different in Cornish usage); the shed had five or six** *tankies*, **the three cossetted Beatties and a couple of 'big uns' for Bodmin.**

T9 at Wadebridge. They were the principal passenger type to the end, one stabling overnight, a second working the early train down from Okehampton and Launceston.

walls of the shed and further illumination came from glazed skylights. Smoke flues and stacks in the contemporary LSW style were supplied and ventilation was assisted by louvres in the gables at either end.

Wadebridge belonged to a period in which the LSWR was at the forefront of development in engine shed layout and practice. It was re-emphasising at major sites the straight shed principles of the 1870s but the Wadebridge shed, of minor importance, was laid out really according to primitive practice, its two roads converging at one end directly on to the 50 ft. turntable. Construction proceeded apace such that on 12th June 1895 the Locomotive Superintendent could put forward one of his staff to run the new establishment:

*..the Locomotive Superintendent....points out.....Necessity for appointing a working foreman for the new Locomotive Depot at Wadebridge and recommend Mr. Connett, a fitter at Exmouth Junction at 40/- a week. Also that a breakdown van and tools be provided at £54. To be considered later.* By the latter part of 1895 the shed was almost ready for use but, it was declared on the 16th October, 'no appointment or provision is required for present'   Someone was eventually put in charge at the shed. Whatever was originally decided it is of interest that the Wadebridge foreman - or at least his position - was a point of contention until the end of steam - Okehampton for decades had more men and engines yet was ever under a 'driver in charge', at very little extra remuneration. Wadebridge was 82 miles from Exeter with an infrequent service, so the man in charge had to stand on his own feet; he was invariably a 'workshop grade promoted'.

1906 heralded the introduction of steam railcars onto the lines around Wadebridge, mainly confined (it was the intention) to Bodmin - Wadebridge services. Their early demise was unforeseen for in 1907 plans were laid before the board for extension of the shed 'to accommodate steam motor carriages'. The extension was carried out in a most sympathetic way embodying the style of the original building. The extra room was sufficient for two of the H13 railcars then allotted to the shed; spare ground at the eastern end of the building was utilised and wood was again employed. Two new pits were built inside with a third outside for the lifting crane, an architects note revealing *.....Lifting road to be removed from present position and refixed here, by the company.* Opportunity was also taken to give a more conventional approach to the shed. The tracks were continued past the eastern coal stage to link with the up side station loop, catch points protecting the neck of the yard. By the

end of summer 1907 the work was complete and the railcars settled in their new home.

Suffering from a variety of drawbacks, including lack of power, firing difficulties and serious maintenance problems led the class to be withdrawn from service at Wadebridge by 1919. Thirteen H13 railcars were built for the LSWR branch lines, with one allocated to Wadebridge but it did not survive World War I. It was incapable of hauling any extra coach without slipping and to carry out boiler repairs involved the removal of the side tanks, hardly the sort of repair for a small shed. One imagines that it was hauled dead to Exeter or Eastleigh Works and a spare railmotor had to be sent to replace it. Meanwhile the service would have needed a spare loco and composite coach. There was a reserve 2-4-0 Beattie Well Tank for the Wenford Bridge branch which no doubt became temporarily a passenger engine. The extra accommodation was nevertheless useful, the engine complement having increased substantially since the first years. Apart from an 'old coach body' for use as a classroom for enginemen and firemen in 1914, Wadebridge disappears from the minutes of most committees for a considerable time. The building survived remarkably well- it was never intensively used and was built to fine specifications as far as the foundations were concerned. However, by the late 'thirties the wooden gables were suffering badly from decay and were decidedly unsafe. The by now traditional remedy was applied - large sheets of asbestos nailed to the original frame (although in this case the sheets were not corrugated). This seems to have been a temporary measure as the whole building was revealed to be in 'urgent need of repair' by 1949. Plans submitted that year required the building to be totally reclad, the old 'Countess' slating giving way to the ubiquitous 'Big Six' durable asbestos sheeting. The walls were largely renewed and made good, everything 'finished with two coats of a quality exterior paint'. In tandem with this work the coal stage, after some fifty years open to the sweeping elements of the lea, acquired a protective canopy.

Passing to the Western Region in 1963 the allocation subsequently gave way to diesel traction, causing many redundancies in the West and elsewhere not least at Wadebridge itself. Diesel shunters still made use of the shed mainly on Wenford Bridge workings until final closure came in 1966. The whole site is now covered by a housing estate and at the time of writing a preservation group has opened a line from Bodmin Road to Boscarne Junction.

## UNCHANGED AND UNCHANGING

The 'bowler hats' down from Waterloo for a summer weekend might penetrate Dorset and Devon at the coast but at Wadebridge the 'inspection' in the early days was a concept dimmed into unreality. By the 1930s the motor car had arrived allowing the 'Exeter Bloke' to make regular trips to his outstations. However, it was still considered unlikely that he would arrive unannounced to do any 'poking about'. The whole place shut down on a Sunday, a phenomenon of the Celtic Fringe which emphasized the distant isolation Wadebridge once had and helped further to set it apart. Sometimes a ballast might be run on the Sabbath, a useful bit of overtime perhaps, when responsibility could be laid conveniently at the foot of 'them at Exeter' - godless and worldly.

Wadebridge remained thus, deep into the BR period, a dreaming which persisted such to make its end only the more shatteringly brutal. Post 1919 'National Agreements' required adherence to seniority in the grades and this was administered throughout the Company. However, at Wadebridge there seemed to be more flexibility and links were never strictly adhered to. Camaraderie and the trust of the 'Guvnor' were highly developed .....*you could do much as you liked providing the job was done*..... The complement of cleaners had been jealously guarded over the years, upheld before periodic staff reviews emanating from up the line. In the mid-1950s there was a gang of four cleaners, given *five* days to clean a Beattie Well Tank. Whilst this did little for Regional staffing quotas it made both for an excellence of cleanliness particularly as far as the 2-4-0Ts were concerned and opportunity for shed work, fire dropping or whatever, and firing out on the line.

Cleaners at Wadebridge gained engine experience more or less from the first, earlier and beyond that enjoyed at some sheds. In the 1950s two of the Wadebridge cleaners lived at Bodmin and it was quite usual to be 'given a go' on the engine travelling to work every morning. Once passed, a cleaner might 'go anywhere' in between a spot of coaling or firedropping. Saturday mornings could often be relied upon to provide a firing turn; the regular fireman would be careful to give the nod if Friday night was anticipated to be a mite heavier than usual and the cleaner, appropriately forewarned, would fire the first Bodmin train. The booked fireman would eventually make it to the shed and await the train's return at some time past 8 o'clock at Wadebridge platform. It could mean at the worst a charge sheet for lateness or a 'tongue lashing from the Guv'. There was no strict system of booking on or off at Wadebridge and provided you knew your next turn and arrived on time to do it 'the guvnor' would be quite happy. The earliest cleaning turn was at 4.30 in the morning and the latest off at 11 p.m. This, however, meant a cycle trip home to Bodmin, the last train leaving at about 9 o'clock. Hurrying though the work invariably it was possible to catch this, stowing the cycles in the van. Reported for this transgression by one less finely tuned than most to the subtleties of Wadebridge life, cycles subsequently would be concealed under mailbags, the fugitives travelling in the engine cab. 'The 9 o'clock' was a Western Region working, St. Blazey - Wadebridge - Bodmin Road - St. Blazey with a 45XX tank. A sympathetic crew would derive great amusement from this, closing the cab doors the better for concealment and going out of their way to make conversation with the vigilant and increasingly puzzled informer.

Wadebridge boys thus gained a considerable line experience of various kinds but to progress it was usually necessary to take seniority transfer, where their advanced knowledge usually caused eyebrows to rise. In 1956 two innocently applied for Reading jobs, unaware there were two sheds, and were astonished to find themselves on *Western Region* workings,

Westbury trains and double trippers *(see for instance Great Western Engine Sheds London Division, Wild Swan, 1987)* with 61XX 2-6-2Ts. The local lads were still on the cleaning gang and remained so, looking on as the Wadebridge boys took their part in the daily pell-mell of the London Division.

The Beattie well tanks and a handful of 02s ('the Bodmin tanks') made up most of the Wadebridge complement. There were T9 4-4-0s over many years - no other type can be said to have so characterized the line, especially the Padstow road, but the 'main line' engines, increasingly light Pacifics and 'Woolworth' moguls, were in the BR period less likely to be part of the official allocation. Engines for the main passenger jobs, principally in summer, were based essentially at Exeter and an overnight stay at Wadebridge for coaling/servicing was part of the diagram. The work of these sheds in the west was carefully slotted together and crew changes were mostly expedited where trains crossed at stations. Engines off Exeter, Okehampton, Launceston and Wadebridge sheds were on the work, increased greatly in intensity over the summer season. Many of the jobs involved a stopover, a night or a few hours at Wadebridge and this work provided for what might be thought of as the senior link.

**Wooden interior at Wadebridge, made spacious be the departure of the ill-starred steam railcars. Nos.0472, 0329 and 054 on 30th May 1922.**

*H.C. Casserley*

The busiest time for Wadebridge came in 1940 as a result of the bombing of Plymouth. GWR trains from South Devon and Cornwall were only able to make their way to London by way of Boscarne Junction and thence over the Southern's North Cornwall line. This of course required several reversals and change of engines at Wadebridge; but given the absence of locos powerful enough to haul trains of any length and too few drivers available, Great Western men (and engines) had to work to Exeter, and without pilotmen.

The 'North Cornwall' or 'No. 2' Link, encompassed much of the passenger and goods work between Launceston and Padstow. Exeter men would work the trains to Launceston where Wadebridge men took over. The engine would be returned the next day and another taken on at Launceston, the crews simply swapping footplates. In summer there was work through to Okehampton; Launceston men also came down to Wadebridge, often with a 'Woolworth', returning later in the day. The 'Bodmin Tanks' occupied another couple of crews at Wadebridge, worked in leisurely fashion on the basis of 'one in, one out'. The engine 'in' for a week was put aside for cleaning but seldom received much more than a 'lick'. Two crews manned the 'out' engine, early and late, trundling to and from Bodmin - Wadebridge and Padstow.

## LOCOMOTIVES

Wadebridge, apart from being the last town of any size on the North Cornwall line, was for years home to the three Beattie well tanks, the little 2-4-0s which had worked the Wenford Bridge line for over seventy years.

A variety of other locomotives were used on the local passenger and mixed traffic work over the years; Adams O2 0-4-4Ts handled the Bodmin branch and Padstow locals could be headed by anything from an S11 or T9 to latter day Bulleid Pacifics and Moguls. The T9 *Greyhound* 4-4-0s, like the Beattie tanks, found a long association with Wadebridge shed and were reliable workhorses remembered fondly by shed staff. Used mainly on Okehampton and Exeter duties, the last days found them trundling between Padstow, Wadebridge and Launceston.

The first locomotive to work the isolated line was *Camel* - a 12 ton 0-6-0. It was not long before a second locomotive was required and *Elephant* came to the line in 1836. The two small engines handled all traffic until they were joined, in 1864, by LSWR 0-4-2s No.42 *Atlas* and No.44 *Pluto*. 0-4-0 tank *Bodmin* came to work the line the same year, and over this period of isolation from the rest of the LSWR system both *Scott* (2-4-0T) and *Jumbo* (0-6-0ST) helped out with local services.*

Railcars Nos. 8,10,13 and 14 were later tried out on Wadebridge - Bodmin work but proved unsatisfactory due to lack of power (drivers experienced dreadful slipping at times) and stayed only a few years. Two Adams 415 Radial tanks took over the duties and were most useful on the heavy grades and tight curves of the branch and performed much of the work until replaced by Adams O2s 0-4-4Ts after World War One. North Cornwall Line trains were dominated by the Adams classes in the early years and 460 4-4-0s handled the bulk of Okehampton and Exeter passenger work until the introduction of the larger and more powerful Drummond types. S11s were allocated to Wadebridge to handle services and were not replaced until after Grouping by the highly successful N 2-6-0s.

After 1947 the larger Bulleid Pacifics were introduced on services to Wadebridge and Padstow in particular the heavier passenger and *Atlantic Coast Express* duties. The reign of the Beattie Tanks eventually came to an end in 1962 with the introduction of GW 1366 0-6-0PTs which in turn were replaced on Wenford Bridge work by the powerful O8 diesel shunters. DMU sets gradually took over the work to Wadebridge, Padstow and Bodmin.
*(Bodmin and Wadebridge 1834 - 1978, Fairclough and Wills, Bradford Barton 1979)*

**Exmouth Junction Pacific** *Budleigh Salterton* **taking coal on 7th July 1949. The 'throw' was long an institution at the shed but the new engines were beyond what could be achieved with a shovel, thus 'the little 'opper'.**
*H.C.Casserley*

**Grand new coal shelter at Wadebridge, a great luxury indeed, on 29th June 1960. It was welcome enough, but BR never really sorted out the turntable; it was too small for Pacifics and these travelled on to Padstow. This was very much in the nature of the sheds in the West, locos 'always goin' somewhere else for sumin'.**
*W. Potter*

# LOCOMOTIVE ALLOCATION 1933

## SALISBURY

**Class A12 0-4-2**
606, 621, 649, 650, 652, 654

**Class C8 0-4-0T**
290, 292, 296, 297

**Class D15 4-4-0**
470, 471, 472

**Class G6 0-6-0T**
162, 238, 275

**Class H15 4-6-0**
330, 332, 333, 334

**Class K10 4-4-0**
382, 389

**Class L11 4-4-0**
408

**Class N 2-6-0**
1405, 1834, 1851

**Class N15 4-6-0 (King Arthur)**
450 *Sir Kay*
451 *Sir Lamorak*
452 *Sir Meliagrance*
453 *King Arthur*
454 *Queen Guinevere*
455 *Sir Launcelot*
456 *Sir Galahad*
457 *Sir Bedivere*
749 *Iseult*
750 *Morgan le Fay*
754 *The Green Knight*

**Class S11 4-4-0**
387

**Class S15 4-6-0**
828, 829, 830, 831, 832

**Class T1 0-4-4T**
74, 75, 80, 365, 366

**Class T6 4-4-0**
684

**Class T9 4-4-0**
121, 285, 713, 727, 729

**Class X2 4-4-0**
586, 592

**Class X6 4-4-0**
665

**Class 0395 0-6-0**
3441

**Class 700 0-6-0**
306, 317, 691, 696

**Class Z 0-8-0T**
957

**Total: 63**

## YEOVIL

**Class A12 0-4-2**
612, 616

**Class C8 4-4-0**
295

**Class D1 0-4-2T**
2295*, 2361*

**Class G6 0-6-0T**
276, 349

**Class K10 4-4-0**
143, 145, 150, 340, 345

**Class L11 4-4-0**
158, 167, 405, 407, 435

**Class O2 0-4-4T**
218

**Class S11 4-4-0**
398, 402

**Class U 2-6-0**
1790, 1791, 1792, 1793, 1794, 1795

*\* Push & Pull air controlled*

**Total: 26**


## EXMOUTH JUNCTION

**Class A12 0-4-2**
611, 640, 643, 644

**Class D1 0-4-2T**
2359, 2633

**Class E1/R 0-6-2T**
2096, 2135, 2695

**Class G6 0-6-0T**
237, 259, 267, 278

**Class K10 4-4-0**
392

**Class L11 4-4-0**
135, 154, 159

**Class M7 0-4-4T**
35, 37, 41, 42, 44, 45*, 133, 247, 253, 320, 328, 356
374, 375, 669, 671

**Class N 2-6-0**
1406, 1826, 1827, 1828, 1830, 1831, 1832, 1835
1836, 1837, 1838, 1839, 1840, 1841, 1842, 1843
1844, 1845, 1846, 1847, 1848, 1849, 1852, 1853
1854, 1855, 1857, 1858, 1859, 1860

**Class N15 4-6-0**
448   *Sir Tristram*
449   *Sir Torre*
740   *Merlin*
743   *Lyonnesse*
744   *Maid of Astolat*
746   *Pendragon*
747   *Elaine*
768   *Sir Balin*
769   *Sir Balan*

**Class O2 0-4-4T**
187, 195, 198, 199, 214, 228, 232, 236

**Class S11 4-4-0**
396, 399, 401, 403

**Class S15 4-6-0**
823, 824, 825, 826, 827

**Class T9 4-4-0**
117, 283, 703, 710, 711, 717, 719, 723, 732

**Class 700 0-6-0**
326, 689, 693

**Class 0395 0-6-0**
3029, 3083, 3433, 3436

**Class 0415 4-4-2T**
3125, 3520

**Class Z 0-8-0T**
954

**Total: 109**

## BARNSTAPLE

**Class E1/R 0-6-2T**
2094, 2095, 2124, 2608, 2610, 2696, 2697

**Class M7 0-4-4T**
36, 242, 250, 256, 377, 668

**Class N 2-6-0**
1829, 1833, 1850, 1856

**Total: 17**

## PLYMOUTH

**Class B4 0-4-0T**
84, 92, 99, 100

**Class O2 0-4-4T**
182, 185, 194, 203, 212, 225, 231

**Class T1 0-4-4T**
9, 71, 361, 363, 364

**Class T9 4-4-0**
116, 280, 289, 709, 714, 715, 718, 722, 733

**Class 757 0-6-2T**
757, 758

**Total: 27**

## WADEBRIDGE

**Class L11 4-4-0**
134, 170

**Class O2 0-4-4T**
216, 221

**Class '0298' 2-4-0T**
3298, 3314, 3329

**Total: 7**

# Summary of Locomotive Sheds
# April 1901

## WESTERN DISTRICT

| Engine Shed. | Opening Date. | No. of Locos. |
|---|---|---|
| SALISBURY (Milford) | 1847 | Closed |
| SALISBURY (Fisherton) | 1859 | Closed |
| SALISBURY | 1901 | 36 |
| Gillingham | 1859 | Closed |
| YEOVIL | 1861 | 17 |
| Templecombe | 1863 | 1 |
| Chard | 1863 | 1 |
| EXETER Queen St. | 1860 | Closed |
| EXMOUTH JUNCTION | 1887 | 60 |
| Seaton | 1868 | 1 |
| Lyme Regis | 1903 | Not Open |
| Axminster | 1860 | Closed |
| Sidmouth | 1874 | 1 |
| Budleigh Salterton | 1897 | 1 |
| Exmouth | 1861 | 1 |
| Okehampton | 1894 | 1 |
| Holsworthy | 1879 | 1 |
| Bude | 1898 | 1 |
| BARNSTAPLE | 1854 | 7 |
| Bideford | 1855 | Closed |
| Crediton | 1851 | Closed |
| Torrington | 1872 | 3 |
| Ilfracombe | 1874 | 1 |
| PLYMOUTH (Devonport) | 1876 | 2 |
| PLYMOUTH (Friary Sta.) | 1891 | 9 |
| PLYMOUTH FRIARY | 1908 | Not Open |
| WADEBRIDGE (B&W) | 1834 | Closed |
| WADEBRIDGE | 1895 | 7 |
| Launceston | 1886 | 1 |
| Delabole | 1893 | Closed |

Total locomotives in Western District 152
Total LSWR locomotive stock 707

# ACKNOWLEDGEMENTS

This book is for Reg Randell, a Southern Railwayman. His help, advice and friendship has been a guide through many strange Southern matters and his specialised knowledge has very largely rendered this book possible.

The story of the sheds in the West has been pieced together from a daunting body of archive material, including plans and records held by the Southern Region, Waterloo and Croydon and Western Region, Swindon. The Minutes and documents preserved at the Public Record Office, Kew have been of invaluable help and further information has been gleaned from published work, acknowledged where appropriate.

It is now over twenty years since the engine shed was extinguished as an institution and this unique workplace, and its all-too obvious drawbacks and deficiencies, is now only distantly recalled by the preservation movement. This book attempts to bring back, briefly, the working life of some of these sheds, most now utterly vanished; even the very earth has forgotten them but for every brick-strewn patch of ground there is a rich seam of human recollection, and often, regret.

To Whatever degree this book has succeeded in bringing back those times, it has only been possible through the indulgence and good heart and remarkable kindness and generosity, of a number of railwaymen, to whom very special thanks are due..... Ken Ley, Henry Ford, Charlie Stone, Neil Taylor, Nobby Clarke, Arthur Westington, Harold Short, Ted Crawforth, Charlie Humphries, Jack Tiley, Rodney Bailey, Ken Davey, Ralph Bartlett, Don Lee, Don Macey, Gordon Nicholson, Alec Swain and a special thanks to Stephen Townroe for his generous contribution and informative critique.

Thanks must also go to the South Western Circle members for their assistance especially Peter Swift, Gerry Beale, David Wroe, Ted Fry and Roger Plumbley.

Special thanks go also to Derek, Doug and Dennis, to John and Mavis, and to Christine and Michelle, and R.C.Riley and Roy Brown, to Dave Banks, Bernard Matthews, Dave Faulkener, Dave Barrett and Gordon King.

The many photographs warrant especial gratitude and are credited appropriately. This account more even than previous efforts has leant upon the work of H.C.Casserley and once again it is a pleasure to acknowledge this absolutely invaluable contribution, and the good offices, too, of R.M.Casserley.

The base motives behind all those West Country long weekends and holidays now revealed, thanks last of all to Beverly and Wendy.